IMAGES OF THE
'MODERN WOMAN'
IN ASIA

IMAGES OF THE 'MODERN WOMAN' IN ASIA

Global Media, Local Meanings

EDITED BY

Shoma Munshi

Routledge
Taylor & Francis Group

LONDON AND NEW YORK

First Published in 2001
by Routledge-Curzon
2 Park Square, Milton Park,
Abingdon, Oxon OX14 4RN

270 Madison Avenue, New York, NY 10016

British Library Cataloguing in Publication Data
A catalogue record of this book is available from the British Library

Library of Congress in Publication Data
A catalogue record for this book has been requested

ISBN 0–7007–1343–3 (Hbk)
ISBN 0–7007–1353–0 (Pbk)

For my Guruji, Swami Jagat Pal; my parents, Anil and Sreela Munshi; and the memory of my grandmother, Renuka Bhattacharya – all of whom believe the best of me

TABLE OF CONTENTS

ACKNOWLEDGEMENTS

I would like to thank all the contributors to this volume for staying on with the book despite their time pressures and busy schedules. I thank them all for keeping their faith in me and I would like to let them know that I could not have done it without them.

I would like to express my gratitude to the International Institute for Asian Studies (IIAS) in Leiden, the Netherlands, where I began my post-doctoral research work; and the Research Centre Religion and Society, University of Amsterdam, where the work on this volume was completed, for their stimulating work atmosphere and facilities. Some people deserve special mention. Cathelijne Veenkamp and Elzeline van der Hoek have been instrumental in keeping the links with Curzon Press alive and active; and I thank Dick van der Meij for his superb support in copy editing and preparing the manuscript. My gratitude is also due to the people at Curzon Press who participated in the production of this book.

I am deeply grateful to the many friends and colleagues who have offered me their valuable suggestions, criticisms and advice, and also warmly given me their time and support over the years, particularly Dale Eickelman, Dipesh Chakrabarty, John Knight, Deborah Tooker, Cynthia Chou, Laurie Sears, Jean Gelman Taylor, Giovanni Vitiello, and David Birch. Others who lent their advice and assistance to my research and this project at an early stage include Nick Dirks, Lorraine Gamman, Purnima Mankekar, Ann Gray, Ien Ang and Krishna Sen. I thank them warmly for their help and guidance. Kishore Singh deserves my special thanks for his continued friendship and help over the years, as well as for supplying the cover illustration for this book.

My greatest intellectual debt is to Professor Peter van der Veer, not only for his advice on my work, his scholarly rigour and input which makes even the most difficult things appear crystal clear; but also for his continued support of my work.

My family has always been there for me in whatever I do. I can never repay the debt of love and support that I owe my parents, Anil and Sreela Munshi, and my sister Poroma Rebello.

EDITOR'S PREFACE

In a break from tradition, I have decided to dispense with the Index. This was not an easy decision to arrive at, but I feel strongly that the information contained in this book should not at any stage be viewed in piecemeal fashion since it is the whole which completes the picture. To ensure this isolation of references was not viewed out of context, I was forced to eliminate the Index. For this and other liberties taken, I seek the forgiveness of my fellow academic community.

NOTES ON CONTRIBUTORS

SARAH CHAPLIN is a qualified architect and Senior Lecturer in Architectural and Design Theory at Middlesex University. She has published papers on Japanese culture, technology, gender, identity, consumption and spatiality She is co-author of *Visual Culture: an Introduction*, with John A Walker, and co-editor of *Consuming Architecture* with Eric Holding; and is currently researching Japanese theme parks and love hotels for a forthcoming book on post-urbanism/post-orientalism.

STEPHANIE HEMELRYK DONALD is Senior Lecturer in Media Studies at Murdoch University, Western Australia. She is the author *of Public Secret, Public Spaces: Cinema and Civility in China*, the co-author of *The State of China Atlas*, and co-editor of *Picturing Power in the People's Republic of China: Posters of the Cultural Revolution*. Her research interests include children and the media, children in diaspora, and the visuality of politics.

RACHEL HARRISON lectures in Thai language and literature and London's School of Oriental and African Studies. She has published papers on contemporary women's writing with particular reference to the issues of sexuality and to representations of prostitution in modern Thai literature.

PERRY JOHANSSON is a Research Fellow at the Center for Pacific Asian Studies at Stockholm University. He is currently working on nationalism and identity in Chinese popular culture.

CHRISTINA H.P. LEE completed a Bachelor of Arts in Communication Studies (Honours) at Murdoch University in 1999 on representations of gendered identity in contemporary Chinese cinema, specifically the concept of the 'ambiguous woman'. Her research interests centre upon the female body politic, identity and displacement, and the relationship between the social context and cultural artifact of film.

REINA LEWIS is Senior Lecturer in Cultural Studies at the University of East London. Her publications include *Gendering Orientalism: Race, Femininity, Representation* and the co-edited *Outlooks: Lesbian and Gay Sexualities and Visual Cultures*; as well as other journal articles. She is currently completing a project on Ottoman women writers and postcolonial theory.

MARK LIECHTY is Assistant Professor in the departments of Anthropology and History at the University of Illinois at Chicago, USA. He is co-editor of the journal *Studies in Nepali History and Society*, and is working on a book on media consumption and class culture in Kathmandu, Nepal.

SHOMA MUNSHI is a Research Fellow at the Research Centre Religion and Society, University of Amsterdam and an affiliated Fellow at the International Institute for Asian Studies, Leiden. She has published papers on consumption, gender and the media. She is currently working on a project on 'Transnational Society, Media and Citizenship'.

KEVIN ROBINS is Professor of communication studies in Goldsmiths College, London. His publications include *Into the Image*; and the co-authored *Times of the Technoculture* and *Spaces of Media*. He is currently undertaking research into media and Turkish communities in Europe.

PATRICIA UBEROI is Reader in Social Change and Development at the Institute of Economic Growth, Delhi. She has edited *Family, Kinship and marriage in India, Social reform, Sexuality and the State* and co-edited *Tradition, Pluralism and Identity*. Editor of *Contributions to Indian Sociology*, her chief interests are in the fields of family, gender, social policy and popular culture in India and China.

Chapter 1

INTRODUCTION

SHOMA MUNSHI

This book is about women and the media in certain Asian contexts. The chapters presented here examine some of the relationships between gender and the fluctuations of power by concentrating on the reach of global media and its reworking(s) in local contexts. In examining the links between gender and the media, the contributors discuss questions involving the relationship between global media flows, gender and modernity in the region.

As the title of the book suggests, this volume intervenes into the current debates in the field of media and cultural studies, global/local and the transnational, feminist scholarship, Eurocentrism and multiculturalism. One of the ideas driving this volume is how media texts and the politics of consumption construct versions of a 'modern' woman in Asian contexts. Second, the book attempts to examine how this is a highly charged and contested terrain across which individuals, social groups and political ideologies struggle for expression through the images and discourses which the media provides. In other words, studying media representations of the 'modern' woman's identity in Asia (or anywhere else for that matter) is not rewarding in its own right, but gains further substance when contextualised within a broader framework of the characteristics of contemporary culture. In a world which is becoming seamless due to transnational media flows, theories of media and the construction of an identity of a 'modern' woman are best developed through specific case studies of concrete phenomena. Third, and perhaps most importantly, how do we define and interpret the feminine as understood in an Asian context?

Our attempt here is to 'cross borders' of disciplines, methods and approaches and build bridges, in examining how the 'modern Asian woman' is represented and understood in various forms of media today. We begin by examining the dynamics of global media and its inevitable interaction with the local. The global-local nexus as mutually interactive and interdependent lays the context for the empirical analyses which follow. In this context, by bringing together a number of case studies located in certain Asian contexts, we ask how does media represent women in the countries under study? What does gender, as exemplified by the 'modern' woman, signify in these contexts? How do women respond to particular images of themselves? Whose voice speaks for whom, and from which space? Does Western theorising on women and media culture make contributions to understandings of 'Asian' identities? Do our analyses of the 'modern woman in Asia' further develop or challenge this theorising developed (at least in the beginning) in Western academia?

GLOBAL MEDIA

First, and inevitably, the papers raise questions about the role that global communications media play in constructing ideas about the world today, and in particular the complex nature of cultural identities in Asian contexts. The globalisation of media and communications industries – including not just television, films, advertising radio and newspapers, but very importantly today, the Internet, have led to a situation in which communication networks, rather than physical, geographical limits have become the new permeable boundaries of our times. These will help create what Marshall McLuhan thought of in the 1960s as the 'global village.'

Robertson has defined globalisation as 'the concrete structuration of the world as a whole' (1990:20), whereby the world becomes one united place. The image that this evokes is a multi-levelled interaction of social forces leading to an all-encompassing sweep of global political, economic and cultural interdependency (cf. King ed 1991). One of the areas where this process of globalisation finds its most potent expression is in the information and communications media. Due to its rapidly evolving mechanisms and speed of transmission, especially of electronic media, notions of the linear chronology of time have been disrupted. Witness the death and funeral of Princess Diana in 1997. It was estimated that her funeral was watched by over a billion people worldwide. It was impossible not to feel the public outpouring of grief, to be a participant. No matter where one was, one felt as though one was *there*, amongst the millions who had poured into London to pay their last respects. Globally disseminated details of the accident and the funeral cut across multiple time zones as the whole world watched the events simultaneously.

The global movements of peoples, cultures, ideas, goods, products and information are all pointers to the fact that one must think more and more in terms of networks of communication as providing the all-importantly linking, yet penetrable boundaries of the times. In the context of global capitalism today, the foundations have been laid for a new global media order, in which mega corporations like Sony, CNN, Time Warner, STAR, and others battle it out for supremacy. Their professed, publicly stated goal may well be that of a closer knit world community. In truth, the driving logic is of course to reach an ever increasing audience worldwide, and consequently, increased profits. 'Driven now by the logic of profit and competition, the overriding objective of the new media corporations is to get their product to the largest number of consumers. There is, then, an expansionist tendency at work, pushing ceaselessly towards the construction of enlarged audiovisual spaces and markets ... audiovisual geographies are thus becoming ... realigned on the basis of the more 'universal' principles of international consumer culture' (Morley and Robins 1995:11).

In this context, Schiller has rightly argued that in today's atmosphere of globalisation, 'transnational corporate cultural domination' is seeking to create a world in which 'private giant economic enterprises pursue ... historical capitalist objectives of profit making and capital accumulation, in continuously changing market and geopolitical conditions' (1991:20). Morley and Robins illustrate this point and put forth a compelling argument about the logic of the new global media order. They write, 'What we are seeing is the construction of the media order through the entrepreneurial devices of a comparatively small number of global players, the likes of Time Warner, Sony, Matsushita, Rupert Murdoch's News Corporation and the Walt Disney Company ... we have now the proliferation of generic channels (sport, news, music, movies) ... Global corporations are presently manoeuvring for world supremacy' (1995:13).

As early as the 1980s, Theodore Levitt's arguments towards an increased global outlook were being used by transnational corporations in strategising for positioning and marketing their products worldwide. Levitt supported his thesis by saying that 'the global corporation looks to the nations of the world not for how they are different but for how they are alike ... it seeks constantly in every way to standardise everything into a common global mode ... .' Such marketing strategies which are deployed by the transnational corporations 'are not denials or contradictions of global homogenisation, but rather its confirmation ... globalisation does not mean the end of segments. It means, instead, their expansion to worldwide proportions' (1983:28-31).

The range and sweep of global flows of mass mediated culture, especially the visual image industries, is not something which can be easily controlled. But this does not imply that it has a global, homogenising effect on particular local situations which respond in their own culturally diverse ways. In this respect, Featherstone's view (1990) is that one should view globalisation in terms of complex processes of global integration rather than in polarised terms of global and local, by which 'what becomes increasingly 'globalized' is not so much concrete cultural contents ... but, more importantly and more structurally, the parameters and infrastructure which determine the conditions for the existence of local cultures' (Ang 1996:153). In other words, this complex process can best be understood as the distribution and spread of certain economic, political and ideological imperatives which determine the ways in which media, production, circulation and consumption are organised throughout the world today.

Transnationalisation of media flows is by now well under way. For its supporters, such global media flows offer the expansion of 'good' ideas such as democracy to a wider public and an escape from restrictive tendencies of nation-states. But their implications still remain a homogenising one. We argue that it remains firmly centred in the West (the threat of Americanisation is a very real one even in the countries of the European Union, notably France for example). Thus, while global media culture acknowledges differences and diversity at one level, its primary task lies in the absorption of distinctiveness to produce a kind of stratified homogeneity (Hall 1991). Which is why we question such a totalising view of global media flows and ask whether such systems, however powerful they may be, really fuse national cultures or overlay them with a new 'cosmopolitan' culture. As Smith argues, 'it is not enough to imagine the global community; new and wider forms of political association and different types of cultural community will first have to emerge. It is likely to be a piecemeal movement, disjointed and largely unplanned' (1991:160). Appadurai has argued that models of global culture which look at a simple centre-periphery tension are analytically inadequate, and he proposes instead a more sophisticated framework of five dimensions of global cultural flows – ethnoscapes, mediascapes, technoscapes, financescapes and ideoscapes – which 'are not objectively given relations but deeply perspectival constructs, inflected very much by the historical, linguistic and political situatedness of different sorts of actors: nation-states, multinationals, diasporic communities, as well as sub-national groupings and movements ... the multiple worlds which are constituted by the historically situated imaginations of persons and groups spread around the globe' (1990:296-7).

THE GLOBAL / LOCAL NEXUS

How do forces of globalisation however, fare, when they encounter the *real* world of different social formations and cultures? It is here that the homogenising, unifying tendency of globalisation start to unravel as one faces the inescapable fact that 'the spatial matrix of contemporary capitalism is one that, in fact, combines and articulates tendencies towards both globalisation and localisation' (Morley and Robins 1995:30). What needs to be carefully considered then is the complex relationship between global media and local meanings, their connections as well as their disjunctions (cf. Appadurai 1990; Morley 1992; Martín-Barbero 1993, García Canclini, cited in Lull 1995). All these scholars, in one form or another, theorise that there can be no trend towards a linear, homogenising development. Such a trend is always, and necessarily upset by opposing forces of differences and social and cultural discontinuities.

Keeping the issue of the transnational media system as crucial to our argument here, we acknowledge (like others before us) that the global and the local therefore cannot be understood in terms of dichotomised, binary oppositions. Nor can it be said that the global tends to erode local cultures while the latter tries to maintain its authenticity. Rather, the global/local nexus has to be understood in *relational and relative* terms, i.e., how one relates to the other relatively, and interacts with the other. On the one hand, technological and market shifts are leading to the emergence of global image industries, while on the other hand, there have been significant developments towards local production. New technologies facilitate the fragmentation of mass markets and the targeting of particular audience segments by large media and advertising corporations: *'the issue is not one of global media or local media, but of how global and local are articulated ...* One possibility is global homogeneity. Another ... offers the possibility of reinventing and rearticulating international and local cultures and identities' (Morley and Robins 1995:1-2, emphasis mine).

Inevitably, the papers in this volume raise questions about the role that the communications media play in constructing ideas about the world today, and in particular the complex nature of local cultural identities in Asian contexts. 'Audiences derive meaning from audio-visual media by using a perspective orientated by belief, common sense and local everyday practices in which visual codes play an important role ... as visual *representations*, images are embedded in a codified vocabulary inextricably linked to 'local' culture. Although recent developments in communication technology and software distribution are a global phenomenon, the ways in which audio-visual media are established and integrated into local practices can be linked to culture-specific traditions, aesthetics, narratives and rhetorics' (Brosius and Butcher 1999:12, emphasis in original).

Kevin Robins' paper on changing spaces of global media suggests that the development of the media has always been aligned to the idea of the national imaginary and imagined communities. This way of thinking about culture has tended to overlook and shut out other complexities such as race, ethnicity, religion, gender, diaspora, etc. What he examines in his paper is how the discourse of global media flows can potentially break down the homogenising nature of the 'imagined community' and allow for an examination of developments in which possibilities of other cultural complexities exist. Robins rejects the corporate ideology of global media corporations in their ideals of creating 'an international media community.' He suggests that what in fact happens here is the creation of a global consumer order. The global-local nexus offers more possibilities, in Robins' opinion, to examine complexities, in that global media flows as experience has shown, have to negotiate with local cultural complexities. In his paper, Robins examines the model of diasporic communication, and within that, suggests that the contested processes in the development of 'new femininities,' is one of the possible areas where potential for taking into account differences in discourse exist. He suggests moving beyond community closure to recognition of cultural complexities, involving the awareness of gender, sexuality, class, ethnicity, family and social structures, because it is in struggles around these sites that cultural expressions and reformulations of ideas of the 'modern' take on increased significance.

IMAGES OF THE 'MODERN WOMAN' IN ASIA

Terms like the 'modern woman in Asia' are fraught with contradictions. The 'modern woman' is not a 'real' but a potential subject position, one that is always in progress. The 'Asian modern woman' may be no more than a discursive ideological space for identification created by the global/local media, but her image interacts with so many other social forces that compete for space in female imagination, that historically and cross-culturally she continues to be a powerful dream or female fantasy. Social theorising about the 'modern woman' continues to influence so many cultural forms and processes of popular culture from organisation of dress and space to participation in advertising and pornography.

How do we define and interpret the feminine as understood in an Asian context? This question becomes even more difficult to tackle when in addition, Euro-American theories of feminism are relocated on to contemporary Asia. In attempting to situate feminist theories as applied to the representation of women in media cultural artefacts, I hold that there can be no fundamental feminist position (cf. Sears 1996). Dialogues on transnational feminist practices which have opened up avenues cutting across national, political and cultural boundaries have resulted from the call towards specificity and a feminist politics of location (see, for instance, Kishwar and Vanita 1984; Barrett and McIntosh 1985; Mohanty 1987; Amos and Parmar 1987; Spivak 1987; Donaldson 1992; Frankenberg and Mani 1993; Rey Chow 1993; Grewal and Kaplan 1994; Ghosh and Bose 1997). I would like to suggest that feminism is a global phenomenon in modernity, but that it has to reproduce itself in local contexts and is thus subject to the same processes as the globalisation of media images.

Of course the discourse about the 'modern woman,' particularly in Asian contexts, is underpinned by ideas of social progress, improvement and 'acceptable modernity.' Indeed, there is a debate on whether there are several different versions of modernity or a single one which finds its origins in the Enlightenment project (for a recent discussion on this debate, see Zurndorfer 1998; Sen and Stivens 1998; Eisenstadt 1996; Stivens 1994). We agree with the view that while there is a common 'modernity' rooted in the European and

American enlightenment, enabled and universalised by imperialism, there are also a great variety of historical trajectories in the world, in which modernity is produced and engaged with; that ' ... it might be preferable to speak of a single modernity and a multiplicity of histories' (van der Veer 1998:285).

Gender issues in Asia[1] are closely tied to contemporary processes of modernity The idea of 'femininity' in Asia has been produced through a wide variety of discourses including those of patriarchy, colonialism and capitalism, and two aspects follow from this. First, the construction of feminine identities in Asia is a reflection of certain ideological positions that seek control over women's lives; and secondly, these ideologies do not go uncontested, and alternative versions of feminine identities continue to be offered by Asian women.

There is one other aspect to bear in mind in terms of the present context: just as we should avoid the tendency to homogenise Asia, we should also remember that the situation of women in Asian societies can also differ markedly. Indeed, the category 'third world woman,' so current now in Euro-American theorising, may be far too monolithic; in that of presenting a homogenised idea of non-western femininity which is too generalised to capture the nuances and complexities of any particular situation. The position of women and their participation in the 'public life' of their community in Asia varies greatly from country to country.

Almost all the papers in this volume are set in the context of the proliferation of global media flows, the creation of public and private spheres and the consumption practices of the particular Asian countries under scrutiny. There are several ways to approach the contested space within which 'modernity' as represented through the feminine, is visible in contemporary Asia. We privilege consumption as ' ... central to the constant search for and the construction of the 'new,' including new identities, that is the hallmark of modernity ...' (Sen and Stivens 1998:5; cf. de Grazia 1996 and Friedman 1990). Furthermore, the contributions examine consumption as an activity, a way of social life, and as 'the work of the imagination' (cf. Appadurai 1996). This finds expression in different ways in the contributions of Mark Liechty, Sarah Chaplin, Perry Johansson and Shoma Munshi. Liechty's paper in this volume examines how in Kathmandu today, media artefacts, in particular imported pornographic videos with their versions of the 'modern woman,' are being increasingly consumed in the private sphere. He further explores how women themselves reconcile class and gender interests in their own attempts to understand, critique and appropriate representations of women and modernity in these media texts. Chaplin's paper argues how the evolving characterisations of the woman in Japan have typically been spatially inscribed, and how public and private spaces determine her image as a *moga* (modern woman). She discusses how in 1920s and '30s Japan, women themselves, by their progressive manoeuvrings, created the conditions necessary for modernity in Japan through a re-negotiation of interior and exterior spaces. These changes were not just modernising spatial practices on the part of women, but more importantly, also acts of spatial transgression. Johansson's paper, set within the background of a developing capitalist culture in China, looks at editorials and advertisements from two official women's magazines – *Chinese Women* and *Marriage and Family* – in examining the politics of gender and identity. Munshi's paper, set within the background of post-economic liberalisation in India and an increasing urban consumer culture, examines the growth of the 'beauty industry' as investment in appearance makes representation of one's looks and bodies a crucial area for (re)defining femininity.

Discussions on the deeply implicated relations between consumer culture, individualism and modernity, of how particular (Asian) societies become locations of intricate and specific negotiations between the global and the local are found in the accounts of Johansson, Chaplin, Munshi and Liechty. All of them look at how representations of the 'modern' woman as they circulate through local consumer culture are constantly shifting, being reworked and redefined by economic, political and ideological forces. Johansson deals with changing images of the feminine in Chinese magazine women's advertising in post-Mao China. Chaplin surveys Japan from the 1920's to present times. Both investigate how in an initial phase of an emergent mass culture and consumerist tendencies, and exposure to media artefacts from the West, patriarchal value systems were transgressed. In Chinese magazine advertising, this translated into large numbers professionally created ads of Caucasian models in Western clothes, pursuing careers, leisure and entertainment. In Japan, during the inter-war period, the identity of the *modan garu* (modern girl) or *moga* developed - a fully heterogeneous individual who rejected her spatially restricted lifestyle. Associated with the coffee house rather than the genteel tea house, women's suffrage, jazz and fashion, the *moga* became a spatially liberated emblem. In the growing middle class consumer economy of today's Kathmandu, Liechty relates women's experiences and reactions as consumers of commercial pornography as they find themselves lodged in the contradictions of a consumer modernity, grappling with contradictory images of the 'modern' woman. Similarly, in today's urban middle class consumer culture in India, Munshi examines how advertisers are targeting women for makeup and fitness items in what has become a profitable industry; how many of these media discourses are influenced by global media flows; yet how, such global discourses remain contained within discourses which are classified as traditionally Indian.

Foucault (1980) and Elias (1978) have written about the complex relationship between the interplay of bodily practices, disciplinary institutions and discourses of knowledge. Stephanie Donald and Christina Lee as well as

Rachel Harrison focus on representations of the woman's body through the deployment of images of women in film and television documentaries in China and Thailand. Harrison examines the complex and often misguided relationship that the producers of television documentaries and the Thai prostitutes they film have with each other. She argues that western documentaries on Thailand is more often than not on the theme of prostitution; and that this dominant perception of Thailand is both reflected in and stimulates a particular flavour of media coverage of the country, which in turn perpetuates pre-existing views. Both at the global and local level, the degree of public interest and media attention is constructed over the silence of those who work within this industry. The representation of the prostitution industry in Thailand, Harrison argues, is a highly complex one, involving numerous players, each with their own interests. Rather than clarifying matters however, the position of the Thai sex worker tends to be obfuscated by the perspectives which media producers have to offer with their greater power, voice and access to modes of representation; and the voice of the Thai female sex worker – the subject of these media representations – remains silent and disempowered.

Using the lens of cinema, Donald and Lee track the feminine cinematic image of Chinese female stars as they evolved from the films of early modern cinema to 1990s films, and examine the ambiguity of the filmic woman and how women in real life can use this space of ambiguity as a means of 'coming home' to their bodies as a collective though diverse population. They argue that the cinematic image of the 'modern' woman in China is not entirely discrete from older images of Chinese femininity. The tensions between social expectations and the performed female body are visible in examples of cinema before the advent of modernisation through capitalism and the associated international engagement with China. They however push their point further in arguing that the condition of ambiguity continues to be a positive marker in the cinematic treatments of the 'modern' woman. It is not the case that images of women are especially radical. Rather, the performance and corporeally experienced aspects of film can translate into memories carried in the woman's body which produce the knowledge of 'coming home.' But with an important advantage: because while contradictions in their representations can be painful, the ambiguity formed and understood through these contradictions can, as a marker of feminine subjectivity, be a political motivation, refusing assimilation into the mores of society.

Furthermore, Donald and Lee as well as Harrison rely on Castoriadis' (1975) notion of the social imaginary in how the symbolic structure of visual media texts is a creative space of the social, the historical, the sexual and the political in human life. The imaginary may not be an exact reflection of real life, but it is important in how real life is shaped and experienced. For Harrison, the understanding of the Thai woman's position as a whole in this imaginary, is at best obfuscated, and at worst obliterated. For Donald and Lee, while contradictions in women's lives as depicted in filmic representations are painful, the ambiguity formed and understood through these contradictions can translate into a shared and public comprehension of women's contemporary conditions.

Another area which this volume investigates is how gender implications are produced and administered in particular (Asian) locations and at particular socio-historical junctures. To this end, the papers of Reina Lewis and Patricia Uberoi both critique the concept of a Western modernity and Western feminism as providing answers for Asian contexts. The area of enquiry for Uberoi is India. She tracks the narrative structures and characteristics of a set of romantic short stories on courtship and marriage, in conjunction with editorials and non-fictional articles, in the English language women's magazine *Woman's Era* from March 1994 through till October 1995. She examines the manifold and intricate trajectories which these stories follow, and unravels why and how romantic courtship is constituted as problematic in contemporary Indian society, the criteria of a suitable 'match' which the stories construct, and the circumstances that are expected to be the final outcome, i.e., the marriage of the chief protagonists. The emphasis on how the notion of 'falling in love,' whether before or after marriage, needs to be circumscribed into wider familial and kinship structures, is seen by Uberoi as a reaction to the fact that *Woman's Era* perceives Indian family systems and values to be under attack from an alien (Western) value system and irresponsible (Western-inspired) feminist movement. Uberoi concludes by asserting that for the contemporary Indian context, we need to understand relations between larger themes of culture and cultural construction of the ideal life cycle for the woman. The image of the 'modern' woman entails complex and multiple negotiations of larger familial, kinship and societal relationships, and the placement of their own, individual lives within that context.

Examining autobiographies and popular fiction written in English by Ottoman women writers between 1872-1926, Reina Lewis' contribution in this volume examines the historical and multiple ways in which Middle Eastern women engaged with western feminism. Concentrating on three sets of authors writing in English primarily for an Occidental European and north American audience – Halide Adivar Habib, Demetra vaka Brown and the sisters Malek and Zeyneb Hanum - Lewis looks at how these women writers presented their struggle for emancipation in the early twentieth century to western onlookers. Her chapter is an account of how the struggle to create a narrative voice that can speak as an Oriental and as a woman without being subsumed under various stereotypes in operation is in itself part of the political fight for emancipation at home and understanding abroad. She compares memoirs, romance and travel writing, and analyses these cultural forms used by the women writers to differently narrativise the questions of gender, ethnicity and nationality facing 'Oriental' women. Lewis comments on how the image of the Western 'new' woman recurs over and over again in the writings of these authors and the repeated emphasis on how differences between Occidental and Oriental women mean that their liberation must follow separate paths.

The nature of class in Asia and the question of national identity as premised on the image of the 'modern' woman in Asia is another theme of our book. The ways in which national societies now create their own versions of modernity have been written about (see, for instance, Siegel 1986; Ivy 1988; Holston 1989; Miyoshi and Harootunian 1989; Niranjana et al 1993, Breckenridge 1995). The arguments forwarded in this volume show that the image of the 'modern woman' implicitly carries with it not only ideas about 'acceptable' modernity and femininity but also ideas about national identity. On the one hand, she has an important role to play in cultural politics against the 'West'; and her position in society is premised upon ' ... a difference with the perceived forms of cultural modernity in the West' (Chatterjee 1997:117). All the contributions to this volume touch upon the theme of the tensions and contradictions of modernity and the trouble which women experience in their daily lives in coming to terms with it as they engage and negotiate with it at various levels and in various ways. Imagined constructions of women in media cannot lie wholly outside the reality that women experience in their daily lives. Rather, it is a field which is open to constant negotiation and changing interpretations. Media texts on the one hand influence the creation and representation of the 'modern woman.' But at the same time, this productive space is constantly challenged by the way that such texts are appropriated by audiences. Women continue to be over-burdened with workplace and domestic responsibilities as well as gendered social demands. Furthermore, the contributors to this volume all document how for instance in China, Japan, Turkey, Nepal and India, the traditional aspects of life are being recontextualised and how the woman is increasingly caught up within networks of projecting a distinct national identity. They underline how the image of the woman is reconfigured by the state through their control of cultural resources as an 'invention of tradition' (Hobsbawm and Ranger 1983). The more traditional aspects of national life are reterritorialised and recontextualised, and the image of the woman is increasingly caught up within networks of projecting a distinct national identity. One only has to recall Wright's (1985) observation about how tradition is very much a part of contemporary politics, and of the manner in which powerful institutions work in selecting particular values from the past for mobilisation in contemporary practices.

The 'modern woman' appears to show us the female face of 'tomorrow' transposing the female face of 'yesterday.' The 'modern woman' may be articulated or constructed by the codes and conventions of global technology;

but her face is constantly being localised to provide a hybrid female figure. This volume stresses the need to replace emphasis on passive reception of global flows, with an emphasis on active, culturally specific, and contextually variable transformations, 'specific historio-discursive determinations' (Ivy 1993:245-7). This volume looks at how media texts and the politics of consumption is a highly charged and contested terrain across which individuals, social groups and political ideologies struggle for expression through the images and discourse which the media provides. We examine the role that media communications play in women's lives and ' ... demonstrate how these artifacts serve as instruments of domination, but also offer resources for resistance and change (Kellner 1995:28). In a world which is becoming seamless due to transnational media flows, theories of media and identity construction are best developed through specific case studies of concrete phenomena. What all the papers attempt to do throughout is not to examine global and local media flows as such, but the practices through which they are represented. Representational practices are part of cultural and historical contexts which have to be understood. They do not arise from some given cultural repertoire for the interpretation of events, but they are contests for the definition of contemporary reality, and hence for control over cultural resources. What the contributors to this volume invoke in their notion of a feminine identity in different Asian contexts is a dialectical engagement wherein the feminine subject positions herself, or is placed in social reality ' ... within those relations – material, economic and interpersonal – which are in fact social, and in a larger perspective, historical (de Lauretis 1986:159).

Multicultural and multiperspectival studies such as these are necessarily political in their implications. All the contributions have questioned, whether explicitly or implicitly, if the concept of a 'Western modernity' is comparable to an 'Asian' one. As Breckenridge rightly argued (1995:2), 'Modernity is now everywhere, it is simultaneously everywhere, and it is interactively everywhere. But it is not only everywhere, it is also in a series of somewheres ... .' It is through a series of a few 'somewheres' that this volume has examined these questions. We have taken a modified Foucauldian approach in locating the subject of the 'modern woman' in Asia not only as constituted and formed by discourse, but also one which resists, ' ... a subject which is neither transcendental in relation to the field of events or runs in its empty sameness throughout the course of history' (Foucault 1980:117). It appears that ideas of an Asian femininity and a 'modern' woman are perceived, constructed and consumed differently from a 'Western modernity,' and that women are part of particular historically and socially constituted relationships of power and knowledge. I concur with Kumar's lucid analysis that ' ... there can be no escape from challenging Western-based theories, whether colonial or post-, continuously, and looking at actual ... Asian data to interpret what these are saying ... Asia has its own discourses of gender and power (the particular configurations of which have been always historically constructed, in the last two centuries partly by colonialism), and it is the complex notion of *discourse* with its attendant connotations that we apply, not any *particular* conclusions regarding modernity (Kumar 1994:12-13, italics in original).

To return to the beginning, this volume has attempted to present a critical, multicultural and multiperspectival study. We hope that readers try and fashion their own reading practices on these interdisciplinary issues, so that ongoing dialogues may be better maintained. Lastly, what all of us who contributed to this volume wanted and hoped for was what Trinh T. Minh-ha put so eloquently when she said, .'.. there is no space really untouched by the vicissitudes of history, and emancipatory projects never begin or end properly' (1991:8)[2]. We too hold out the same hope that we have provided some disruptions, requestioning and rethinking on issues of women in the media in Asian contexts, and that this project too continues to be an ongoing one, resisting closure and never ending properly.

NOTES

1   I find it useful to cite Laurie Sears' classification of Asia here: 'For those who are not familiar with the somewhat arbitrary ways in which Asia is divided into both economic and academic terms, Southeast Asia includes Burma (Myanmar), Thailand, Cambodia, Laos, Vietnam, Singapore, Malaysia, Indonesia, the Philippines, and Brunei while South Asia usually includes Pakistan, India, Nepal, Bangladesh, Sri Lanka, Bhutan, and, importantly, Tibet. Sometimes Afghanistan and Iran are also included in South Asian Studies programs, but they are more often considered to be part of the Middle East. East Asia usually includes China, Japan, Taiwan, Hong Kong, Korea, and Mongolia' (1996:13, footnote 20). My definition of Asia is broader and I have extended the definition to incorporate Turkey as well.

2   See also Laurie Sears (ed.) 1996, who with her beautifully-crafted project on the feminine in Indonesia hoped to '(disrupt) images of 'Indonesia' and 'women.'

REFERENCES

Alexander, M. Jacqui and Chandra Talpade Mohanty (eds) (1997) *Feminist Genealogies Colonial Legacies, Democratic Futures.* New York and London: Routledge.

13

Amos, V and P. Parmar (1984) Challenging Imperial Feminism, *Feminist Review* 17: Autumn, pp. 3-19.

Ang, Ien (1996*) Living Room Wars: Rethinking Media Audiences for a Postmodern World*. London and New York: Routledge.

Appadurai, Arjun (1996) *Modernity at Large: Cultural Dimensions of Globalization*. Minneapolis: University of Minnesota Press.

--(1990) 'Disjuncture and Difference in the Global Cultural Economy,' in: Mike Featherstone (ed.) *Global Culture: Nationalism, Globalization and Modernity*. London: Sage, pp. 295-310.

Barrett, Michèle and M. McIntosh (1985) 'Ethnocentrism and Socialist Feminist Theory,' *Feminist Review*, 20: June, pp. 23-47.

Breckenridge, Carol A. (ed.) (1995) *Consuming Modernity: Public Culture in a South Asian World*. Minneapolis: University of Minnesota Press.

Brosius, Christiane and Melissa Butcher (eds) (1999) *Image Journeys: Audio-visual Media and Cultural Change in India*. New Delhi: Sage.

Castoriadis, Cornelius (1975) *L'institution imaginaire et la société*. Paris: Seuil.

Chatterjee, Partha (1997*) The Nation and its Fragments: Colonial and Postcolonial Histories*. Delhi: Oxford University Press.

Chow, Rey (1993) '"It's You and Not Me": Domination and "Othering", in: Theorizing the Third World,' reprinted in Linda S Kauffmann (ed.*) American Feminist Thought at Century's End: A Reader*. Cambridge, MA: Blackwell.

Donaldson, L. (1992) *Decolonizing Feminisms: Race, Gender and Empire-Building*. Chapel Hill: University of North Carolina Press.

Eisenstadt, Shmuel (1996) *Japanese Civilization: A Comparative View*. Chicago: University of Chicago Press.

Elias, Norbert (1978) *The Civilizing Process*, trans. Edmund Jephcott, Oxford: Basil Blackwell.

Foucault, Michel (1980) *Power/Knowledge*. New York: Pantheon.

Frankenberg, Ruth and Lata Mani (1993) Crosscurrents, Crosstalk: Race, 'Postcoloniality' and the Politics of Location,' *Cultural Studies* 7: Spring, pp. 292-310.

Friedman, J. (1990) 'Being in the World: Globalization and Localization,' in Mike Featherstone (ed.*) Global Culture: Nationalism, Globalization and Modernity*. London: Sage.

Ghosh, Bishnupriya and Brinda Bose (eds) (1997) *Interventions: Feminist Dialogues on Third World Women's Literature and Film*. New York and London: Garland Publishing.

De Grazia, Victoria (1996*) The Sex of Things: Gender and Consumption in Historical Perspective*. Berkeley: University of California Press.

Grewal, Inderpal and Caren Kaplan (eds) (1994) *Scattered Hegemonies: Postmodernity and Transnational Feminist Practices.* Minneapolis: University of Minnesota Press.

Hall, Stuart (1991) 'The Local and the Global: Globalization and Ethnicity,' in: A. King (ed.) *Culture, Globalization and the World System.* London: Macmillan, pp. 19-40.

Hobsbawm, Eric and Terence Ranger (eds) (1983) *The Invention of Tradition.* Cambridge: Cambridge University Press.

Holston, James (1989) *The Modernist City: An Anthropological Critique of Brasilia.* Chicago: University of Chicago Press.

Ivy, Marilyn (1988) 'Tradition and Difference in the Japanese Mass Media,' *Public Culture* 1(1), pp. 21-9.

Kellner, Douglas (1995) *Media Culture: Cultural Studies, Identity and Politics between the Modern and the Postmodern.* London and New York: Routledge.

King, A. (ed.) (1991) *Culture, Globalisation and the World System.* London: Macmillan.

Kishwar, Madhu and R. Vanita (eds) (1984) *In Search of Answers: Indian Women's Voices from 'Manushi.'* London: Zed Books.

Kumar, Nita (ed.) (1994) *Women as Subjects: South Asian Histories.* New Delhi: Stree.

De Lauretis, Theresa (ed.) (1986) *Feminist Studies, Critical Studies.* Bloomington: Indiana University Press.

Levitt, Theodore (1983) *The Marketing Imagination.* London: Collier-Macmillan.

Lull, James (1995) *Media, Communication, Culture: A Global Approach.* Cambridge: Polity.

Marcus, G.E. and M.M.J. Fisher (1986) *Anthropology as Cultural Critique.* Chicago: Chicago University Press.

Martín-Barbero, J. (1993) *Communication, Culture and Hegemony.* trans. E. Fox and R. A. White, London: Sage.

Miyoshi, Masao and Harry D. Harootunian (eds) (1989) *Postmodernism and Japan.* Durham, North Carolina: Duke University Press.

Mohanty, Chandra Talpade (1987) 'Feminist Encounters: locating the Politics of Experience,' *Copyright* 1: Fall, pp. 30-44.

Morley, David (1992) *Television, Audiences and Cultural Studies.* London: Routledge.

Morley, David and Kevin Robins (1995) *Spaces of Identity: Global Media, Electronic Landscapes and Cultural Boundaries.* London: Routledge.

Niranjana, Tejeswini, Vivek Dhareshwar and P. Sudhir (eds) 1993) *Interrogating Modernity: Culture and Colonialism in India.* Calcutta: Seagull.

Robertson, Roland (1990) 'Mapping the Global Condition: Globalization as the Central Concept,' in: Mike Featherstone (ed.) *Global Culture: Nationalism, Globalization and Modernity*. London: Sage.

Schiller, H. (1991) 'Not Yet the Post-imperialist Era,' *Critical Studies in Mass Communication* 8, pp. 13-28.

Sears, Laurie J. (ed.) (1996) *Fantasizing the Feminine in Indonesia*. Durham, NC and London: Duke University Press.

Sen, Krishna and Maila Stivens (eds) (1998) *Gender and Power in Affluent Asia*. London and New York: Routledge.

Siegel, James T. (1986*) Solo in the New Order: Language and Hierarchy in an Indonesian City*. Princeton, NJ: Princeton University Press.

Smith, A (1991) *National Identity*, Harmondsworth: Penguin.

Spivak, Gayatri Chakravarty (1987) *In Other Worlds: Essays in Cultural Politics*. New York: Methuen.

Stivens, Maila (1994) 'Gender and Modernity in Malaysia,' in: A Gomes (ed*) Modernity and Identity: Illustrations from Asia*. Bundoora, Melbourne: La Trobe Asian Studies, LA Trobe University Press, pp. 69-95.

Trinh T., Minh-ha (1991) *When the Moon Waxes Red*. New York: Routledge.

Van der Veer, Peter (1998) 'The Global History of 'Modernity,' *Journal of the Economic and Social History of the Orient* (JESHO), 41(3), pp. 285-94.

Van Zoonen, Liesbet (1994) *Feminist Media Studies*, London: Sage.

Wright, P (1985) *On Living in an Old Country*. London: Verso.

Zurndorfer, Harriet T (1998) ed *Journal of the Economic and Social History of the Orient* (JESHO), 41(3).

CHAPTER 2

CHANGING SPACES OF GLOBAL MEDIA

KEVIN ROBINS

FROM IMAGINED COMMUNITY TO GLOBAL MEDIA

In this chapter, I am concerned with cultural developments associated with 'globalisation' and 'transnationalism.' The focus of my discussion will be on the media industries - and particularly the audiovisual sector - and the significant transformations that they have been undergoing over the past decade or so. The objective is not so much to elaborate a theoretical framework, but rather to try to explore some of the political and policy issues relating to 'post-national' media and the emergence of transnational media spaces and audiences. In trying to address these issues, I want, as much as I can, to open up some of the potential that may be inherent in developments going on at the present time in the media industries. At the same time, however, I shall also be concerned with some of the difficulties in the way of change, because I don't by any means want to suggest that transformations in media industries and cultures are automatically going to lead to new kinds of transnational spaces. It is a question, then, of balancing a sense of possibilities against a recognition of some of the real dilemmas to be confronted in the globalisation process.

Let me begin with a brief historical perspective, and say something about broadcasting up until now, or, more accurately, up until the mid-1980s. In media studies, a great deal of research has pointed to the paramount significance of radio and television to the imagination of national societies or communities within Europe - and I think that is a very important starting point for any discussion of new media spaces. This research, of course, picks up on an agenda that that was initially elaborated in the influential work of Benedict Anderson (1983), who considered the implication of earlier generations of media - the print and publishing media - in the promotion of vernacular languages and the creation of national consciousnesses. Following the important insights of Anderson, media researchers sought to demonstrate how, through the twentieth century, the institution of broadcasting - in the classic form of 'public service' broadcasting - has been crucially implicated in the production and reproduction of the national imaginary. It is a question of how television, for example, has made visible to each other people who believe that they are part of the same (national community), but who would otherwise not have been aware of each other. And the key point is that broadcasting does not simply reflect the nation - it isn't as if there is a pre-given national community which television simply reflects - but, rather, that it has been central in actually producing that community, in *instituting* the imagined community of the nation.

The national significance of broadcasting has been apparent from the very early days. And in the decades since its emergence, audiences comfortably came to believe that broadcasting was somehow 'in its nature' a national medium, a national institution - they came to accept the hegemony of the national broadcasting culture. For a great period of time through this century, we have tended, I think, to be unaware of its constructedness and hence, in a certain sense, its arbitrariness. And, by the same token, we generally failed to take account of how much the national system of broadcasting has also, since its origination, been a contested system - of how, right from the early days of broadcasting, there have been significant challenges to the national paradigm.

First, we must note, national media regimes had to resist the challenges to the national hegemony that came from within. For there have been possibilities, and frequently demands, for broadcasting to function as a medium that is responsive to the internal diversity of the nation - responsive to its ethnic, gender and territorial complexities. So, the national system was forged at the expense of recognising the claims of ethnic groups, of women, and also of particular regional and local cultures. The internal complexities within the national territories, along with the various frictions and disagreements between different parts of the country, have generally been suppressed, in favour of a broadcasting policy and strategy that emphasised the cultural elements that were held in common across the national space. The subordinated elements have then generally been designated as 'minority' interests within the national formation, and catered for on that basis.

It is also important to recognise that radio and television signals have never had any respect for national frontiers - indeed they have a natural tendency to confound the ordered arrangements of state boundaries. So, the history of broadcasting has also been the history of the development and implementation of legal and regulatory mechanisms that would work to inhibit the transnational possibilities inherent in the medium. Broadcasting had to be forcibly nationalised: signals from outside were always regarded as invasive and treated as potential threats to the 'integrity' of national cultural life. Nation states defended the principle of what may be regarded as audiovisual sovereignty for the national culture.

So my introductory point is simply to emphasise that broadcasting came into existence as an imaginary institution articulating a national culture and serving as the communications medium for a national public space. Media cultures have been historically grounded in the national imaginary and have supported the project of binding together national communities. They have been implicated in the vision of nation as family. And, of course, particular cultural values are implied in this familial imagery. The overriding objective was to promote national coherence and cohesion - Prasenjit Duara (1996:164) refers to it as 'the social process of community closure,' a process, that is to say, in which the complexities of culture, gender, class and place have always been subordinated to the national cause.

What has of course become ever more clear since the mid-1980s is that the national model for broadcasting has been increasingly undermined - first, as a consequence of new technological innovations, (the development of satellite systems and of network technologies - the Internet and the Information Superhighway); second, in the face of a whole array of economic developments, involving the unleashing of competition within the broadcasting, media and telecommunications industries; and, third, as a result of the regulatory transformations that occurred when national governments began to come to terms with what they saw as the inevitability of transnational commercial broadcasting. Over the past ten to fifteen years, then, we have seen a real challenge to the hegemony of national media and communications regimes across the world, in the context of a gathering corporate push to build transnational markets and audiences - a push which national governments have been unable to significantly resist.

What, we must now ask, have been the consequences of this global corporate push? What are the implications of the ongoing processes of transnationalisation and globalisation in the media industries? In what ways might they impinge on questions of cultural rights and political/democratic organisation? (on this, see Robins 1997). In the following discussion, I shall identify different possible scenarios for transnational media spaces - possible scenarios because we should regard the trajectory of globalisation as contestable, and therefore open and variable. In certain cases, I shall suggest, global projections do not in fact offer a significant alternative. What I shall argue is that these agendas for a new transnational media order - these logics of globalisation - do not offer a meaningful way forward. And the reason that they do not, I believe, is because they do not succeed in breaking with the national imaginary. They remain committed to the institution of imagined community, and to its logic of community closure. Then, as the argument develops, I shall try to explore some developments that do, in my opinion, open up certain possibilities for a more meaningful transnational media order. Here I shall be concerned, particularly with what have been called 'diasporic media,' the emergence of diasporic spaces, and how this deals with questions of women's identities to raise just one possibility of research. These represent an interesting new development, in my view, complicating the global media map in ways that could be culturally productive.

THE CORPORATE IDEOLOGY OF GLOBALISATION

The prevailing scenario for a future media order may be described as the corporate ideology of globalisation. Large media conglomerates - like Time Warner, News Corporation, Sony, Disney, and so on - have become the champions of this agenda for global cultural empire. Driven by the pure logic of profit and competition, the strategy of these corporate giants is clearly to try to get their products to the largest number of consumers that is possible. The overriding imperative is to break down what are now perceived and presented as the arbitrary boundaries and frontiers of national communities - national borders have come to seem to impose arbitrary limitations on the expansion of markets, and are regarded as anachronistic and unreasonable obstacles to the corporate imperative of rationalising business practices and strategies. Since the 1980s, then, we have consequently seen a corporate offensive intended to undermine the authority of the national and public service model of broadcasting. Under the slogans of the 'free flow of information' and 'television without frontiers,' freewheeling media businesses have claimed the right to market their audiovisual products and services across borders, wherever they can find welcoming and paying cultural consumers. The aim is to dissolve the old order of national boundaries and particularities in the cause of the new universalism of a global consumer culture.

What we have, then, in this new corporate agenda is a particular model of transnationalisation and globalisation, and one that we should take seriously. We need to consider it carefully because, however problematical it might be, it has a powerful resonance, and because it threatens to impose itself as the hegemonic vision of cultural globalisation. Consider the clarion call made, at the beginning of the 1990s, by the late Steve Ross, who was then head of Time Warner. In his so-called 'World Address' to the Edinburgh Television Festival in 1990, Ross argued forcefully on behalf of the benevolent and progressive potential of post-national media systems. 'The new reality of international media is,' said Ross, 'driven more by market opportunity than by national identity.' And the culture of the market - imagined in terms of market harmony - can work to dissolve the conflictual legacy of national cultures. 'The competitive market place of ideas and experience,' Ross continues, 'can only bring the world together. With new technologies, we can bring services and ideas that will help draw even the most remote areas of the world into the international media community... It is up to us, the producers and distributors of ideas, to facilitate this movement, and to participate in it with an acute awareness of our responsibility as citizens of one world.' So, the market institutes a common agenda and a common set of values - it becomes the means to counter the divisiveness of national cultures and to bring us all together in 'one world.' On the basis of what he calls 'consumers' tastes and desires,' then, Ross envisages a new global order characterised by the 'interconnection of cultures' - the new universalism and ecumenicism of a global consumer culture.

This is an agenda that has developed and gathered pace in the ten years since Ross's keynote address, extending from broadcasting to new media. Thus, the idea of a global or transnational community - the idea of 'one world' culture - has come to be taken up in many of the debates around the Internet and the project for a global network society. So, Bill Gates (1995) believes the transnational information superhighway will 'make all communication easier,' and he tells us of how 'bulletin boards and other on-line forums allow people to be in touch, one-to-one, or one-to-many, or many-to-many, in very efficient ways.' I don't know what 'efficient ways' means, but here again there is the conviction that global commercial media can provide a common focus for the people of the world to come together in a transnational electronic community. Or, as Al Gore (1994) puts it, in relation to the US information superhighway project, the new networks make possible 'a kind of global conversation in which everyone who wants can have his or her say.' In the idea of a global conversation, we have the sense of a community of interest, a global community of shared values and common objectives.

This vision that is being projected by Steve Ross, in relation to broadcasting, and, more recently, by Bill Gates and Al Gore, for the future of the information Superhighway, is about creating what seems to be a post-national universalism, a new market-driven cosmopolitanism, if you like, across the planet. We must all surely be sceptical about this corporate 'vision.' And there are good reasons, it seems to me, for being sceptical. For this ideal of globalisation, which claims to be instituting something new and even revolutionary, actually turns out to be a rather banal project in the end - promoting what is, in fact, a very familiar and conservative political agenda. But rather than simply denouncing the corporate hype, I think it is worth considering what precisely this familiar and conservative message is - worth considering in order to establish precisely wherein the undoubted appeal of the corporate ideology of globalisation might reside.

Here I want to draw attention to three ideological themes that run through this kind of discourse - with respect to both the audiovisual media and the new technologies of the Internet and Information Superhighway. The first theme concerns the idea of a community. It is there in the idea that the new transnationalism is about building something that can be called an 'international media community'; a future community where all of us could have our say in a single global conversation. I think that it is highly significant that transnational developments are being imagined now in terms of community. And what I want to suggest is that what we are being offered is really no more than a perpetuation and extension of the national imaginary. What is perpetuated is we the homogenising way of thinking about culture and identity that has been proper to national communities - but simply scaled up. As if its not possible to think about transnationalism other than in terms of a bigger version of a national imaginary, with all of its emphasis on shared values, its common culture, its common objectives.

The second theme picks up on the very old and familiar idea - or ideal - of communication. The idea is that the new media technology will facilitate and promote communication among those who live in the international media community. And, furthermore, that the promotion of what Gates believes is more 'efficient' communication will be associated with greater social consensus at the international level. What we have here, then, perfectly complementing the ideology of community, is what might be called the ideology of communication. It is an ideology that goes back way into the nineteenth century, and, it has been mobilised every time that a new communications or media technology has been developed. In the twentieth century, we may say that it has almost come to rival the ideology of progress itself. Who could possibly object to (more efficient) communication? In this ideological frame, communication is linked to increased intelligibility; intelligibility is linked to mutual comprehension; and greater comprehension is then further linked to some kind of international mutual solidarity and agreement. It is precisely on the basis of (more efficient) communication, it is suggested, that it will be possible to sustain the sense of community on an international scale.

The third of the themes running through the whole global media agenda is closely related to these two. It has to do with the imagined potential of new media technologies for overcoming what is regarded as the problem distance. What is at issue is the technological transcendence of distance- on the basis, it seems, that it is distance that prevents cultures from successfully communicating with each other - distance that 'keeps us apart' - and distance also, therefore, that stands in the way of transnational imagined community. The new technologies, it is assumed, both audiovisual media and new network technologies, will bring people closer together, at a global scale. They will help to finally create what Marshall McLuhan thought of as the 'global village.' Through these new technologies, it becomes possible to overcome the barriers of distance and for people across the world to communicate directly with one another, just as they would in a face-to-face community. And, with this, we are back to the agenda of community - the corporate ideology of mediated global community.

This is one vision, then, of a new media order. It is a vision that we should take seriously, however much we find it problematical (as I clearly do). For it can have a certain popular resonance, with its idealistic anticipation of a one-world future (what is effectively a global consumer order). And it is able to mobilise established discourses of electronic utopia, suggesting that the electronic media will allow us to create some kind of new communicative order. But it does all this - all this futuristic rhetorical work, we might say, - whilst at the same time sustaining the comforting and conservative discourse of imagined community, albeit on the basis of a new global geography. In this scenario, which privileges the identity of the global consumer, the principles of community closure remain operative. The global community is a unitary community, and - as with all such communitarian visions - it seeks to ensure that the differences associated with ethnicity, gender, culture, religion or class are fundamentally neutralised. The corporate vision of (media) globalisation is fundamentally a difference-blind vision.

GLOBAL MEDIA AND LOCAL CULTURE

Now I come to a second discourse on global media. It is one that corresponds better to the reality of contemporary developments, and one in which certain possibilities may be opened up - though not, I suggest, in any really radical way. This perspective recognises that the dynamics of global change are in fact more complex the ideological vision of Steve Ross or Bill Gates would have us believe. It is more in touch with the realities of what we might call actual globalisation, and sensitive, particularly, to those aspects of contemporary society that might resist and obstruct and make difficult the market expansion of organisations like CNN, News Corporation, Time Warner or MTV. For it is clearly the case that there are certain factors of complexity and inertia in the real world that make corporate marketing strategies and scenarios for simply expanding markets extremely difficult on a day-to-day basis. The world of actual cultures does not readily, or sometimes willingly, comply with the corporate blueprints for media globalisation.

In thinking about actual globalisation, we have to acknowledge the continuing force of geocultural and geopolitical borders. Thus, we have to recognise that many (national) cultures throughout the world are reacting extremely defensively with respect to transborder broadcasting. Iran is perhaps the most obvious example of active resistance, with its strategy of self-reliance in relation to broadcasting (Mowlana 1997). But there are other countries - and Asian ones provide particularly good case studies (for example, Malaysia, Singapore, China) - that, rather than resisting outright, are seeking to negotiate the new global order in such a way as to achieve some kind of 'domestication' of transnational satellite broadcasting (Richstad 1998; Chua 1997). We have been made particularly aware recently of these difficulties through the problems that Rupert Murdoch has been having with the intransigent Chinese Government.

But, if principled opposition and the politics of domestication represent one kind of challenge to aspiring global media operators, there are a great many other factors that work to resist and inhibit the pure drive for global-scale markets. These are the factors of cultural diversity and difference in the world - factors that may severely complicate global marketing strategies. Here I am signalling the everyday realities of religious difference, ethnic and cultural identity issues: problems, particularly, of language; problems of historically evolved tastes and preferences; problems of cultural sensibility and sensitivity. These are also factors that inhibit global marketing strategies. And, in the last few years, media organisations have come - have had to come - to recognise their significance. A whole new kind of corporate discourse has consequently begun to emerge, concerned with the relation between the global and the local - between global media, with their universalising aspirations, and local cultures, with their particular histories and identities. Corporate strategists have had to look for some kind of adjustment and accommodation between their attempts to achieve economies of scale, on the one hand, and the need to recognise certain cultural borderlines and frontiers, on the other. Thus, a self-styled global organisation such as CNN is having to recognise that, particularly as it seeks to a broader audience base, it becomes necessary to take account of cultural differences - the trick being to recognise which can be modified and which are, for the moment at least, non-negotiable. Similarly, Rupert Murdoch's strategies in Asia, with STAR Television, are having to come to terms with regional and linguistic differences. And MTV has had to adjust and target its music programmes for Asian, European, Latino, and other specific markets.

And what we should also note here, as yet another factor of resistance to global strategies, is the continuing importance, and perhaps still even the centrality, of national broadcasting systems and spaces. National (broadcasting) cultures still exert a very powerful attraction within the changing media order. Indeed, in particular contexts, it may even be gaining a certain momentum. In certain parts of the world, there have been mobilisations for regional and small-national television services. What these represent is actually a re-vitalisation of the imagined community model. And, again, we may say that these efforts to sustain local cultures also work as a (partial, at least) counterforce to the corporate strategies that have been geared up to build geographically expansive markets. We might say that if some kind of new media order is being brought into existence, it is also the case that the old order is not disappearing. The national organisation of broadcasting remains highly significant, and the new order is having to construct itself through a process of negotiation with that older order.

When we consider the realities of new broadcasting developments, then, we have to say that there are factors that considerably inhibit the logic of corporate globalisation. It becomes very clear that the vision of creating global programming and global markets has been rather overstated. The global marketing ideologues face real complications, and they are having to negotiate the real complexities of cultures across the world. We might note the observations of Theodore Levitt, who was one of the big advocates of global advertising in the 1980s, in a book called *The Marketing Imagination* (1983). Levitt was very much concerned with achieving scale economies at the global level. But he also (reluctantly) acknowledged the reality principle whereby corporate strategists should adjust to the dynamics of the actual cultural order - 'the respectful accommodation,' as he puts it, 'of multinational corporations to what they believe are fixed local preferences.' According to Levitt, there are cultural dynamics - what he calls 'vestiges of the hardened inherited past' - that simply cannot be done away with. There are established cultural contours that the global advertiser or broadcaster has to build around.

So, in this global/local scenario for media transnationalism, what is recognised is that there are significant obstacles in the way of the pure ideology of globalisation. What it makes clear is that cultural diversity and difference will not be eroded - that there will have to be some kind of negotiation and accommodation between global media and local cultures. There is, then, a much greater pragmatism in this perspective. And we must surely feel that it offers more interesting, and more realistic, possibilities for a new (global) media order. In its most positive variant, it has put a strong emphasis on 'local' cultural complexity. In the case of India, for example, attention has been brought to the cultural, ethnic, class/caste and linguistic complexity of this vast 'imagined community.' Commentaries on Indian media policy and programming on the multiple channels now available have focused attention on the complexity of the Indian cultural space (Thussu

1998; Brosius and Butcher 1999) - which is a space that is no longer confined to the sub-continent (Jain 1998). Broadcasters, like Rupert Murdoch, who had plans to create a pan-Indian English-language channel, have had to come to terms with the new mediatic flourishing of regional languages.

But, at the same time, let us also note that, if the global/local scenario opens up certain possibilities through its recognition of cultural particularities, it often turns out to be no more radical in the possibilities that it offers than the first scenario. For it is an agenda that is still generally predicated on the idea of imagined community. In part, it is concerned with the transnational or global community, and in part it comes to terms with 'vestigial' communities, acknowledging the continuing significance of nationally and regionally organised cultures, but also ethnic or religious communities. In the case of this second scenario - with its 'global-local' slogan - the agenda is still about broadcasting for imagined communities - which are now recognised as existing on a more geographically complex basis. There is still a logic of community closure at work. And we should note that certain types of diversity may prevail, whilst others are disavowed. Thus Leela Rao (1999:10-11) observes that, whilst 'regional language programmes appear to have expanded the television universe and caused a migration of audiences from national to regional realm' - which may be interpreted as from one kind of imagined community to another - Indian audiences for the new television channels must still wait for broadcasters to 'articulate and present a woman in all the hues of diversity this country lays claim to.'

A NEW POSSIBILITY SPACE IN TRANSNATIONAL MEDIA?

I now want to go on to consider a particular development within the process of media globalisation - we might regard it as one particular variant of the global/local dynamic. And in this development, I want to suggest, there may also be certain cultural possibilities - possibilities that are to do with moving beyond the confines of imagined community and the processes of community closure. What I am offering is certainly not a blueprint for a new order - that is not what interests me. It is a consideration, rather, of certain developments in the process of media transnationalisation that I think have not been acknowledged in terms of their potential to open up alternative agendas for (more multicultural) broadcasting futures.

Where are there possibilities in the globalisation process, I want to ask, possibilities for elaborating more complex, and interesting, new cultural spaces? I start from what I see as a certain disorderliness in the way that transnational media are developing across the world. I use the term 'disorderly' very deliberately, drawing on the kind of associations that Richard Sennett (1970) evokes in various writings about the city and urban culture, where he is concerned with 'the uses of disorder.' What I want to suggest, without being too idealistic, is that there are certain developments occurring in transnational broadcasting now - often as a consequence of commercial developments - which are not associated with a new media order, but rather with a new disorder - which may actually be a productive disorder. Transnational developments, particularly through new market dynamics, are throwing up all sorts of changes, I suggest, which political debates on the future of broadcasting need to take into account. The possibilities are to do with moving beyond the national framework and the discourses of imagined community. They are to do with the institution of what could be an interestingly new global media map, with new kinds of possibility spaces. As Sinclair, Jacka and Cunningham put it in their book *New Patterns in Global Television*, 'global, regional, national and even local circuits of programme now overlap and interact in a multi-faceted way, no doubt with a great variety of cultural effects, which are impossible to conceptualise within the more concentric perspective appropriate to the previous decades.' (1996:5). This complexity is something we should hold on to.

The global development I am concerned with here is generally referred to in terms of the emergence of new 'diasporic' media and media spaces (Karim 1998; *Javnost/the Public* 1999), and it provides a particularly intense version of the global-local encounter. Over the last decade or so, we have seen the establishment of a whole array of new television channels, distributed through satellite links, and targeting particular ethnic, national or religious groups around the world. There is Zee TV, for example, an Indian broadcaster targeting Indian viewers in various parts of the world (Europe, North America, Africa, West Asia). MBC is a London-based company that broadcasts to transnational Arab audiences. Medya TV (formerly MED TV) is a (now) Paris-based organisation which is broadcasting to Kurdish communities across Europe and the Middle East. This development of diasporic communication is, in my view, an important development. These new forms of 'diasporic communication' seem, to me at least, to open up all kinds of interesting possibilities for multicultural broadcasting arrangements, of a kind that could not be envisaged under the broadcasting regimes of imagined community (see Lavie and Swedenburg 1996). Within this, the development of 'new femininities' is a contested process. Questions of gender, sexuality, domesticity, family, social structures are central sites for the cultural expression and reformulations of ideas of the 'modern.' The participation of women in the struggles around these issues - as producers,

27

consumers, objects and critics of these representations (cf. Sen and Stivens 1998:24) becomes an important object of study.

Let me illustrate what I mean with reference to one particular example, the one I know best, that of transnational television from Turkey, aimed at Turkish populations living outside the country. It is now possible for Turkish populations in Europe, in Australia - and soon in North America - to watch Turkish channels. And there is a proliferation of Turkish channels reaching out to the 'Turks abroad' (more than twenty at the present time). These include the state television service, TRT, with its more 'official' programming, as well as a great variety of commercial operators (Show TV, Interstar, ATV, KanalD, and religious stations, such as Kanal 7. This development of Turkish transnational television has been in part ideological, with both the Turkish State and a number of religious organisations keen to reach Turkish communities. But it also has strong commercial dynamics, too, with Turkish media organisations conscious of the possibilities of adding these widely dispersed diasporic populations to their existing market base.

Quite how the transnationalisation process will work out in the longer run - how the ideological and commercial dynamics will adjust to each other - remains far from certain. But we are, I think, in a position to identify certain interesting possibilities - ones that are precisely to do with productive disorder - and to suggest a certain cultural potential. First, there is the existence now of a new Turkish audiovisual space across the globe, making it possible for Turks 'in diaspora' to be involved in Turkish cultural life on a day-to-day basis. Turkish populations in different parts of the world are now able to connect back to their 'homeland,' but also they have the possibility of connecting horizontally, as it were, with other parts of the diaspora. The new Turkish cultural space takes Turkey as a key reference point, of course, and so there are possibilities for it to be just a geographical extension of the Turkish imagined community. But there are also possibilities for it to become de-linked, and for the meanings of Turkishness to be opened up through a new kind of cultural mobility.

The development of this new cultural space also has significant cultural and political implications for the parts of the world in which the 'Turks abroad' are living. Previously - to take the example of Germany, where the biggest Turkish population exists - it was the remit of the national broadcasters to provide programming to the minority Turkish audience. This raised a whole set of issues to do with finances, resources, and cultural policies towards 'minority' populations. Now suddenly this past framework has become almost completely redundant, because Turkish audiences don't want 'minority' German programming now that they can switch on their televisions and watch 'real Turkish television,' straight from Ankara or

Istanbul. Suddenly, then, there has been a shift from a situation in which the national broadcasters of the host culture were struggling for the resources to provide 'minority' services, to one where the Turkish broadcasters can add this new audience to their existing one, and create new advertising markets as well. This has profound implications for the cultural relationship between Germans and Turks. The logic of German community closure - involving the cultural and political management of the 'minority' Turks - has been severely disrupted. The national cultural order has been disordered.

Through this process of transnationalisation of Turkish culture, then, there are some quite interesting and significant transformations in cultural life identity. For the Turkish migrant viewers, there is now a new cultural fluidity, whereby they can be mentally and imaginatively switching their perspective between (at least) two places. There is a shift in the way in which these migrant groups relate to cultural time as well. Ten years ago, migrant communities would remember the 'homeland' that they had come from and left behind, either as refugees or as economic migrants. If they had been abroad for ten years, they had a frozen, monochrome image of the Turkey that they had left behind, and of all the cultural and political agendas that were current at that time. Now, with the advent of satellite broadcasting, they are suddenly in a new situation, one in which they are synchronised with day-to-day politics back in Turkey. Now, Turkish migrants are using television to think between and across spaces of the world (Aksoy and Robins 2000).

Moving between cultural spaces, they are sensitised to cultural difference. One might consider how they have become more alert to ethnic or religious differences, for example. Or one might think about how women's identities have become a newly salient issue. One of the issues that confronts transnational Turkish audiences is precisely is precisely what Leela Rao calls the hues of diversity in women's identities. For the proliferation of commercial channels from Turkey has brought a greater variety of women's images and voices to the screen. In the old broadcasting order, the predominant representation was of the modern, Kemalist woman, the ideal image of the 'modern,' 'civilised' woman. With commercial and religious television, however, it became possible for the first time to see other kinds of women, and particularly women with headscarves. And through this confrontation of images, audiences have been invited to reflect on women s roles and identities (Saktanber 1994; Göle 1998). They see 'traditional' women, but also 'modern' women of different kinds (both secular and Muslim). Women (and men) living in the Turkish diaspora then have an even more complex agenda, as they seek to connect changing representations of women on Turkish television with their experience of gendered identities in the places in which they live. Women's identities are particularly salient in the transnational Turkish experience of global change.

Of course, there are bound to be all kinds of problems in these developments, and we shouldn't disregard these problems. But what I want to argue that there is also something positive in what is going on here. I would see it in terms of a kind of confounding of the old order, of the old nationally structured order of broadcasting. It is part of a much bigger process, in which new cultural flows are complicating and confusing old cultural sovereignties. A process in which new cultural spaces being mapped out, across old national structures (that do not actually disappear), creating new kinds of cultural juxtapositions and encounters. I think these developments can be productive in so far as they make us think about questions of cultural co-existence and encounter - in relation to gender, ethnicity, class - in the new transnational spaces that are being created. But the point is that for them to be productive, we have to think beyond imagined communities, and towards the elaboration of more complex cultural ensembles appropriate to the times we are living through. We have to think against the grain of community closure.

TRANSNATIONAL MEDIA: BEYOND IMAGINED COMMUNITIES?

What I have been inferring, in a theme that has run right through this discussion, is that we have to think about the cultural forces and factors that might inhibit change. What is particularly at issue here is the question of community, and particularly imagined community, the appeal and force of which I have been regarding as a very fundamental obstacle to any transformation of audiovisual cultures. My point is that imagined community implicates us in a particular way of relating to cultural identity. The imagined community - or what better refer to as the group illusion - has insisted on a particular way of thinking and inhabiting the cultural order. Above all, the imagined community presents itself as a singular, unitary and coherent entity - community closure is what the imagined community of the nation has stood for. What it has emphasised are the elements that people within the community hold in common, at the expense of recognising their internal diversity - the differences within. The ideologues of imagined community have always argued that the attributes that are held in common are the primary elements - the bonding elements - in the cultural life of that kind of group. The imagined community therefore works towards maintaining the continuity and (relative) stability of those attributes. It works towards sustaining and reinforcing the significance of the shared culture over time. And it also emphasises the demarcation of that culture from other cultures, which also exist - and have the right to exist - as other imagined communities - the imagined community exists as part of a world system of sovereign communities.

That is how the imagined community of the nation has worked. It has existed as a particular kind of cultural order, in terms of a particular way about thinking about identity, belonging, attachment. What I am arguing is that this kind of thinking - with its rather closed and defensive objectives - is a highly problematical way of thinking about identities in times that are throwing up new kinds of cultural complexity. And what I want to emphasise, in a context that is said to be all about (global) cultural change and upheaval, is that this kind of thinking about identity and belonging is being sustained and preserved, beyond the frame of the national community. It seems as if there are considerable difficulties in the way of thinking about identity in terms other than those underwritten by this paradigm of the imagined community. So, for example, what are often thought of as new expressions of localism simply reproduce this mentality of imagined community at a more fragmented level (and, of course, there may well be less space for accommodating ethnic, cultural or religious differences as communities become scaled down). And at higher levels, too - in terms of global regions, such as East Asia or South Asia; or in terms of the space of the globe as a whole, as in Steve Ross's world market scenario - there is the same tendency to think through the mental template of imagined community. In all the contemporary scenarios for global cultural change, we seem to find the same recourse to the discourses of imagined community - the same inability to think about change alternatively, through more complex discourses.

In all of these scenarios, the ideal is to have, at whatever geographical scale, some kind of unified collective, with shared values and shared objectives. And what I am arguing is that this way of thinking about culture and identity is now deeply problematical, in times that are throwing up much more complex forms of cultural experience - times that require much more open and inventive ways of responding to change. My concern is with how - and whether - it might be possible to move beyond the ideal of community, and beyond its problematical illusion of cultural self-containment and self-sufficiency. It is a question of moving beyond community closure to a recognition of cultural complexity, -involving the awareness of differences based on gender, class, ethnicity, and so on and an engagement with what Nira Yuval-Davis (1997:131) calls 'transversal politics' in which 'perceived unity and homogeneity are replaced by dialogues which give recognition to the specific positionings of those who participate in the as well as to the "unfinished knowledge" that each situated positioning can offer.' What I have been suggesting is that the globalisation

31

of the media industries is now producing a new cultural disorder, and that we should be trying to work with this disordering logic, working to render it culturally productive. For the challenge is for us to come up with richer possibilities than those of the mainstream global media operators - richer visions of what a genuinely transnational or global media order could be. In looking at so-called 'diasporic media,' and the question of women's identities therein, I have tried to hint at some of the possibilities that may be inherent in the processes of media transnationalism - if we have the capacity to recognise their significance.

REFERENCES

Aksoy, Asu and Kevin Robins (2000) 'Thinking across spaces: transnational television from Turkey,' *European Journal of Cultural Studies* 3 (forthcoming).

Anderson, Benedict (1983) *Imagined Communities: Reflections on the Origin and Spread of Nationalism*. London: Verso.

Brosius, Christiane and Melissa Butcher (eds) (1999) *Image Journeys: Audio-visual Media and Cultural Change in India*. New Delhi: Sage.

Chua, Beng-Huat (1997) 'Invading State Control: Global Broadcast Communication in South-East Asia,' in: Kevin Robins (ed.) *Programming for People*. Rome: RAI, pp. 240-7.

Duara, Prasenjit (1996)'Historicising National Identity, or Who Imagines What and When,' in: Geoff Eley and Ronald Grigor Suny (eds) *Becoming National: A Reader*. New York: Oxford University Press, pp. 151-77.

Gates, Bill (1995) *The Road Ahead*. London: Viking.

Gore, Al (1994) 'Forging the New Athenian age of Democracy,' *Intermedia* 22(2).

Göle Nilüfer (1998) 'Islamism, feminism and post-modernism: women's movements in Islamic countries,' *New Perspectives on Turkey* 19.

Jain, Ravindra K. (1998) 'Indian diaspora, globalisation and multiculturalism: a cultural analysis,' *Contributions to Indian Sociology* n.s. 32:2.

Javnost/The Public (1999) Special issue on Globalisation and diasporic media, *Javnost/The Public* 6:1.

Karim, Karim H. (1998) *From Ethnic Media to Global Media: Transnational Communication Networks Among Diasporic Communities*. Hull, Québec, International Comparative Research Group, Department of Canadian Heritage.

Lavie, Smadar and Ted Swedenburg (eds) (1996) *Displacement, Diaspora and Geographies of Identity*. Durham: Duke University Press.

Levitt, Theodore (1983) *The Marketing Imagination*. London: Collier-Macmillan.

Mowlana, Hamid (1997) 'Islamicising the media in a global era: the state-community perspective in Iranian broadcasting,' in: Kevin Robins (ed.) *Programming for People*. Rome: RAI, pp. 204-14

Rao, Leela (1999) 'The elusive identity: woman on Indian television,' Unpublished paper.

Richstad, Jim (1998) 'Asian values and transnational television,' in: Anura Goonasekera and Paul S. N. Lee (eds) *TV Without Borders: Asia Speaks Out*. Jurong Point, Singapore, Asian Media Information and Communication Centre, pp. 287-306.

Robins, Kevin (ed.) (1997) *Programming for People: From Cultural Rights to Cultural Responsibilities*. Rome: RAI

Ross, Steve (1990) 'Worldview address,' delivered at the Edinburgh International Television Festival, 26 August.

Saktanber, Aye (1994) 'Becoming the "other" as a Muslim in Turkey: Turkish women vs. Islamist women,' *New Perspectives on Turkey* 11.

Sen, Krishna and Maila Stivens (eds) (1998) *Gender and Power in Affluent Asia*. London and New York: Routledge

Sennett, Richard (1970) *The Uses of Disorder*. New York: Knopf.

Sinclair, John, Elizabeth Jacka and Stuart Cunningham (eds) (1996) *New Patterns in Global Television*. Oxford: Oxford University Press.

Thussu, Daya (1998) 'Localising the global: Zee TV in India,' in: Daya Thussu (ed.) *Electronic Empires: Global Media and Local Resistance*. London: Arnold, pp. 273-94.

Yuval-Davis, Nira (1997) *Gender and Nation*. London: Sage.

CHAPTER 3

WOMEN AND PORNOGRAPHY IN KATHMANDU: NEGOTIATING THE 'MODERN WOMAN' IN A NEW CONSUMER SOCIETY

MARK LIECHTY

For many people around the world modernity is an experience, first and foremost, of life in emerging local consumer societies, an experience tied to the steady encroachment of global capitalism and its cultural logics into ever more communities and ever more domains of life. This welding of the modern and the material is perhaps even more powerful in Nepal (and other 'Least Developed Countries' (LDCs) on the Third World periphery) where decades of state-sponsored and internationally-funded 'development' initiatives have left a thick ideological residue (if little else) that mires understandings of 'progress' in a calculus of quantity (Pigg 1992:499). In a 'developing state' like Nepal, 'modernity' seems to be a largely external condition: its arrival - most often packaged and for a price - from a 'developed' and 'modern' elsewhere constitutes progress. This paradox of Third World modernity, of perpetually being on the 'becoming' or 'receiving' end of the development spectrum, is one of the greatest conceptual challenges that Kathmandu's emerging middle class faces as it carves out a new cultural space that is at once modern and Nepali (Liechty 1999). For these people the equation of the modern and the material - progress and possession - is an often painful, but inescapable, reality (Liechty 1998a).

Parallel to, though largely subsumed within this material mode, is a sub-discourse or rhetoric of freedom, equality, independence, and empowerment associated with modernity. For many Third World women these promises are among the most appealing aspects of what 'modernity' has to offer, regardless of whether one views them as universal human aspirations, or as the ideological trappings of a Western-driven, bourgeois 'Enlightenment Project.' These emancipatory themes were much on the minds of women in Kathmandu during the early 1990s. Following the *Jan Andolan* ('People's Movement') of 1990 - in which a mass uprising of Nepali people forced the Nepali state to adopt a multi-party democratic constitution - women paid close attention to slogans touting democratic rights, equality, and freedom.[1]

In the heady, hopeful months following the 'People's Movement,' women in Kathmandu embraced 'freedom' as a key element in their understandings of self as modern, even while they condemned the contradictions between rhetoric and reality that they continued to experience in their daily lives (Liechty 1996b). Indeed many women viewed the establishment of democracy less as an empowering moment than as a threat to their own personal security. One woman in her mid-thirties noted that it was no longer safe for women to walk the streets. 'Since the multi-party system began,' she complained:

> people seem to be willfully harassing women. Before people felt safe. The police would take action. But now nobody cares.
> Some people say it's because of the multi-party system. The multi-party system has come so who can do anything about it?
> Everybody's shouting 'We have the right of speech!' They say, 'One can do whatever one wants [*je paeyo tyahi garna huncha*]!' So now it's difficult for us women.

For this woman and others, democracy and freedom are very much gender issues. Another young woman had a similar view. When asked why she felt unsafe on the streets she replied haltingly:

> Because, ... because the boys think that ... After the multi-party system [the boys think] 'We are *free*. There is *freedom* now.' They think that to do anything is OK. That's why the girls have to look out for themselves.[2]

In the political ferment following the 'People's Movement' (*Jan Andolan*), the challenge for women in Kathmandu was to construct a new femininity that claimed the ostensibly non-gendered promises of freedom (individual rights, educational advancement, achievement, and merit) in the face of on-going and even re-entrenched forms of patriarchy.

Women's efforts to claim the promises of modernity are never easy, but they become even more difficult in the context of Kathmandu's materially-oriented middle-class consumer culture. Here the contradictions between dominant political rhetoric and women's social reality are compounded by the even more insidious contradictions between women's class and gender interests. In the ongoing processes by which social boundaries in Kathmandu are being redrawn in terms of class (Liechty 1994, 1998a), gender identities also must be reconstructed. Thus negotiating new class identities is intimately tied to the parallel challenge of negotiating new gender identities even though the two (class and gender) do not always involve compatible interests. For example, local fashion practice often pits class interests against gender interests. Ironically fashion has become one of the main *material* components of claims to middle-class status, even while emerging as one of the most *morally* denigrated practices of modernity. Not surprisingly Kathmandu's middle-class men bask in fashion's significations of material prosperity, while women risk its moral condemnation. In Kathmandu, as elsewhere, commercial interests target middle-class women as the primary objects of fashion (in films, magazines, fashion shows, etc.) even while saddling them with the burden of maintaining 'traditional morality' (cf. Liechty 1996b).

Another dimension of Nepali women's efforts to reconcile class and gender interests revolves around their attempts to understand, critique, and appropriate representations of women and modernity in mass media. In their daily lives women must confront both the ever-changing images and objects that circulate through the local consumer culture, and the unstable meanings that accompany them. This semantic instability is particularly challenging in dealing with representations of the 'modern woman.' As others have noted (e.g., Chatterjee 1989), for generations South Asian women have had to struggle to construct a suitably-modern yet suitably-local femininity from dominant discourses and representations of modernity that are tainted by their associations with colonial or foreign powers, or 'westernized' elites. In Nepal too, middle-class women find themselves stuck in a bind between needing to claim modernity in order to distinguish themselves from those 'below' them on the social scale, and needing to critique modernity as it is associated with elite lifestyles which the middle class views as corrupted by foreignness and consumer excess (Liechty 1999).

Perhaps nowhere is the challenge of negotiating (or domesticating) images of 'modern women' more difficult than the case of imported video pornography.[3] In pornographic images Nepali women come face to face with the 'modern woman' in her most terrifying avatar. Making sense of these consumer-erotic[4] images of women and female sexuality is an intimidating task because they force Nepali women to make difficult decisions about their own identities as 'modern' - and Nepali - women. This chapter examines Kathmandu middle-class women's experiences and reactions as consumers of commercial pornography. The stories that women tell illustrate some of the ways that they find themselves lodged in the contradictions of consumer modernity. This chapter describes middle-class Kathmandu women's efforts to grapple with the profoundly contradictory images of the 'modern woman' as depicted in political rhetoric and consumer culture. The challenge for women is to select what they identify as the positive aspects of modernity (freedom, independence, equality, empowerment) from the 'dark side' of modernity (new forms of patriarchy and sexual objectification, harassment, etc.). As these women's voices indicate, the images of women and female sexuality depicted in commercial pornography are particularly difficult to process. Judgements as to whether these images are 'good' or 'bad,' suitable or unsuitable, 'natural' or perverse, intriguing or sickening, shifts depending on the subject position women assume at a given moment. When dealing with the multiple levels of meaning with which pornography confronts women in their everyday lives - from issues of gender equality and emancipation, to the imperatives of participating in the local middle-class consumer society and the 'modern' world of goods, to debates over national identity and the association of modernity and foreignness, to threats of sexual assault and harassment, to the visceral experience of having strange, threatening, and bewildering images of presumably 'modern' sexuality thrust into the most intimate spaces of their domestic and marital existence - the contradictions among the meanings of 'modernity' become almost impossible for women to reconcile.

BACKGROUND AND CONTEXT

Although Kathmandu has been a national capital since the state of Nepal's founding in the eighteenth century, it is only since 1951 - when the country emerged from a century of isolationist, dictatorial rule - that the city has veered into the powerful political, economic, and cultural currents of global modernity. The fact that Nepal was one of few nations at the dawn of the 'post-colonial era' without a legacy of direct colonial occupation has for the past fifty years made the country a veritable laboratory for modernisation theory and a prime site for experimentation with wave upon wave of aid and development projects.[5] With a state apparatus designed largely in response to the sudden influx of foreign aid (Fujikura 1996), since 1951 Kathmandu has been the conduit for an estimated 3.7 billion U.S. dollars in grants and loans from foreign countries and international banks (Joshi 1997). By the time the money filters through the maze of centralized bureaucratic bodies and their affiliated Non-Governmental Organizations (NGOs) in Kathmandu,[6] often very little remains for projects at the rural 'grass roots' (Justice (1986), Blaikie, Cameron, & Seddon (1980)).

In addition to international development aid, in the past few decades other industries centered in Kathmandu - most notably international tourism and carpet exports - have contributed to the surprisingly large volume of cash flow within the valley. With several hundred million dollars funneled into the local economy each year one begins to understand how a considerable number of people in the national capital may be cash-rich even in a 'Least Developed Country' (LDC) whose annual average per capita income was only 190 US dollars in 1993 (Central Bureau of Statistics 1996:303). For every person with their hands in one of these business or bureaucratic cash boxes, many more enjoy the 'trickle down' benefits, even if the trickle rarely reaches beyond the rim of the Kathmandu valley.

It is this kind of local monetary economy - where cash is relatively plentiful and where there are limited opportunities for investment - that forms the context for the consumer patterns and social formations that are described in this chapter. Elsewhere I discuss Kathmandu's 'middle-class' and its cultural dynamics in considerable detail (Liechty 1994, 1998a). Here I will simply note that the Kathmandu valley's large number of government offices, educational institutions, NGOs, financial institutions, and businesses have created a sizeable middle class between the large mass of urban poor, and the nation's small transnational elite. Although by in the context of Nepal as a whole this middle class would qualify as an urban elite, within the socio-economic milieu of the Kathmandu valley they constitute a social middle.

PORNOGRAPHY IN KATHMANDU

Hard-core screen pornography has been available in Kathmandu (on a small scale) for decades, but with increasing buying power among middle-class families and the wide-spread availability (since around 1980) of VCR technology (Liechty 1998b), viewing 'blue films' has become a more and more common experience for men and women, young and old. Of those people that my co-workers and I interviewed, a large majority had seen pornographic magazines and films, and many, people including women, spoke frankly about their experiences and impressions.[7]

In spite of the fact that it is illegal to buy or sell pornography in Nepal, Kathmandu's ubiquitous video rental shops stock a wide array of pirated pornography from around the world as well as local productions. In 1991 a Kathmandu-based vernacular weekly newspaper confirmed my own observations, reporting that,

> In the Nepali capital thousands of pornographic films are easily available in the video shops. In Kathmandu these days even though [pornographic] films shot in foreign countries are easily available, the desire of local people to see Nepali young men and women in *blue* films is growing [*ruchauchan*] (*Saptahik Nepali Awaj* Asoj 11, 2048 v.s. (Sept. 27, 1991), p. 7).

Although its proliferation and availability seem extraordinary, for Kathmandu residents pornography has become so common as to be unremarkable.

WOMEN AND '*BLUE* FILMS':
'WE SHOULD ALSO KNOW THESE THINGS.'

Elsewhere I have described the wide-spread consumption of pornographic mass media on the part of men and boys in Kathmandu (Liechty 1994:439ff). But even after realizing that '*blue* film' viewing was common among males, I was surprised to find that many middle-class women and girls had also seen pornographic media, and were willing to speak candidly about their experiences with a female co-worker. Others who said that they had not seen pornographic films were willing to talk about what they had heard and what they thought. These interviews indicate not only that women are fully aware of the pornographic media that males around them are consuming, but that these films were the subject of active debate between women. Younger and older, women were trying to come to terms with the kinds of sexuality depicted in these media: trying to determine what these images meant for themselves and their relationships with men.

For young (usually unmarried) women, pornography was something that all had heard of and many were curious about. In schools and on campuses '*blue* films' seemed to be a common topic of conversation. For example one young woman, an 18 year old college student at Kathmandu's all female campus, spoke of how she knew about '*blue* films.' After noting that she herself had never seen one, she continued,

> My friends have talked about it and from hearing this it sounds like I had better not watch these films. They say 'There is kissing, and touching, and .. Oh! don't watch!' Those who have told me this have already seen these things. Some of them are married and some aren't.
> You know the trend of girls these days is that they want to know more than the boys. The girls today think they must watch everything, they should like everything. They say 'We should also know these things. Is this only something the boys should watch? Why not the girls?' Those who have watched these are very frank about this.

Later in the conversation she explained why she thought women were so interested in watching pornographic films.'

> I think they take interest in this because they want to know about the relationship between boys and girls. They want to really understand. They might have heard about this but that's not enough. They want to see and find out about this. People watch this to know what it is like.

39

As with many others, this young woman's critique focused mainly on matters of gender access to pornography, not on the representations themselves. Indeed for her pornography seemed to offer a largely unproblematic representation of heterosexuality. Significantly though, this young woman discussed women's interests in '*blue* films' in terms of 'the trend of girls these days' and 'girls today think ...' For her, women's access to and knowledge of pornography is a matter of women's desires to be up to date and on equal footing with men, that is, modern and progressive. For young women and girls pornography is alluring (even if they haven't actually seen it) because if offers them the chance to 'see and find out,' 'to really understand.' Here consuming pornography is a matter of women's empowerment and claiming equality with men.

While school girls were often curious about '*blue* films,' among the women interviewed by my female co-worker, married women were more likely to have had first hand experiences watching pornographic videos. Of the four married women who spoke most openly of their experiences, in each case the woman's husband had brought a video home and suggested that they watch together. These women responded with varying degrees of hesitation and embarrassment.

At one extreme was a woman in her mid thirties; the mother of several children, she had some college-level education. When asked if she had ever seen a '*blue* film,' she replied,

> I haven't seen many but sometimes my husband brings them home. I watch alone since I'm a little shy. I don't watch with my husband. He watches them first, then I do. He says 'Let's watch together' but I say 'No.'
>
> The *blue* films are too extreme [ek dam *over* bhyo]; they're toooo much! So the two of us together watching is too embarrassing. I get sooo embarrassed, so after him, then I watch it!
>
> I don't see that many because he doesn't bring so many. But usually when he's not here I watch. When he's gone away I feel that I can watch freely. But when he's in the valley, I don't feel comfortable.

Her first experience with such a film had come several years after her marriage when her husband put a video in the VCR in their bedroom after both of them had gotten into bed. As her husband watched, she caught glimpses of the film while pretending to sleep. She felt extremely uncomfortable but a few days later she had the opportunity to see the film by herself. Although she spoke of disliking the films, since that time, every few months - 'by chance' - she watches a '*blue* film' that her husband has left in the house. Good or bad, she pointed out that many other women are also watching pornographic films, with or without their husbands. 'These things' she said, 'are happening all over, all the time.'

Later in the conversation she explained in more detail what she found troubling about '*blue* films.'

> Well, there are *natural* things that are already in one's *mind*. But watching that kind of thing I feel disgust [ghin lagyo]. In that it happens in all kinds of ways. For me, I think it shouldn't be like this.
>
> This kind of *love* I don't like too much. Using their mouth and all that, it makes me feel disgusted. I mean, the mouth should be used for food so it seemed very *dirty* to me. It should be done *naturally*.
>
> It's a matter of one's own interests and I hear that some people are watching these films and then after that the husband and wife go to bed. But just because one watches, that doesn't necessarily happen.
>
> If these things happen from the inside, then that's good. But without interest, just because you have the *feeling*, that shouldn't necessarily happen. That's what I feel so there's nothing in me that makes me want to see the film.

In her remarks this woman seems torn between her own subjective dislike of the pornographic videos she has seen, and her need to acknowledge the wide spread consumption of these products by others around her, including other women, and even herself. She struggles to contrast her own experience of sexual intimacy - an innate, '*natural*' mode of sexuality that comes 'from the inside' and is 'already in one's *mind*' - with a pornographic '*love*' in which sexual relations occur 'in all kinds of ways' that are not just perverse, in her opinion, but also somehow shallow, external, or false. But ultimately she neither criticizes her husband for bringing '*blue* films' home, nor condemns the films themselves, in spite of the fact that they disgust her. Similarly one part of her refuses to watch these videos with her husband - refuses to let this 'extreme' sexual behavior become part of her own experience of intimacy - while another part is almost irresistibly drawn to '*blue* films' when her husband is far away. Her conflicting attitudes reflect a deeper split in her subjective experience. As a wife she is unwilling even to acknowledge pornographic sexuality in her husband's presence for fear of legitimizing it and allowing her husband to recast her in its image. But as a modern woman - well educated and aware of events and trends around her - she is compelled to come to terms with this artefact of modernity that has been cast into her bedroom and her life.

Indeed this woman's remarks can be read as a kind of subtle, internal dialogue on modernity. At one level they represent her efforts to come to grips with an inescapable element of the modern consumer society that is growing up around her and which has now invaded even the inner domain of domestic sexuality. Images of pornographic sexuality force her to weigh her own understandings of self as a modern woman against the images of presumably 'modern' female behavior that she sees on her screen.

At another level her choice of words also points to an ongoing, and unresolved, struggle with 'the modern.' Her use of English words in an otherwise Nepali conversation indicates a kind of 'code switching'[8] in and out of an arguably 'modern' epistemological space. English words like 'natural,' 'dirty,' 'mind,' 'feeling,' and perhaps most tellingly, 'love,' point to her awareness of a different kind of subjectivity in need of special linguistic marking. This new way of being and knowing is signified as modern by the use of English words even when in all cases formally equivalent Nepali words could have been used. In one case she contrasts 'the *feeling*' (in English) of sexual arousal that she assumes these videos is supposed to produce (and she assumes *is* produced in other women), with her own *feeling* of disgust which she expresses using the very different Nepali passive verb construction *ghin lagyo*. So too her use of the English word '*love*' - and her implicit comparison of 'this kind of *love*' with another love that she *does* like - indicates her awareness of a different, 'modern' world of male/female sexual intimacy (depersonalised, decontextualised, extra-marital, gratuitous) that has nothing to do with the kind of love that the Nepali noun *prem* would connote.[9] In short, by using English to mark off the space of pornography, artificial arousal, and 'unnatural' sexuality, this woman is marking off and critiquing 'the modern.'

Another woman who spoke of her experiences with pornography continued the theme of separating pornographic sexuality from her own experience, but added a new dimension of gender critique. A twenty-three year old part time college student, this woman lived in her husband's parental home. Having been married in her late teens it was several years before her husband started asking her to watch '*blue* films' with him. 'The first few times I said 'No' but then he told me, 'You can watch if you want, or not if you don't want. It's up to you.'' She went on to explain,

The first time I saw one, I felt very awkward and uneasy [*apthyaro lagyo*]. But after that I got into kind of a habit. I mean, I became able to watch.'
How did you feel?
'The first time I watched, *emotion* came. But since then, well, nothing really happens.'
What do you think of these films?

'I'm not really interested in these. I feel like this is something that people shouldn't really be watching. I mean, it's just not worthwhile. But, I guess it's a matter of each person's interest.'

What does your husband think?

'Well, he must have interest in them and that's why he keeps bringing them home!

Expanding on the topic of her husband's interests, she went on to explain that his predilections were far from unique. She described long waiting lists at video rental shops for the most popular pornographic films. 'People must watch these things sooooo much!' she said. 'I've heard that if a shop doesn't have this kind of film, they'll soon *flop* [go out of business].'

A bit later in the conversation she discussed why she thought '*blue* films' had become so popular. She made it clear that, in her opinion, it is not people in general, but men in particular who want these films.

I don't know, but it seems to me that we women aren't that interested in *sex*. Because various things are always happening in our lives we can't go around just thinking about *sex*. When we live in a joint family lots of distracting things are happening so the issue of *sex* doesn't come up very often.

But for men it doesn't happen like this. It seems like the men want *sex* all the time. If we don't have interest in *sex* then the men don't get any fun. And for that reason they bring this kind of thing hoping that we will also get some enjoyment from this.

That's how it seems to me. Maybe they think that if we watch it, it will *affect* us. They're hoping we'll also feel the *emotion*. Women aren't so interested in this so that's why they bring it to show to us.

Here again the English words 'sex' and 'emotion' demarcate a new or modern set of sexual practices and conditions from another more familiar mode of sexuality and gender relations. But here word choice contrasts not only a modern from some other space, but also aligns those spaces with gender. Here 'men want *sex* all the time' and men 'feel the *emotion*' whereas women 'aren't so interested.' Implicitly she links pornography with male (heterosexual) arousal. She identifies pornography as a consumer item that capitalizes on and/or produces male erotic desire, not female. Whether the nature, intensity, or frequency of this male erotic desire is new or modern is unclear. But the fact that husbands 'keep bringing [pornographic videos] home' in hopes that the modern visual medium will '*affect*' their wives, points to the fact that this woman, like many others in Kathmandu, is increasingly expected to supply the sexual gratification demanded by a new electronic commercial means of sexual arousal. Like all mass commodities pornography sells not by producing gratification, but by inflaming and shaping male desire, again and again. For this woman pornography is, above all, boring. Its significance lies in its role in transforming the bedroom into a new space of mediated male sexual fantasy: fantasies that implicate wives in new patterns of female objectification and male gratification.

The other two women who spoke in detail of their personal experiences watching pornographic videos focused on the social repercussions of this new intense male sexual desire being fanned by pornography. One of these was a twenty-four year old seamstress whose income, when combined with her husband's family's small manufacturing business, afforded them a lifestyle that was, by local standards, well within the middle-class. The family owned several televisions and VCRs, one of which was in her and her husband's private bedroom. When asked if she had ever seen a '*blue* film' she replied,

> Yes, I've seen two actually, with my husband. And that was only in the night when we were completely alone. My husband turns off the sound completely. I found these people [the actors] are in the habit of making a lot of noise!
> *So what did you think?*
> Um, what can I say? Some scenes were like in our own experience, but some weren't like anything I've ever done. So, I mean, some of them were just like our own events, but others were, um, you know, like 'that' [_ tyahi].

When my co-worker asked if she thought it was very common for women to watch '*blue* films' the woman responded with surprise,

> Are you kidding? Even girls [ketiharu] are watching this all the time.
> *Of what age?*
> Oh, eighteen to twenty year olds, but also married women. I've been meeting sooooo many women who have seen them. Only we women know about women's things.
> It's like the husband will go off to work, the kids have gone to school, then women get together in a group of friends and watch them. Also sometimes the female members of one family will watch together, without showing the children and without letting anyone else [e.g., the mother-in-law] know.
> Doing like this is fine for the married people but not for the unmarried ones. For them I think it's bad.

The next question - about why women preferred to watch these films with other women - led the conversation to a more critical level.

Well, if it's your own husband, then there's no reason to be uneasy. It's like your own experience [*ghatana*]. But with others it can be very difficult. I mean, for example, there are some men who can forget who their own relatives are when they get very emotional.

This woman's remarks are important because they allude to (among other things) new, emerging forms of female sociality organized around media consumption (Liechty 1998b, cf. Gillespie 1989). Groups of women watching pornographic videos lefty lying about by their husbands are no doubt important forums for making sense of, coming to terms with, and critiquing this mediated form of modernity. But perhaps more important is this woman's (apparently shared) fear of the social effects of pornography on men. Under the 'emotional' influence of pornography, even female family members might become objects of male sexual aggression. She went on to describe a conversation she had had with her husband on the topic.

Some boys are like this,' he says. They are thinking 'How can I force her to submit to me?' 'They do all these things,' he said. When he explained all this to me, it really bothered me.
So what do you think about these films?
Now that I know about this, they make me sick to my stomach [*waka lagyo*].

Here the 'price' of stirring up male sexual desire is paid not simply by the wife who is asked to provide more (and different forms of) sexual gratification. Instead male desire threatens to break out of the confines of marital sexuality to endanger not only strangers, but even kin. As she begins to associate pornography consumption with growing rates of sexual abuse and rape (Liechty 1996) this woman's attitudes toward '*blue* film' viewing went from relative indifference to revulsion.

The fourth woman who spoke of watching '*blue* films' shared many of the experiences of the others. She too worried about the increased potential for violence against women by men who were consumers of imported pornography. This twenty-four year old woman's husband's family ran a successful business producing gear for Nepal's large tourist trekking industry. Among other prestige goods, the joint family owned two televisions and a VCR. Describing her opinion of '*blue* films,' she remarked,

It may be good for others but not for our family. I mean, for the
tourists, maybe it is good. Otherwise, why would they make them?
But for we Nepalis, films like that are not good. Many girls will be
spoiled by this.
I mean, while watching these films, in what a bad manner they [men]
think of others! Even their own sisters they begin to look at in this way!
This is what they do once they become like that. That's the way men are.

Again the fear is about how men behave after 'watching these films.'
Having watched '*blue* films' men 'begin to *look* at' women in a new, and
sexually threatening way. Once men have seen these films, women *look* a
different way in their eyes, but it is the men's eyes - their sexually-
objectifying visions and erotic images of women - that have changed, not
the women themselves.

Yet from this woman's remarks it seems that she understood the images
of women in '*blue* films' to be not merely male fantasies, but the realities
of some other place. Pornographic films must be 'good for the *tourists*' -
a generic term used for Caucasian Westerners (Hepburn 1993). If not, 'why
would they make them?' Although I think similar ideas are implicit in many
of the remarks by other women recorded above, this woman explicitly
distinguishes a Nepali female 'we' (that includes herself, the interviewer,
and other women like them), from a foreign female 'them.' Whereas the
other women had constructed their ideas around a distinction between their
own individual experiences and those shown in the modern media, here the
same distinction is made but in terms of a generalised Nepali us and a
foreign '*tourist*' them. Not surprisingly, the modern and the foreign come
to be largely interchangeable categories.

This same 'us'/'them' theme came up at another point in the
conversation. Here the woman being interviewed confided that her marriage
was not in good shape; her husband visited prostitutes and had threatened to
bring home a second wife. Once again she turned to the topic of
pornography noting that in the '*blue* films' people are always 'doing like
this, like that. You know, the boys [ketaharu] will watch that kind of thing
immediately.' When my co-worker asked if she was suggesting that her
husband's growing interests in pornography were behind his use of
prostitutes and wishes for a new wife, the woman replied,

Maybe that's right. Maybe that's what he wants. Well, that's not
possible from us, no? Maybe for this reason he's talking about getting
remarried.

This woman implied that the foreign sexuality she had seen in pornographic films might be available from tourists (and perhaps prostitutes), but was 'not possible from us': self-respecting and respectable Nepali women. The same kinds of sexual behaviors that other women had identified as unnatural, dirty, and sickening were for this woman foreign. By relegating these threatening forms of sexual behavior and objectification to a space of foreignness, she attempted to preserve a subjective space in which she could maintain a sense of self as a dignified, Nepali, woman.

One thing that these women's accounts of their experiences watching '*blue* films' with their husbands makes clear is that in Kathmandu pornographic sexuality is playing an increasingly common role in 'everyday' sexuality. One additional piece of information that sheds light on the issue of domestic sexuality and pornography came in the course of an interview I conducted with a Nepali psychologist whose practice in Kathmandu included marriage counselling for middle class couples. This counsellor noted that men who would never permit their wives to view pornographic films do so themselves, and then come to expect certain behaviors from their wives. 'What happens,' he explained,

> is that, like for people my age, in their thirties, we see these cassettes and know about the different styles, positions, and postures. But let's say I want various types of postures and styles, *with my wife.*
>
> Well, I *never* allow her to see that kind of posture, that kind of cinema, but I expect that she must do those things.
>
> Particularly, you know, what you say, sucking, in English. Sucking. I have found two or three marital conflicts and divorces centering on this problem. The wife refused. 'I can't' [the women say].
>
> So many questions come from my clients' side; 'I want *this*,' [the men say] 'but my wife is not serving me.

From pornographic media men learn to desire new forms of male sexual pleasure which they expect their wives to provide. Yet it is the very form of one-sided male sexual gratification that these men most desire that the women were most likely to single out as 'dirty' and 'unnatural.' This new form of male sexual pleasure - so closely associated with foreign pornography in South Asia that it is known as 'English sex' among sex workers and their clients in Calcutta (Dell 1997, 1999) - has clearly become a disruptive part of a new domestic sexual economy in Kathmandu.

If this marriage counsellor had encountered 'two or three' marital conflicts tied to these demands for new sexual 'services,' it seems very likely that there are many similar instances in other middle-class homes in Kathmandu. Indeed he seemed unaware of the trend reported by the women in this chapter of men more or less forcing pornographic videos onto their wives in their own marriage beds. It is likely that for every woman like those described here, many more women may not have seen pornography, but find themselves drawn into its erotic economy through the expectations of husbands who have become consumers of this global commodity form. As a new mediated erotic sensibility permeates and expands the realms of male sexual experience, new sexual desires and demands arise such that wives too are expected to make possible the new forms of male sexual gratification. With the experience of modernity in Kathmandu so intimately caught up in the capitalist commodity form, the experience of modern intimacy is extraordinarily difficult to negotiate, especially for women.

CONCLUSION

How are we to understand middle-class women's responses to modern commercial pornography in the capital of a Third World 'developing' country like Nepal? The material presented here, though very limited, points to a number of significant themes. One of these is a kind of sexual relativism that emerges in most of the remarks recorded here. Even if they condemned the contents of pornographic videos based on their own identities as individuals or Nepalis, all of these women conceded the validity of pornographic sexuality for *other women* ('I guess its a matter of each person's interest') and/or people from *other places* (.'.. for the *tourists* maybe it is good'). Because pornographic videos were almost by definition foreign imports depicting foreigners ('tourists'), the us/them interpretation of '*blue* films' was common among women in Kathmandu. Speaking of the sexual mores in foreign places where pornographic films come from, one women noted, 'It's said that they're *free* like that in those countries.' Another woman explained,

> I don't like *blue* films, I'd have to say, because our society doesn't allow that, and we don't have any desire to watch this because we have been raised in this kind of society.
> If we had grown up in a *free* type society we might have liked this. So because of this there is no reason to watch *blue* films.

For these women, the '*free* type society' found in foreign countries that produce '*blue* films' - the modern materialist society *depicted* in those same films - may be suitable for 'them,' but not for 'us.' While this compromise is one way for Nepali women to both comprehend pornographic images, and to shield themselves from the objectifying gaze of pornographic sexuality, it comes at the expense of granting reality (even if a foreign reality) to the sexual culture of the '*blue* film,' of surrendering the concept of 'freedom' to this realm of alien reality, and of allowing barriers to be constructed between 'foreign' and Nepali women.[10]

For women in particular the challenge of pornographic sexuality becomes one of reconciling what seem to be modern foreign freedoms with an acceptable *Nepali* female sexuality, and a legitimate role in an emerging middle-class public culture. If the women in pornographic films represent 'the modern woman' as she exists in modern, foreign, 'free-type' societies, what does this mean for Nepali women who also wish to stake out claims in the new terrain of modernity and freedom in Nepal? In the heady days of post-*Andolan* ('People's Movement') Kathmandu in the early 1990s talk of democracy, freedom, progress, and modernity saturated the public sphere. But for middle-class women, forced to deal with the sexual objectification implicit in new consumer regimes (and regimens) ranging from 'fashion' to 'blue films,' the challenge was to prevent 'freedom' and 'modernity' from becoming simply new modes of male dominance.

This middle-class conflation of modernity and the commodity form - and the contradictions that such a conflation spawns - relates to a second theme that emerges from these women's voices. On the one hand women recognize and critique the sexual objectification that propels most commercial pornography. By characterizing these products as 'dirty,' 'unnatural,' 'worthless,' and a threat to women's security these women place consumer sexuality - with its fetishization of male sexual gratification - outside the bounds of acceptable marital intimacy. Yet on the other hand, this critical perspective is often neutralized because of pornography's association with an equally fetishized cult of consumer prestige goods (VCRs, TVs, and videos notably among them): a cult that privileges imported 'modern' consumer goods and their associated lifestyles (Liechty 1998a). To the extent that much of the middle-class experience of modernity in Kathmandu revolves around a consumer ethic that tends to be outward-looking - equating 'foreign' or 'developed' with 'modern' - many women seemed forced to concede that pornographic sexuality must be the acceptable norm elsewhere in modern, 'free-type' societies. In this way women are lodged in the contradictions between two related but conflicting forms of modern consumer desire: a commercially-driven economy of male erotic desire literally embodied in consumer pornography, and the non gender-specific consumer longing generated in Kathmandu's new class-based commodity culture. For these women it is difficult to reconcile a middle-class cultural practice that privileges the foreign/modern commodity form, with a commodified sexuality that threatens their own gender status.

At stake is their ability to construct unified identities as modern, Nepali, women.

Finally a third theme that emerges in these women's remarks concerns how this general consumer ethos is not something limited to the street, market, or other arenas of public display, but that works its way into even the most private domestic settings and intimate interpersonal relations. In effect even marital sexuality has become a mass mediated domain, or at least threatens to become so. When men bring new commercially-generated desires into their bedrooms and into their marriage relations, women are confronted with modernity in ways that are as threatening, baffling, and shocking as they are viscerally intimate and even unspeakable. Perhaps it is these often profound disjunctures among the multiple subject positions that middle-class women in Kathmandu embody - between public and private, between class, gender, and national identities, between political rhetorics of freedom and daily experiences of harassment - that may begin to account for the difficulties they face in negotiating the 'modern woman.'

NOTES

1 For discussions of the Nepali 'people's movement' and its aftermath see Hutt (1994), and Raeper & Hoftun (1992). Elsewhere I discuss middle-class Kathmandu women's debates over, and critiques of the new democratic 'freedoms' (Liechty 1996).

2 Asterisks designate English words used in statements otherwise made in spoken or written Nepali and presented here in translation.

3 Whereas representations capable of inciting sexual desire are strictly neither modern nor Western, I agree with Lynn Hunt who argues that the origin of 'truly modern pornography' is concurrent with the development in Europe of 'mass-produced texts or images with the sole aim of producing sexual arousal in the reader or viewer' (Hunt 1993:305). As a mediated, mass-produced commodity, pornography (perhaps more than any other media genre) transcends locality in its transnational search for markets. A mode of representation that constructs and confines (largely male) erotic desire, pornography has become a notably successful global cultural commodity.

4 I use the words 'consumer-erotic' to characterize commercial pornography to distinguish it from erotic representations found in, for example, medieval Nepali temple statuary. As Linda Williams argues, an erotic sensibility can never be understood 'independent of its production in social discourse' (1989:118). Medieval Nepali eroticism has to be understood as part of a religious (Tantric) 'social discourse' that

(whatever its patterns of sexual or gender objectification) is distinctly different from the consumer-driven logic of commercial pornography. Whereas Tantric eroticism may fetishize sexuality in the achievement of spiritual union with the creator/cosmos, pornographic eroticism fetishizes sexuality in order to drive the consumer to the point of purchase, again and again. As a commercial genre, pornography is characterized by a number of ideological, narrative, and representational conventions (Williams 1989) that construct erotic desire according to the needs of capital. Modern pornography, I suggest, is part of a new universe of generalized consumer desire that is perhaps the key cultural dynamic of middle-class societies around the world (cf. Sklair 1995). To view medieval erotic representations as 'pornographic' is to impose our own 'modern' mediated sensibilities onto a very different 'social discourse.'

5 For overviews of, and views on, Nepal as a 'development laboratory' see Stiller and Yadav (1979), Skerry, Moran, and Calavan (1992), and Fujikura (1996). For a critical history of shifting development policies world wide since 1950 see Escobar (1995).

6 According to one recent reckoning, around 70% of Nepal's total annual budget goes simply to running the Kathmandu administration (*The Independent* (Kathmandu) 27 November, 1996, p.5).

7 Research for this article was carried out in the Kathmandu valley between 1988 and 1991, and in 1996. This paper draws on a set of over 200 open-ended, tape-recorded interviews with a cross-section of urban residents conducted by four Nepali co-workers (see acknowledgements) and myself. Discussing experiences with pornographic media was a sensitive topic, especially for women. I am therefore heavily indebted to Ganu Pradhan for most of the excellent interview material used in this paper.

8 Gumperz defines code switching as 'a discourse phenomenon in which speakers rely on juxtaposition of grammatically distinct subsystems to generate conversational inferences' (1982:97). I would argue that the 'subsystems' may also, even more importantly, be epistemologically distinct.

9 Elsewhere I discuss the use of the English word 'love' in colloquial Nepali to designate a kind of commercialized, mediated form male/female relations among young people in Kathmandu (Liechty 1994:422ff).

10 Concerning the meanings of 'foreignness' as they relate to pornography in South Asia, it is instructive to compare these Nepali women's views with those of middle-class women in India where foreignness is

associated less with a privileged domain of modernity (as it is in Nepal) and more with the historical legacy of India's colonial past. Heather Dell (1999) describes how middle-class women in Calcutta critique pornographic video (and 'english sex') on the basis of its foreignness. These women flatly reject pornography, and the inroads it is making into domestic relations, by adding it to the long-established middle-class narrative of anti-Indian, foreign depredations and moral perversions (cf. Chatterjee 1989). But for women in Nepal, where foreignness and modernity are in many ways fused, finding the space for an outright critical subject position is more difficult, compromised, and contradictory.

Acknowledgements: Research for this paper was conducted between 1988 and 1991, and in 1996 with the help of the Departments of Anthropology and South Asia Regional Studies of the University of Pennsylvania, a Fulbright-Hays Doctoral Dissertation Research Abroad grant, and a faculty travel grant from the Department of Anthropology at the University of California, Santa Barbara. Special thanks go to research co-workers Som Raj Ghimire, Krishna and Ganu Pradhan, Ang Tshering Sherpa, and Surendra Bajracharya. Thanks also to the International Institute for Asian Studies (IIAS), in Leiden, The Netherlands, for a post-doctoral research and write-up grant, and Beulah S. Hostetler for helpful editorial comments. Earlier versions of this paper were presented at the conference 'Images of Women in Media,' International Institute for Asian Studies, Leiden, The Netherlands (Nov. 6-8, 1995), the Cultural Analysis Colloquium, University of California, Santa Barbara (Jan. 17, 1996), the Wisconsin Conference on South Asia, Madison (Oct. 17-19, 1997), and the Annual meeting of the American Anthropological Association, Washington, DC (Nov. 19-23, 1997).

REFERENCES

Blaikie, Piers, John Cameron and David Seddon (1980) *Nepal in Crisis: Growth and Stagnation at the Periphery*. Delhi: Oxford University Press.

Central Bureau of Statistics (1996) *Statistical Pocket Book Nepal*. Kathmandu: HMG.

Chatterjee, Partha (1989) 'Colonialism, Nationalism, and Colonialized Women: The Contest in India,' *American Ethnologist* 16:4, pp. 622-33.

Dell, Heather (1997) '"English Sex", Middle-Class Wives, and Prostitutes:

Sexual Consumption as Deterritorialization in Colonial and Post-Colonial India,' paper presented at the 96th annual meeting of the American Anthropological Association, Washington, DC, Nov. 19-23, 1997.

--(1999) '"Ordinary" Sex, Prostitutes, and Middle Class Wives: Sexual Practice, Liberalization, and National Identity,' paper presented at the 28th Annual Conference on South Asia, University of Wisconsin, Madison, Oct. 15-17, 1999.

Escobar, Arturo (1995) *Encountering Development: The Making and Unmaking of the Third World*. Princeton: Princeton University Press.

Fujikura, Tatsuro (1996) 'Technologies of Improvement, Locations of Culture: American Discourses of Democracy and "Community Development" in Nepal,' *Studies in Nepali History and Society* 1:2, pp. 271-311.

Gillespie, Marie (1989) 'Technology and Tradition: Audio-Visual Culture Among Asian Families in West London,' *Cultural Studies* 3:2, pp. 226-39.

Gumperz, John (1982) *Discourse Strategies*. Cambridge: Cambridge University Press.

Hepburn, Sharon (1993) 'Fashion and ethnic Tourists in Nepal: Whose Authenticity is This?', paper presented at the 22nd Conference on South Asia, Madison Wisconsin, Nov. 1993.

Hunt, Lynn (1993) 'Pornography and the French Revolution,' in: Lynn Hunt (ed.), *The Invention of Pornography*, New York: Zone, pp. 301-39.

Hutt, Michael (ed.) (1994) *Nepal in the 1990s*. New Delhi: Oxford University Press.

Joshi, Bikas (1997) 'Foreign Aid in Nepal: What do the Data Show?', *Himal South Asia* 10:2, pp. 70-1.

Justice, Judith (1986) *Policies, Plans, and People: Foreign Aid and Health Development*. Berkeley: University of California Press.

Liechty, Mark (1994) *Fashioning Modernity in Kathmandu: Mass Media, Consumer Culture, and the Middle Class in Nepal*. Ph.D. dissertation: University of Pennsylvania.

--(1996) 'Paying for Modernity: Women and the Discourse of Freedom in Kathmandu,' *Studies in Nepali History and Society* 1:1, pp. 201-30.

--(1998a) 'Consumer Culture and Identity in Kathmandu: "Playing with Your Brain",' in: Debra Skinner, Alfred Pach and Dorothy Holland (eds), *Selves in Time and Place: Identities, Experience, and History in Nepal*. Lanham, MD: Rowman & Littlefield, pp. 131-54.

--(1998b) The Social Practice of Cinema and Video Viewing in Kathmandu,' *Studies in Nepali History and Society* 3:1, pp. 87-126.

--(1999) 'Class as Cultural Practice: Middle-Class Experience in Nepal,' paper presented at the 28th Annual Conference on South Asia, University of Wisconsin, Madison, Oct. 15-17, 1999.

Pigg, Stacy (1992) 'Inventing Social Categories Through Place: Social Representations and Development in Nepal,' *Comparative Studies in Society and History* 34:3, pp. 491-513.

Raeper, William and Martin Hoftun (1992) *Spring Awakening: An Account of the 1990 Revolution in Nepal.* New Delhi: Viking/Penguin India.

Skerry, Christa A., Kerry Moran and Kay M. Calavan (1992) *Four Decades of Development: The History of U.S. Assistance to Nepal.* Kathmandu: USAID/Nepal.

Sklair, Leslie (1995) *Sociology of the Global System, second edition.* Baltimore: Johns Hopkins University Press.

Stiller, Ludwig F. S.J. and Ram Prakash Yadav (1979) *Planning for People: A Study of Nepal's Planning Experience.* Kathmandu: Sahayogi Prakashan.

Williams, Linda (1989) *Hard Core: Power, Pleasure, and the 'Frenzy of the Visible.'* Berkeley: University of California Press.

CHAPTER 4

INTERIORITY AND THE 'MODERN WOMAN' IN JAPAN

SARAH CHAPLIN

In this chapter I will show a moment in Japanese history when a woman's identity was in the process of being newly constructed, through a re-negotiation of interior and exterior spaces. The moment comes in the wake of the great Kanto earthquake which wiped out most of Tokyo on 23 September 1923, after which Japan entered a frenzied period of rapid rebuilding, of modernisation and westernisation (seen then as synonymous processes). At the same time, the image of women was undergoing its own process of modernisation/ westernisation, in terms of gender roles, sexual relations and spatial practices. Indeed, as Gail Lee Bernstein has stated, the 1920s was a period when 'the nature, status and proper sphere of women became the preoccupation of bureaucrats, journalists and women alike' (Bernstein 1991:65).

I will characterise these changes taking place throughout the 1920s and into the 1930s not just as modernising spatial practices on the part of women, but more importantly as acts of spatial *transgression*, which themselves generated much media attention and produced various sites of abandonment, in terms of attitudes to the home, language, appearance, and occupation, the latter two being loaded terms, as will become apparent. I will also attempt to show that space is a technology of gender - although I am not speaking as a spatial imperialist by asserting that space governs our lives entirely - it is just a necessary and potent agent in this scenario. I am using the term transgression with deliberate ambivalence: by their very progressive manoeuvrings, women created the conditions necessary for modernity in Japan, and yet from the point of view of the patriarchal state, their spatial transgression was regarded by the outset of the second world war as a chief cause of the slide towards cultural and moral degradation, at which point Japan's identity had plunged into an austere, reactionary nationalism. As one writer has stated, 'The Japanese woman was an important stake in the... struggle between cosmopolitanism and nativist reaction' (Darrell William Davis 1996:54).

MODERNISATION AND IDENTITY

The new persona to emerge in this period was that of the 'modern' girl, or *modanu gaaru*, a neologism probably coined in 1920 and shortened to *moga* as the stereotype became established. The *moga* epitomised the cosmopolitan lifestyle, and according to Akira Miura's dictionary of ''English' in Japanese,' refers to 'young girls of the 1920s who wore bobbed hair, high heels, and long skirts' (Miura 1985:102). This superficial description belies the very profound effects these women had on society, and trivialises their impact on Japan's self-image. Darrell William Davis accords the *moga* more political power: 'The *moga* was a fashionably liberated symbol of women's rebellions against a stifling patriarchal order ... she was a hotly disputed figure on the streets of Tokyo, as a frank embodiment of feminine sexuality,' and he argues that 'in the Japanese context, she signified the 'advances' of westernisation to old Japan' (Davis 1996:53).

The way in which the construction of the 'modern' woman' is inextricably caught up with the formation of a modern nation state in Japan is of particular interest, and is recorded by the fickle opinions of prominent male novelists and intellectuals of the period, who were unable to embrace the West without clinging to patriarchal notions of tradition, and the belief that these were necessarily founded upon motherhood and the internalisation of women. Inevitably, the only way 'out' of this situation for women was to externalise their goals and values, and to fight for them on their own terms of universal suffrage, which took as its major issue, over and above matters concerning the vote, birth control, and other rights, the right to occupy public space, which had hitherto been effectively denied women in Japan. Japanese men responded by saying that the whole of the domestic interior was effectively women's space, but this was clearly not the point: the right to occupy public spaces without fear of judgement, and the ability to command respect and status in the world outside their closeted homes was the real issue.

Women tackled this primarily by aligning themselves with the dominant *other* of the day - the West - thereby moving outside the fixed categories assigned to women at the time. Significantly, in the context of Japanese culture, which is disdainful of direct vocal articulation, 'finding one's voice,' the standard metaphor in championing the silenced *other* in post-colonial discourse, is inappropriate. Expressing opinion through the occupation of space was therefore the radical option for Japanese women.

The 1920s really marks the second of three significant periods of modernisation in recent Japanese history which historian Ann Wasuro has identified, the first being the 1880s and 90s, the period after the Meiji

Restoration of 1868, when Japan opened up trading links with the west after two centuries of self-imposed isolation and introspection, and the third period being the 1970s and 80s, a time of industrial re-engineering of Japan's standing in the global market economy. The arrival of Commander Perry's American ship into Yokohama in 1853 was in itself an aggressive and decisive act of spatial transgression, an intrusion into the previously internalised island-nation of Japan, and marked the beginning of a period of comprehensive self-appraisal for the Japanese. As Western architects, politicians, teachers and military leaders were brought over to restructure the very institutional basis of Japanese society, Japanese intellectuals began to ask themselves how far reform should be taken. One voice at the time, Kozaki Hiromichi believed, 'We must not simply adopt the externals of Western customs; we must go further and reform people's minds as well' (quoted by Ann Wasuro 1996:39). This extends and in some ways reverses the prospect of spatial transgression to the very habits of thought of the Japanese people: it was deemed necessary by reformers to rework the inner world of the Japanese psyche as well as altering external received notions, in other words there was a need to rearrange *honne* (true feelings) as much as *tatamae* (public front). Despite this active search for new habits, some of the old samurai tendencies were reinforced: Ian Buruma comments on the 'samuraisation' of the Meiji period, which gave fathers greater powers to control their families and property' (Ian Buruma 1995:200).

INSCRIBING SPATIAL BOUNDARIES

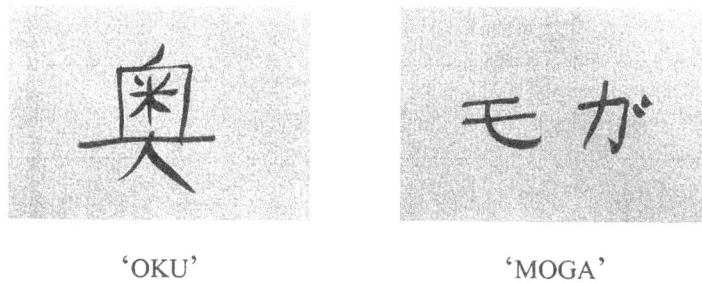

'OKU'   'MOGA'

Notions of interiority and exteriority, insideness and outsideness dominate the discourse of Japanese cultural history, particularly the status of women when considered in the context of debates about nationalism and identity. It is immediately noticeable how much a sense of belonging to a group is ingrained conceptually and historically through even a cursory examination of the Japanese characters for country, home, wife and mother. As Chinese-derived calligraphic ideograms or *kanji*, these convey graphically notions of spatial confinement and boundedness as a condition of identity: the box enclosing a figure, the roof over the family home, and a combination of roof, enclosure and elevation above the ground is evident in the character for *oku*, the polite term for wife, which carries also the meaning of a deep interior space in a temple, and literally translates as 'honourable lady within.' In fact the core character enclosed within this complex *kanji* is that of rice, implying a wife's household duties to provide sustenance.

By contrast, the way *moga* is written reveals its significance in terms of women's emancipation: the Chinese character system is one of three written scripts in Japanese, the other two being phonetic syllabaries, *hiragana*, and *katakana*. The former is used for Japanese words which do not derive from Chinese, and the latter is used for foreign or 'loan' words which have been incorporated into spoken Japanese as transliterations. *Moga* is written in *katakana*, and from this it can be inferred that there was a deliberate intention to conceive of *moga* as *other*, positioning it outside the boundaries of patriarchal Japanese thought and traditional notions of female identity, although the degree of appropriation and ownership of the term, indicated by its abbreviation, effectively appends it to the Japanese language. Linguist Miura regards it as a pseudo loan-word rather than a true loan-word, in that it is a term invented and understood only in Japan. Other writers are critical of the notion 'loan-word,' arguing that its connotations of borrowing are false: the word will not be 'returned' to its donor language. However, the idea of a loan-word preserves its status as a 'visitor' to the Japanese language, and its rendering in *katakana* has a similar effect as placing a word in English in inverted commas: setting it apart as not quite belonging to the author.

It is well known that the Japanese demarcate these spatial boundaries of belonging not only in written communication, but also in conversation, marking out others with more polite forms of address, and using more humble language when speaking to or about one's own family. The foreigner, or *gaikokujin*, person from outside, can never transgress the familial boundary of *ie*, the 'in group,' to become Japanese, even if they are Korean or Chinese. Once an outsider, always an outsider. Likewise, once a Japanese, always a Japanese: leaving home, the family, the group, or the country cannot ensure a departure from this commitment.

This sharply defined social delineation makes women's spatial transgression all the more apparent, but there are other factors worth highlighting to do with geography, history and demographics: Tokyo in the 1920s was a huge, densely populated metropolis, and one which since Edo times had been geared towards the lives of men: as the city to which samurai were sent for long periods as retainers without their wives and children, it became known as a city of bachelors, its urban development dedicated to their patterns of work and play. Today, the samurai is replaced by the *salariman*, referred to colloquially as a 'corporate warrior,' who sees the bright lights of entertainment districts such as Shibuya and Shinjuku as exclusively serving his bachelor 'needs' before returning home to wife and family in the suburbs. In other words, bachelor urbanisation continues to inform the development and use of many parts of the city.

Until relatively recently, the focal point for an evening's entertainment was the old pleasure quarter or *yukaku*, known as the floating world, or Yoshiwara. This was a large walled enclave, in which prostitutes were confined for the whole of their short lives (average life expectancy was about 25 years), in wretched conditions, for the service of men. Oblivious to the women's quality of life within, writers in the early twentieth century, such as the Baudelairean Kafu, described by Nicholas Bornoff as 'a recluse and an inveterate nostalgic,' (Bornoff 1992:322) romanticised Yoshiwara and lamented its decline:

There was a sad, plaintive harmony in the life and scenes of the Yoshiwara, like that of Edo plays and ballads...but time passed, and the noise and glare of the frantic modern city destroyed the old harmony. The pace of life changed. I believe that the Edo mood still remained in the Tokyo of thirty years age. Its last, lingering notes were to be caught in the Yoshiwara. (Buruma 1995:93)

There was a single entrance to the pleasure quarter, a black gate, which functioned as a control point: men visiting were expected to leave their swords outside, the same symbol of submission as that required upon entry to a traditional Japanese tea pavilion. This gesture does not however signify a shift in the control of power to the women inside Yoshiwara, and the modus operandi of men in search of a prostitute was no less combative: the complex choreography of sexual proximity did not end with admission at the gate to Yoshiwara: a liaison with a prostitute was expected to develop over time, until the woman accepted the client as a customer, at which point the couple would perform the same *sake* ritual, drinking from a cup three times, as is the custom in a formal marriage ceremony. (This was known as a 'visiting marriage,' and dates back to the Heian period in Japan.) Throughout this 'courtship,' the dynamics of flirtation, submission and conquest were spatially determined, where the ideal, promoted by many historical commentators and philosophers, was the perpetual maintenance of an erotic distance, referred to as *iki* - considered the only decorous way of conducting amorous relations. As an ideal, *iki* is perhaps the strongest indication of an invisible boundary that women were not supposed to cross in their relations with members of the opposite sex. Spatial transgression thus amounts to a dishonourable act and would bring considerable disrepute to the woman and her family.

'TEA SHOP, GINZA'

Other distinctions were clearly drawn: in Edo literature, a professionally trained *geisha* of Yoshiwara in this context was regarded as *yujo*, woman of pleasure, which contrasted sharply with *jionna*, woman of the soil or land, which was the standard image for a Japanese man's wife. Chizuko Ueno's sociological research has shown that since feudal times, the mother of a man's children was not thought of as seductive or capable of giving or receiving intimate pleasure, and was often equated with boredom, lack of sophistication, darkness, ugliness, and terrestrial ties (Chizuko Ueno 1996:125). It should also be noted that all the *shunga* or erotic art of the Edo period depicted men with prostitutes or mistresses, not with their wives.

It is clear from this that women were historically cast into two impossible categories, both involving spatial incarceration, either within the home or the pleasure quarter, and that their own needs were not considered, let alone attended to. Only in folklore were other identities for women allowed for, all of which lay outside the bounds of society. These stories cast women into even uglier, more demonic roles - witches with supernatural powers, ghosts and wicked temptresses, who rendered men helpless. This is of course a familiar male fantasy encountered in many myths around the world, but in the Japanese context it reveals the extent to which a woman who expresses any form of desire, passion, or power, is regarded as evil or strange. Such stories are, of course, allegorical, underscoring the 'good wife, wise mother' identity imposed upon Japanese women. Susan Napier, analysing these tales in comparison with examples found in modern Japanese literature, finds that there is a perceived equivalence between the demonic woman found in ancient folklore, and more recent depictions of western women: 'western female characters,' she suggests, 'serve to instruct readers to respect the tradition of Japan, and their fear of being overrun by foreigners' (Susan Napier 1996:21). In addition to their cautionary function, all these characterisations of feminine 'otherness' are representative of forms of wish fulfilment, textual signifiers of male anxiety towards change, but Napier also asserts that such female personae also offer potential solutions to change.

NAOMI AS *MOGA*

One figure who demonstrates most clearly the ability to move from a stable, unassuming feminine identity to the embodiment of the 'Other' is the character of Naomi in Jun-ichiro Tanizaki's novel *Chijin no Ai*, 'A Fool's Love,' serialised in a popular journal between March 1924 and July 1925, and which later became known as *Naomi*. The character of Naomi has been identified with the image of the *moga*, in that both represented 'a constellation of heterogeneous cultural influences, including the foreign, the passionate, the extravagant, and the individualistic, all of which militated against the hegemony of traditional social mores' (Davis 1996:57).

Chijin no Ai is an 'I'-novel, written in the first person by a male protagonist, Joji, as an account of his affair with Naomi. He finds her working as a waitress in a popular café, and is attracted to her because she looks like Mary Pickford. He attempts to transform her into an elegant westernised woman, with English and piano lessons and modern clothes, but instead she transforms herself from cute teenager to fully-fledged femme fatale, and Joji's relationship with her becomes increasingly masochistic. These motifs are used satirically by Tanizaki, although it was read at face value by the *moga* of the day, as an encouragement to women who wished to effect a similar re-invention of their image. The novel proved extremely controversial, and produced an atmosphere of panic among male journalists of the day: according to Ian Buruma the resulting concept of 'Naomism' meant 'a breakdown of traditional restraints. The 'Woman' was revealed under the kimono. Raw passion was unleashed' (Buruma 1995:53). In other words, Naomi is synonymous with spatial transgression.

In terms of Tanizaki's literary oeuvre, this novel occurs at an ambivalent moment in his development. Having written enthusiastically about dancing, cinema, cafe society, and the need to adopt Western ways in several earlier works, after the unexpected popularity of *Naomi*, which the authorities actually succeeded in suspending from publication in 1924 for encouraging the adoption of western ways too much, Tanizaki began a shift towards a form of nativism which took hold in the 1930s, which culminated for him in the publication of an essay entitled *In Praise of Shadows* in 1933 (Jun'ichiro Tanizaki 1977). Writing by then in a more nationalistic mode, Tanizaki's basic quest can be identified as the search for a lost tradition of Japan, which is equated with the search for a lost mother, who represents simultaneously the maternal and the seductive woman, *jionna* and *yujo*. As Ian Buruma puts it, 'the flowering of extreme nationalism, resulting in the doomed militaristic adventure, came very soon after the golden age of Naomism' (Buruma 1995:53).

In Praise of Shadows discusses the impact of Western technology, particularly the effect of electric light on the traditional Japanese interior, and suggests that if the Japanese had not had Western technology imposed on them, they might have developed products more appropriate to their needs, lights that were less harsh, radio that reproduced the delicate sounds of Japanese music more sympathetically, etc. It is a wistful lament, in which Tanizaki implicates the woman in his sense of regret, building as Napier has shown a triad of house/garden/wife, in which 'Tanizaki subverts modernity through both presenting alternatives to it in the form of the garden enclosing a traditional woman, and also by contrasting the keepers of tradition with ordinary human beings who belong to a mundane world outside the garden gates' (Napier 1996:45).

SPACES OF TRANSGRESSION

By the time Tanizaki's essay was published, however, women were already moving outside these prescribed limits into their own liminal territories, effectively reterritorialising urban space: 'As an inspiring, iconoclastic figure on the screen and on the street, the *moga* was a strike against the interlocking puritanical impulses towards moral rectitude and conservative cultural impulses to preserve the status quo' (Davis 1996:54). The particular spaces of transgression which the *moga* occupied in the city were the streets, shops, cinemas and cafés of Ginza, a part of Tokyo newly rebuilt by the British architect Thomas Waters after the 1923 earthquake in fireproof eastern-style masonry construction. Café society was flourishing in the 1920s, and by 1933, there were 40,000 cafés recorded throughout Japan. These were the places where popular songs were advertised and where women like Naomi worked as waitresses, creating a situation in which their presence as cultural producers 'reworked everyday relationships between men and women and between Japan and the West' (Miriam Silverberg 1991:68).

Such cafés still exist, and have evolved into their own weekend micro-environment: women in droves flock to Ginza to shop and promenade with their parasols, taking English-style afternoon tea or stopping for coffee and cake in one of the many establishments. The cosmopolitan status of cafés is evident from the signs written in Japanese English: 'Shall we Approach Towards Opportunity?' one sign invites, while another displays a naked classical female statuette beside its name, 'Ginza Pocket Park,' referring to a Japanese urban planning concept, in which new public spaces were created on small plots of land for local residents to meet and children to play. One of the oldest cafés, located at the busiest intersection in Ginza, is owned by Twinings Tea Company, and has a genteel first floor parlour overlooking the street. Almost all the clientele are women, there to please only themselves. Yasuo Takahashi is at pains to point out that this consumer experience is as far from the traditional Japanese teahouse as it is possible to be: in an essay entitled 'Why You can't have Green Tea in a Japanese Coffee Shop,' he describes the polarisation of coffee and green tea in terms of 'rivalry between modern and traditional, or western and Japanese culture' (Yasuo Takahashi 1994:31). This is an important distinction: without it, women's presence in the cafés would not constitute an act of spatial transgression.

In Ginza, another space to which the 'modern' Japanese woman had recently gained access is represented by the great department stores such as *Isetan* and *Takashimaya*, many of which were only constituted in the early 1900s. Originally called *hyakkaten*, or shops which stocked one hundred items, these places became known simply as *depato*, the anglicised Japanese term for department store, a loan word expressed in *katakana*. These were seen as glamorous, prestigious places, whose staff were well versed in the Japanese social graces of present giving and wrapping and yet whose ambience and merchandising were distinctly cosmopolitan.

'GINZA CAFÉ'

'MOGA IN GINZA'

'MOBO IN DEPĀTO'

After the earthquake, many *depato* had to be rebuilt, and were reopened with new rules: Mitsukoshi's customers voted not to have to remove their shoes upon entering the stores any more, thus rendering the interior an honorary external space to which the traditional requirements of Japanese social etiquette no longer applied. Whilst this may well have been a practical step to avoid the operational nightmare of ensuring the safe storage and return of customers' footwear, it also effected a spatial continuity with the outside world, literally and metaphorically, by removing the connotations of domesticity and interiority from the experience of shopping. This departure created an opportunity for female shoppers to construct a new identity at leisure without stigma being attached to this new activity of cultural browsing.

It has been noted that the department stores of Paris and New York played a similar role in the social emancipation of women, and in the introduction of goods from abroad, but in Japan, department stores were responsible for promoting unprecedented trends, such as engagement rings, a taste for western designer clothing and foodstuffs such as coffee and whisky. The first McDonalds fast food outlet was offered in the context of a Mitsukoshi store in 1971, boasting the slogan 'If you keep eating hamburgers, you will become blond' (noted by Millie Creighton 1992:46). Millie Creighton has argued that the *depato* 'imbued western imports with meanings relevant to the Japanese context,' (Creighton 1992:42) making foreign merchandise familiar to their young female clientele. In Miriam Silverberg's view, it was in such richly stocked emporia that 'Men and women in the 1920s and 30s constructed an identity not by bricolage but by a form of cultural code-stitching, whereby aspects of Western material and mass culture were integrated into the experience of everyday practice' (Silverberg 1991:87).

Along with these influential retail establishments, the *moga* also turned to new forms of entertainment as an everyday space of transgression: jazz was big in Tokyo in the 1920s, significantly a form of music which emphasised improvisation and spontaneity, and new forms of dance were being introduced, notably the tango. Not only were the clubs willing to allow women to enter as individuals in their own right, to drink alcohol and smoke cigarillos, but this new high body-contact dance involved a different sort of spatial transgression, in that the very defined and strictly observed personal body space of the Japanese, especially in relation to traditional dance (only performed by trained *geishas* for male suitors who were not allowed to make contact with them), was breached.

Tango was introduced to Tokyo from Argentina via Paris and London by Baron Megata in 1926, and was thought of at the time as 'the representation of courtship and seduction, a public display of passion performed by a heterosexual couple locked in a tight embrace' (Marta Savigliano 1992: 237). The Baron offered free classes to aristocratic young women and men, that is *moga* and *mobo* (modern boys), and for the first time the Japanese were able to explore an acceptably erotic form of public display of emotion. Marta Savigliano describes tango in the Japanese cultural context as 'a saleable exotic commodity,' (Savigliano 1992:237) and notes that it was in fact a toned-down, less passionate, more English-inspired version of the complex steps that was taught in Tokyo, whose choreographic style was more restrained in its sexual connotations. Nevertheless, the close proximity to members of the opposite sex that the tango afforded makes it yet another spatially transgressive practice actively pursued by Japanese women during this period.

Also new to the entertainment scene were Revue troupes and shows, one of which was the 'Takarazuka Young Girls' Opera Company,' formed in 1914 and featuring an all-female cast, who were required to be pure, righteous, and beautiful. Within their ostensibly convent-like existence, with predominantly pink, Disney-like spaces called 'Street of Flowers,' 'Ladybird Café' and 'Ladies' Inn,' the students of the Takarazuka Company were trained in a system of *kata*, or formal patterns, how to dress and behave like men, so as to be able to take their roles convincingly. This notion of *kata* of 'way of art' is central to the Japanese symbolic system, *geido*, much in evidence even today, unlike the more frivolous 'way of spirit,' characterised by spontaneous action, and linked more closely with jazz.

Jennifer Robertson has researched the Takarazuka phenomenon, and has revealed how a lesbian subculture emerged, which was linked to the development of the *moga* identity, in the sense that both issued a challenge to the 'good wife, wise mother' formula which polite society demanded of women at the time. The Takarazuka girls innovated with wild costumes and short-cropped hairstyles, appropriating and manipulating gender roles to suit themselves. Members of this particular troupe referred to women who chose a conventional marriage as the 'boxed-in gals,' inferring that sexual freedom was linked to a new-found spatial freedom, albeit within the confines of their cloistered existence as the so-called 'official angels of paradise' (Jennifer Robertson 1998:48). They too were boxed in, but it was perhaps the nature of their confinement that they were referring to: the boxed-in Chinese character for *oku*, wife, did not apply to these women, who were more liberated in spirit if not in space. However, this innovation was not to last, and the Opera Company was closed down in the mid-thirties, as nationalist fervour grew.

Apart from frequenting new spaces which lay outside the confines of domesticity, *moga* were also able to augment their transgressive excursions into the public sphere by virtue of mass media: in addition to the explosion of cinemas - totalling 1026 theatres in Japan in 1926 - providing another space to which women now had access both physically and intellectually, there was also a wealth of radio stations, a booming publishing industry producing 1 yen books, and a wide range of new magazines aimed at women, some more controversial and progressive than others. The circulation and extent of print culture in the 1920s cannot be underestimated: by 1931 the circulation of *Shufo no Tomo*, 'The Housewife's Friend,' had reached 8 million, but did little perhaps to advance their cause, subscribing as it did to the 'good wife, wise mother' image. Similarly unenlightened was *Fujin Kurabu*, 'Women's Club,' whose editorial stance emphasised moral instruction and conveyed the notion that women were still the property of men.

More progressive, however, was the *Fujo Shimbun*, ('Women's Newspaper'), founded in 1900. featuring a prominent woman activist such as Rosa Luxembourg on the front cover each week, and covering current affairs in some detail. Until 1942 when it ceased publication, the (male) editor, Fukushima Shiro, was committed to women playing a more active role in society, and gave the paper an international and pacifist outlook, believing that educating women would facilitate their equality. The paper was aimed at city women, and gave them a sense of being more fully involved and engaged in public life and politics at a macro level. It would seem that *Fujo Shimbun* recognised that while women had been incarcerated in their homes leading an entirely interiorised existence, they had effectively been denied any insights into the world outside, except for brief, furtive glimpses and overheard conversations. It is difficult to imagine the effect such a publication would have had on a generation of capable literate women, whose life of enforced mental and spatial introspection was suddenly exposed to sights and events about which they had previously had no knowledge.

Sandra Wilson's research on this Japanese women's newspaper shows that what began as a gesture towards the liberation of women veered towards a rather more problematic, intensely chauvinist tendency as the Manchurian Crisis deepened for Japan in the early 1930s (Sandra Wilson 1996). The editor of *Fujo Shimbun*, having always espoused the idea that women were above the petty warring tendencies of their fellow men, and that the women's vote would benefit society by introducing a more ethical, maternal and essentially non-violent bearing to politics, finally conspired with the State and urged readers to put their country first and make personal sacrifices, even featuring a tank on the front cover of an issue in January 1939. Wilson attributes the disappearance of *mobo* and *moga*, and the demise of so-called *eroguro*, or the atmosphere of erotic-grotesque which surrounded their lifestyle, to the war in Manchuria. The editor of *Fujo Shimbun* even claimed that the fascination with western things disappeared with the Manchurian incident altogether, creating a loss of spiritual direction among the Japanese people, who had come to depend on their westernised outlook.

This loss would account for Tanizaki's turning to the past and to tradition for answers, and by implication, women were effectively sent home. Tanizaki's exhortations in *In Praise of Shadows* refer to a dim domestic world which he believed to be 'the very epitome of reality, for a woman of the past did indeed exist only from the collar up and the sleeves out; the rest of her remained hidden in darkness' (Tanizaki 1977:28). Tanizaki reminded a public who had lost their way that 'a woman of the middle or upper ranks of society seldom left her house, and when she did she shielded herself from the gaze of the public in the dark recesses of her palanquin. Most of her life was spent in the twilight of a single house, her body shrouded day and night in gloom, her face the only sign of her existence....our ancestors made of woman an object inseparable from darkness' (Tanizaki 1977:29-30).

Likewise, as the Machurian crisis grew, the editor of *Fujo Shimbun* felt obliged to urge women to return home and 'save the nation' by rebuilding the individual household, by simplifying their domestic sphere, and discarding everything hollow and meaningless, only keeping 'all that is necessary and sincere' (quoted by Wilson 1996:98). With a new emphasis on frugality, the lifestyle of the *moga* came to seem frivolous and unnecessary, and such women acquired the reputation of those who 'flit around like butterflies over a flower.' (Wilson 1996:98)

'NEW WOMAN'

Although this put a brake on the *moga's* pursuit of spatial transgression, it was by no means the end of persistent activity towards the shaping of a Japanese modernity and the image of the 'modern' Japanese woman. In fact, a point of clarification is required regarding the contemporaneous but not quite equivalent concepts of 'modern girl' and 'new woman.' Although these terms are used in many accounts of the period interchangeably, the 'new woman' proved the enduring identity, whose involvement in public life operated on an altogether more intellectual level. Whereas the *moga* was interested in transforming lifestyle at the level of consumption, appearance and behaviour, the 'new woman' was interested in transforming belief systems, and raising consciousness about women's status in society. The *moga* was interested in modern taste, the 'new woman' in modern philosophy. Although both personae were progressive in that they changed the spheres in which they moved, the 'new woman' was not just a recipient of Western ideas, but a mouthpiece for them, actively proselytising. Thus, whereas the *moga* achieved the awakening of individuality, the 'new woman' was responsible for 'the modernisation of the soul' (Robert Bellah 1976:88).

Such was the role played by Baroness Ishimoto Shidzue, a 'new woman' who had been involved in the 'Bluestocking Movement' prior to the 1920s, and had set up business selling knitting yarn at a time when women were not supposed to run their own businesses. She met with considerable public disapproval as well as economic success, but after the Kanto earthquake destroyed this livelihood, she decided to follow her real calling and started giving public lectures to women up and down Japan about education and birth control, presenting her American mentors, Mary Beard and Margaret Sanger, who were pioneers in the field of women's rights. It should be noted at this point that prior to the Constitution of Japan in 1947 women were not allowed to speak publicly, and these honoured guests were only allowed ashore if they promised not to lecture in public. However, the authorities could not prevent them from speaking to gatherings in private residences, and the western women's ideas were still conveyed.

Shidzue published an article entitled *Kimono into Décolleté* in Vogue magazine, which commented on how new women were able to go back and forth easily between traditional Japanese and modern Western culture, inferring the ease with which women could effect spatial transgression by means of what they wore. She herself made these adjustments to her own style of dress, wearing kimonos when speaking in the United States, and western clothes in Japan. This mutating identity was kept in play in order to maintain a certain distance from others and thereby retain her 'otherness,' both in the eyes of her western friends, and to mark herself as an outsider in the increasingly nativist culture of Japan.

Nativism was in fact the stock response to all these acts of feminine spatial transgression, a desire to enfold all this enlightening talk and the exercising of bright new identities into a masculine fantasy of dark interiors and the confinement of women, a desire which is immediately apparent in Tanizaki's fanciful descriptions which equate layers of dress with the architectural layering of a traditional Japanese house: 'This was the darkness in which ghosts and monsters were active, and indeed was not the woman who lived in it, behind thick curtains, behind layer after layer of screens and doors - was she not of a kind with them? The darkness wrapped her round tenfold, twenty fold, it filled the collar, the sleeves of her kimono, the folds of her skirt, wherever a hollow invited' (Tanizaki 1977:35).

SITES OF ABANDONMENT

For Tanizaki, this is not about associating the dark interior with some form of *unheimlich*, it rather suggests an association with the mother as a known space to which to retreat when an external 'otherness' threatens. That is to say, darkness in the Japanese domestic interior evokes rich imaginings, but to the Japanese psyche these are different from a Western sense of the uncanny. Nevertheless, Tanizaki's romanticisation of interior space charts one of the many sites of abandonment which the various acts of spatial transgression created in the early twentieth century: the domestic interior had been sought out by western electric light, the *other* as well as the outside had forced its way inside. *Oku*, the deep, darkened interior space had been discovered and the woman confined there consequently revealed by being cast into western light. This is not so much science destroying the mystery, the poetics of space, but a witnessing of the dependency of that mystery upon a masculine insistence that it is bound up with the feminine.

Other sites of abandonment present themselves upon an examination of where the effects of spatial transgression have literally left their mark: the literal appearance, the unconcealing of women, their presence in the sight of others on the street, makes their domestic identity the first site of abandonment. This gave rise to the appearance of new words, new vocabulary, and the abandonment of older, more traditional terminology in favour of westernised words.

Returning to Tanizaki's narrative, it is obvious that dress is another site of abandonment, leaving behind the difficult restricting layers of the kimono, and adopting looser, freer garments from a western-style wardrobe. This new practice also led to the abandonment of a site for shoes that were once left outside the front of the department store.

In the kitchen, traditional Japanese meals took hours to prepare and emphasised the spatial separation of each individual dish onto plates of different shapes and sizes. During this period, many of these culinary practices were abandoned in favour of methods and gadgets which are less time-consuming - hence the growth in popularity of rice cookers and women's preference for casseroles, cooked all in one pot rather than occupying many separate dishes (Masahiro Hikata 1994:88).

In terms of employment, a woman's occupation, itself a spatially loaded term, is still largely 'decorative' many cases - as witnessed in the function of 'office ladies.' However, Japanese women have taken on new professional roles, a few now occupying spaces hitherto denied them in a corporate hierarchy, and have in the process abandoned some of the older roles. In hostess bars, the modern equivalent of the Yoshiwara, it is tall, blond, western women, eager for the attentions (and generous gifts) of wealthy Japanese businessmen, who have taken the place of *geisha*. In the many *karaoke* bars, Kunihiro Narumi postulates that the *karaoke* machine represents a kind of 'electric geisha,' providing mechanical accompaniment where there was once a Japanese girl playing the *shamisen* (Kunihiro Narumi 1994:60). Narumi points out that *karaoke* is an abbreviation of an expression that actually means 'empty orchestra,' and that its function, once provided by a *geisha* trained in the art of conversation, is to facilitate communication. The female service role is thereby abandoned, and the 'modern' Japanese woman joins her male compatriots singing and being entertained as a customer in her own right.

CONCLUSION

In many of these sites of abandonment, it becomes apparent that modernity in Japan was both shaped by and in turn assisted the progress of both the body image and spatial context of the 'modern' Japanese woman in the construction of her identity, by providing a means with which to mechanise or obviate her previous functions. This is not the whole story, however: the modernisation of the soul is not synonymous with the mechanisation of the body - emancipation demands a great deal more than that.

It would seem that while the 'modern' Japanese woman has achieved in many respects a new liminal position, her current position also highlights the limitation of feminist critique: the impossibility of what to do about the overriding patriarchy. This is one ideological site that in the present context of Japanese culture can neither be wholly transgressed nor abandoned. Westernisation has no real answer to offer on the Japanese question of male superiority and the lack of a genuine site for sexual equality.

Latterly, certain sites of abandonment within Japanese popular culture represent a less than encouraging development of the formation the 'modern' Japanese woman's identity. Fashion advertisements which use only Western models - *gaijin* - to display clothes paradoxically reveal a loss of confidence in the representational power of the Japanese body coupled with an increased self-orientalism. The Japanese body is cast aside, not considered to be the right size or shape, thereby constructing only a fantasy identity based on western bodily proportions and at the same time increasing the marked 'otherness' of Western counterparts (Creighton 1995:135).

What is needed now are signs of a movement beyond the spatially transgressive stage, which is in itself only the first part of overcoming a patriarchal value system, operating as an unspoken critique which deterritorialises certain problematic spaces. The second stage is that the critical spatial practices which were constructed by 'new women' and *moga* alike, are acknowledged, so that a process of ideological adjustment can take place, ultimately effecting a third stage, which is the reterritorialisation of traditional Japanese culture and urban spatiality. This requires a set of tactics with which to oppose the strategies of the state/patriarchy. These could perhaps be constituted by emphasising the 'Way of Spirit' instead of the 'Way of Art,' thereby abandoning the strictures of *kata* for a more open-ended, creative mode described as *asobi no seishin*, which 'at the peak of its development, escapes from religion and is based on the playful spirit...of the common people' (Creighton 1995:135).

Finally, then, a moment to consider what may seem on the face of things too trivial a space to end this discussion, yet easily one of the most playful, most prolific, socially produced spaces in modern Japan: the Love Hotel. As a site of spatial transgression it indicates the abandonment of the home as a place suitable for sexual relations. This form of pleasure palace, which has been a feature of entertainment districts in Japanese urban environments since the 1950s, typically has rooms which can be rented by the hour, or overnight, and is a complex mixture of the discreet and the flamboyant. Nowadays, love hotels are just as often used by young married couples as for extra-marital liaisons, which perhaps shows the extent to which the 'new woman' has made the love marriage a priority (the woman's right to choose a partner was only granted as late as 1947).

As a site of abandonment, in relation to the traditional home there are signs that even the love hotel enables the Japanese woman to modernise through a form of mechanisation: Nicholas Bornoff writes: 'as a machine for sensual pleasure, the love hotel pulls out all the architectural stops. Exempt from having to conform to the norms determining the relentless sameness of the average Japanese home, it is an antidote to humdrum lives' (Bornoff 1992:50). The decor of the love hotel bedroom typically avoided reference to the traditional Japanese domestic interior with all its connotations of servitude, making it a unique space in the formation of the identity of the 'modern' Japanese woman, and as Ueno has notes, one 'in which women can escape the distinction between *yujo* and *jionna*' (Ueno 1996:139). Most importantly, the love hotel indicates that women have achieved a positive space which is outside of the home environment in which to construct their sexuality, which is still an evolving process.

Initially, love hotels favoured romantic western motifs on their street facades, turreted castles with garish neon signs recalling predominantly European precedents. Inside, there were rooms catering for a range of extravagant masculine tastes, complete with a variety of sex aids. In the 1950s and 1960s love hotels were still essentially the product of bachelor urbanism, places in which a man's sexual appetite could be satisfied. What is interesting, however, is that these many of these interiors are now being refurbished, and after careful surveys of 'modern' women's tastes (since it is predominantly the woman now making the choice as to which love hotel to frequent), they are being re-fitted with more bland, impersonal interiors, even sometimes traditional Japanese decor, to replace the previously fantasy-themed rooms. In the case of the bland, generic interior, what is significant is that the male fantasy has effectively been transgressed in favour of an environment which does not objectify women to the same extent as givers of pleasure, enabling them also to play the role of pleasure-seekers. This indicates that connotative values have changed, but rather than interpret this as a sign that 'modern' Japanese women no longer regard traditional Japanese interiority as a site of incarceration, and now feel comfortable in their status and their identity to want to make love in such surroundings, it is more likely that rooms themed on traditional Japanese interiors now carry connotations of historical romance, since their modern occupants feel just as remote from this domestic past as they do from the European fantasy interior.

It is ironic, then, that while Japan once sought to modernise its cultural context by employing a range of Western signifiers, it is now the traditional aspects of Japanese life that are being recontextualised in the same way as new cultural imports from the West were in the past. Department stores are now having to perform the role of mediating traditional Japanese culture to a younger generation which is unfamiliar with older customs and rituals. In this process of recontextualising home-grown culture, which inevitably involves a reinvestment of attention in some of the sites of abandonment I have highlighted, it remains to be seen whether this can be achieved without recourse to old patriarchal definitions of spatiality. There is the potential for newly constructed urban spaces and practices to offer a less gendered approach to the construction of meaning, by avoiding the tendency to privilege the feminine as the site of a specifically Japanese past, as Tanizaki was wont to do. Women's attitudes to the occupation of space have shown themselves to be more flexible than this, and in the next stage of constructing identity in the context of space and culture, it is likely to be this open-mindedness which informs future developments.

REFERENCES

Bellah, Robert (1976) *Beyond Belief: essays on Tradition in a post-traditional World.* New York: Harper and Row.

Bernstein, Gail Lee (1991) *Recreating Japanese Women, 1600-1945.* Berkeley: University of California Press.

Bornoff, Nicholas (1992) *Pink Samurai*. London: Grafton.

Buruma, Ian (1995) *A Japanese Mirror*. London: Vintage.

Creighton, Millie (1992) 'The *Depato*: Merchandising the west while selling Japaneseness,' in: Joseph Tobin (ed.) *Re-made in Japan*. New Haven: Yale University Press.

Creighton, Millie, (1995) 'Imaging the Other in Japanese Advertising Campaigns,' in: James G. Carrier (ed.) *Occidentalism: Images of the West*. Oxford: Oxford University Press.

Davis, Darrell William (1996) *Picturing Japaneseness*. New York: Columbia University Press.

Hidenobu, Jinnai (1995) *Tokyo: A Spatial Anthropology*. Berkeley: University of Califonia Press.

Hikata, Masahiro, (1994) 'Japanese Tableware: a Pottery Museum in every Home,' in: Atsushi Ueda (ed.) *Electric Geisha*. Tokyo: Kodansha

Hiroko, Tomida (1996) 'The Evolution of Japanese Women's Historiography,' *Japan Forum*, vol. 8, no. 2.

Hopper, Helen M (1996) *A New Woman in Japan: a political biography of Kato Shidzue*. Boulder: Westview Press.

Lebra, Takie Sugiyama (1984) *Japanese Women: Constraint and Fulfilment*. Hawaii: University of Hawai'i Press.

Miller, Laura (1995) 'Crossing Ethnolinguistic Boundaries: A Preliminary look at the Gaijin Tarento in Japan,' in: John Lent (ed.) *Asian Popular Culture*. Oxford: Westview Press.

Miura, Akira, (1985) *'English' in Japanese*. Tokyo: Yohan Publications Inc.

Mackie, Vera (1996) 'Equal Opportunity and Gender Identity: Feminist Encounters with Modenity and Postmodernity in Japan,' in: Y Sugimoto and J P Arnason (eds) *Japanese Encounters with Postmodernity*. London: Kegan Paul.

Napier, Susan (1996) *The Fantastic in Modern Japanese Literature: the subversion of Modernity*. London: Routledge.

Narumi, Kunihiro (1994) 'The Electric Geisha,' in: Atsushi Ueda (ed.) *Electric Geisha*. Tokyo: Kodansha.

Pincus, Leslie (1991) 'In a Labyrinth of Western Desire, Japan in the World,' *Boundary 2*, vol. 18, no. 3.

Robertson, Jennifer Ellen (1998) *Takarazuka, sexual politics and popular culture in modern Japan*. Berkeley: University of California Press.

de Sabato, Elizabeth (1995) *The Women of the Pleasure Quarter*. Worcester: Art Musuem.

Savigliano, Marta (1992) 'Tango in Japan and the World Economy of Passion,' in: Joseph Tobin (ed.) *Re-made in Japan*. New Haven: Yale University Press.

Silverberg, Miriam (1991) 'Japan in the World,' Masao Miyoshi (ed.), *Boundary 2*, vol. 18, no. 3, Durham: Duke University Press.

Stevenson, John (1995) *Yoshitoshi's Women*. Seattle: University of Washington Press.

Suzuki, Tomi (1997) *Narrating the Self: Fictions of Japanese Modernity*. Stanford: Stanford University Press.

Takahashi, Yasuo, (1994) 'Why You can't have Green Tea in a Japanese Coffee Shop,' in: Atsushi Ueda (ed.) *Electric Geisha*. Tokyo: Kodansha.

Tanizaki, Jun'ichiro (1985) *Naomi*. New York: North Point Press.

Tanizaki, Jun'ichiro (1977) *In Praise of Shadows*. New Haven: Leete's Island Books.

Ueno, Chizuko (1996) 'Urbanism and the Transformation of Sexuality: Edo to Tokyo,' *Columbia Documents of Architecture and Theory*, vol. 5.

Wasuro, Ann (1996) *Modern Japanese Society 1868-1994*. Oxford: Oxford University Press

Wilson, Sandra (1996) 'Women, the State, the Media in Japan in the early 1930s: Fujo Shimbun and the Manchurian Crisis,' *Japan Forum*, vol. 7, no. 1, April 1996, pp. 87-106.

CHAPTER 5

MARVELLOUS ME:[1]
THE BEAUTY INDUSTRY AND THE CONSTRUCTION OF
THE 'MODERN' INDIAN WOMAN

SHOMA MUNSHI

Once upon a time, a dusky beauty glided down the ramp of London's Albert Hall to be crowned Miss World. The year was 1966, the girl was Reita Faria, who reputedly had entered the contest for a lark with borrowed finery from friends and family - and won. Cut to 1999 and another nubile nymphet sashaying down an aisle in London's Olympia Theatre. But this was no gauche ingenué. Dressed in an ice blue evening gown studded with Swarovski crystals, smiling a pearly white smile, the lady was cool, sophisticated and articulate. Upon being crowned Miss World, the eyes misted over on cue behind the water proof mascara, and Yukta Mookhey became the fourth title holder for India since 1994 on the international beauty circuit (*India Today* 1999). As this book goes to press, the newly crowned Miss Universe 2000 is Lara Dutta, once again an Indian.

This persona has become the face and body of the 'modern' Indian woman of today. Around her has grown a profitable beauty industry which takes care of every aspect of women's appearance in India nowadays. The outside look meets the international blueprint for beauty - glamorous, healthy and beautiful - and it connects India to the outside 'modern' world. This investment in appearance as a key identity marker, particularly in post-liberalisation India, makes representation of one's looks and bodies a crucial area for (re)defining femininity (cf. Macdonald 1995: 192). Since the opening up of markets in 1991, two things have been happening simultaneously: India is perceived as a huge potential market for consumer products, and market research data indicates the changing profile of the 'modern' Indian woman, saying that 'the hedonistic woman has at last come of age' (IMRB 1998).

The focus of this paper is a middle class, urban consumer culture, in which I examine the growth of the 'beauty industry' in India: how marketers and advertisers are targeting women for their makeup and fitness items in what has become a booming industry; how many of these media discourses are influenced by global media flows; yet how, such global discourses remain contained within discourses which are classified as traditionally Indian.

THE INDIAN MEDIA LANDSCAPE

The 1990s in India witnessed sweeping transformations in the information and communications landscapes. Once liberalisation of the Indian economy started up in 1991, the boom in media industries became practically unstoppable. A few landmark events in the sphere of the media which have resulted in an open skies policy, signaling the final break with Nehruvian socialism, need to be mentioned here. One was the introduction of the Prasar Bharati (Broadcasting Corporation of India) Act, 1990, which came into effect in September 1997, and which facilitates the creation of an autonomous body, the Prasar Bharati Corporation, to replace the system of government control over Doordarshan (the government television channel) and Akashvani (All-India Radio). Another was the beginning of live broadcasting of the proceedings of the Indian Parliament 'wherein the saga of democracy at its best in the making and unmaking of governments was witnessed by millions of people ...' (Doordarshan 1997). A third was the Broadcasting Bill of 1997, designed to replace the Cable Television Networks (Regulation) Act of 1995, in order to facilitate and regulate broadcasting services. Most importantly, after the general elections in India in October 1999, Prime Minister Atal Behari Vajpayee, set up a task force for reforms in the telecommunications industry, and for the first time ever in India, a new IT (information and technology) ministry was set up as well.

The media scene in India has changed both quantitatively and qualitatively as a result of these measures. Currently, India numbers more than fifty television channels, a third of which are government owned, and the rest are owned privately, of Indian and foreign ownership. Both the state-controlled Doordarshan and private channels like ZEE, STAR, Sony, EL, ATN etc are vying for viewers, whose numbers have risen from 17 million to over 300 million in less than fifteen years (Zee, n.d.). Indeed, it is said that India's present status now ranks it as 'the world's largest television network - Doordarshan - with a large number of private cable and satellite channels' (Agrawal 1997: 145), which now jostle with each other for viewership ratings, in the world's largest democracy with a population of a billion people as of 15 August 1999 (Internet: 1999). The national channel (Doordashan) is facing stiff competition from both private as well as regional channels.

In the critical area of viewership preferences, the National Readership Survey shows that 'the upper and middle income urban audiences prefer ZEE TV and Sony to the entertainment channel DD2 or Metro. Doordarshan's revenues have dipped as a result - from Rs 570 crores[2] in 1996-97 to Rs 395 crores in 1998-99. Channels less widely received in the country meanwhile have registered increasing profits: ZEE's annual revenue is Rs 325 crores, Sony's Rs 275 crores, and Sun is touching Rs 170 crores (Business Standard: 2000). It is well known that India has the world's largest film industry based in Mumbai (Bombay) popularly referred to as Bollywood.

Therefore, as far as the entertainment industry goes, India is now indeed working overtime. Ever since the Gulf War, when the country opened its doors to foreign satellite channels, the viewer is spoilt for choice. At the heart of everything - advertising, publicity, entertainment, fashion and films - lies the magic mantra of communication. What with Miss Indias now regularly lifting the crown at international beauty pageants, which are telecast live all over the world, the country has entered the portals of the worldwide entertainment industry, and an entry point for Asia. Its size is estimated at Rs 15 400 crores, of which the total spend on advertising is estimated at about Rs 8400 crores (ibid.).

ENTER THE GLOBO-INDIANS:
URBAN CONSUMER CULTURE

Both as a viewer and as a buyer, the Indian consumer is in an enviable position today and is being wooed assiduously. Television viewing has become a veritable smorgasbord with non-stop, high quality programmes being beamed through how-many-channels-are-you-getting-now, and assuring the viewer that they are part of a global lifestyle market.

Televisions serials account for the highest viewership ratings. This is a sea change from the days when Doordarshan's Sunday morning broadcasts of the epics *Ramayana* and *Mahabharata* had an entire nation tuning in to them to the exclusion of everything else[3]. Given the choice on the small screen these days, it is serials like *Amanat* (Property, more in the sense of heritage), *Ashirwad* (Blessings), *Saans* (Breath), *Basera* (Shelter, thereby implying home), *Saath Saath* (Together) and others which dominate viewing time. Perhaps there is a wry truth in the observation that 'today's role models are the Kaamyas, Heenas and Priyas (of television serials) who lead vicarious lives on television ...' (Dash 2000).

The consumer durables and non-durables market has also witnessed many changes. Global lifestyles for the urban middle classes in India have been made possible by the fact that almost all international brands are available locally now. Companies, spurred on by fierce competition, churn out a seemingly never-ending range of products that are top quality, priced at affordable levels, and backed by prompt service. Market research data shows that the Indian consumer has never had it so good.

As far as consumer profiling is concerned, the woman, like before, remains the key decision maker in purchases. Not just that. Qualitative market research data on Indian women indicates that with the increase of women in the work place and the proliferation of global media channels, today's 'modern' woman in India 'crosses behavioural boundaries all the time... she is confident and can hold her own in any place and at any time' (IMRB 1998). The November 1997 findings of P: SNAP, an extensive psychographic and lifestyle study conducted by Pathfinders, the market research bureau, are telling. The study, which covered 11 000 women in 38 centres, showed that 'women are becoming more individualistic and paying greater attention to themselves' (P: SNAP 1997).

And producers of visual media - advertisers, film and television producers - are fast catching up with this. Conscious to the fact of women's changing roles, they have consequently begun to enlarge the range of feminine subjectivities which will increase consumption. For the 'modern' woman, who now in most cases combines both family and career, familial relationships and independence, selflessness and a little (long overdue) selfishness, media discourses now articulate distinct methods of address towards her. As Anvar Ali Khan of Ogilvy and Mather advertising pointed out to me, words like 'style,' 'grace,' 'presence' have become the new buzzwords in advertisement copywriting'[4].

As global media flows become part of the lexicon of contemporary India - especially in the beauty industry - more and more advertisements and films depict a material culture which plays upon the aspirations of a large middle class, numbering over 250 million (Internet 1999) who are caught in the globalisation process as they swing between their Indian traditions and internalising a transnational identity more in keeping with global lifestyles (cf. Murshi 1999).

Such global lifestyles of the urban middle classes in India today are not just 'imagined,' but very real ones. Large numbers of them have some close family member living overseas, either studying, working, or in business. A substantial number of urban, middle and upper middle class Indians also travel overseas at least once a year, whether on vacation or on work. Maintenance of ties with friends and family overseas has been strengthened by the new information and communication technologies (like e-mail, or being able to watch the same television programmes) which allow the possibility of time and space to collapse by their sheer speed and at times, simultaneity of transmission.

Thus, new lifestyle and connected consumption patterns are produced by global flows of information and communication technologies, and these are localised to suit domestic tastes and preferences where the need arises. Indeed, market research shows that with the availability of most global

brand names in India now, Indians no longer feel that 'westernisation equals the best. By extension, global brands are not axiomatic preferences ... it is "internationalised-but-Indian"
moorings of the consumer which have to be examined now' (Youth P:SNAP Polls 1997).

MAKING UP AND MAKING DO

Studies done on visual media flows in the West show how definitions of femininity have been linked to the development of consumer culture and the broad shifts in the ways in which women were constructed: most notably, a shift from the representation of women in terms of their roles as wife and mother to an increasing emphasis on glamour, sexuality and appearance (see for instance, Winship 1987; Wolf 1991; McRobbie 1991; Wilson 1992; Dowling 1993; Macdonald 1995; Lury 1996). A similar pattern can be seen in the representations of femininity in the Indian visual media as well (see for instance, Munshi 1997 and 1998). Advertisements of the 1960s and 1970s in India mainly featured women in their roles as homemaker - as a mother, wife and daughter-in-law (the last being important in the context of joint families in India). Treating motherhood seriously as a vocation was strongly visible in advertising then. At a time when women were generally homebound, being a full-time housewife was the norm whose mothering activities were not to be treated lightly. Advertising discourse, fully aware of this, adopted a serious, almost righteous air, while targeting mothers as consumers (Munshi 1998:578). Not just that. Ads from the 1960s and '70s depicting the woman always showed her anxious for the approval of her husband and mother-in-law. Television commercials for Sanifresh (a household cleaner) in the 1980s depicted the daughter-in-law holding her breath in terrified fear while her mother-in-law checked every corner of the house for any offending dirt. Military music playing in the background clearly underscored the mother-in-law's superior hierarchical position.

Women's preoccupation with what Janice Winship famously called 'the work of femininity' (paying attention to one's appearance) in India has followed a somewhat different route from western representations. As far as advertising went, there were very few beauty product advertisements. If any, they had to do with hair oil: long, thick hair worn braided or in a bun was the general fashion norm; creams and powders with skin-whitening and smoothening properties: a smooth, fair skin was considered a hallmark of good looks. They also underlined the need for masculine appreciation. The herbal soap Margo stressed the natural properties of the product and told the woman that it left her with 'a naturally glowing complexion and exhaustive compliments from your man.' Films sometimes, particularly those with stories of rich landlords, had the women doing *shringar* (dressing up) in long scenes: getting their hair braided by maids, wearing jewellery and expensive saris while waiting for their husbands to come home. It is not that women did not pay attention to their appearance. They did so, but in a very different way, and one which always needed approbation, either from the husband or from the family.

With the gradual decline in the numbers of joint families in urban India, an increase in the numbers of women in the workplace, the wife and mother who lives for her husband and children is morphing into the partner and friend who is carving out her own consumption and self-fulfilment space (P:SNAP Polls: 1997). The cosmetic company, Modi-Revlon for instance is building its brand through a series of profiles of professionally successful women who radiate confidence about their achievements. Maruti Udyog now market their hugely sold Maruti 800 as the care which helps the woman balance both home and career with the byline 'helps you speed between two worlds.' She also seems less dependent on outside approval than before. Indeed, Anne French hair remover's byline has gone from the 1970s 'don't you want his approval?' to the 1990s 'I feel soft and silky and woman all over.'

Standards of beauty have also changed. With the proliferation of global media flows, particularly satellite television, what is considered 'beautiful' and 'modern' has also now undergone a change. It is now far more aligned to westernised representations of what is considered beautiful. The voluptuous film actresses with long hair of the 1970s have yielded to short haired *Baywatch* style bodies on our Bollywood heroines and models.

Nowhere is the influence of global media flows more potently visible than in advertisements for makeup and fitness items. Following television commercials in the West on specialised institutes for skin care (L'Oréal, Pond's, Clinique), India too now boasts of the Pond's Institute where women are now invited to write in with their queries on skin care. In a similar vein, just as beauty counsellors for the international range of Clinique skincare products are present to help women choose the correct products for their skin type in almost all the big departmental stores in the West, Lakme's 'Orchid' and their latest 'On Top of the World' ranges are sold by 'trained beauty counsellors' just 'like they have back on Fifth Avenue.'

International companies like Lancôme, Elizabeth Arden, Vichy, Christian Dior, etc. all liberally incorporate semi-scientific reasoning in marketing their products. Not only do they detail the elements which protect the skin even while using makeup, they also pay great attention to that great fear of wrinkles and other visible signs of ageing. Indian advertising here has fast caught up with the West. Products claiming age-delaying properties like Calope's Evening Primrose oil capsules with 'EFA (essential fatty acids), GLA (gamma linolenic acid) and LA (linolenic acid)'; Nisha's Herbal product's 'Shape Up' tablets, now promise the elixir of looking youthful beyond one's years. Lakme's range of cosmetic products powerfully incorporates scientific discourse for the protection and nourishment of the skin. In their 'Maximum' range, the hand and body lotion's 'special self-adjusting formula ... contains lecithin to balance your skin's pH factor ... and milk, the best known natural emollient to pamper your skin; while the sunscreen lotion acknowledges that ' ... the sun's harmful ultra violet rays damage your skin causing sunburn and leading to fine lines and wrinkles.' The sunscreen factor is 'the umbrella for your skin with the latest in skin care technology with Vitamin E and a sun Protection Factor (SPF). Their 'Ultra' range of blushers and lipsticks has D-Panthenol in its composition and, in advanced western style, a 'shade card' with 'different shades to match your skin.' Whether Lakme, or Modi-Revlon, or Tips and Toes or Elle, expressions used in describing their range of makeup are powerfully reminiscent of western advertising: descriptions like 'lush, smooth, silky, sheer, luxurious, creamy, sheen and lustre' predominate.

Hair care product advertising till the 1990s were mainly for hair oils with herbal ingredients like *skikakai* and *amla* as the basic nutrient properties. But hair then was also generally worn long, braided or in a bun. Married women in fact had their heads covered with the *pallav* (one end) of the sari or the *chunni* (the long scarf) of the churidar kurta ensemble. This has also changed. Hair is worn short and styled in many different ways and even married women (except for an intial period) cover their heads less and less. All hair care products now make references to Vitamin E, Panthenol, Pro Vitamin B5, Byogen, Keratin and Glucasil to retain glossy, shining hair. Created by Laboratoires Garnier, Paris, the Ultra Doux 'hair care beauty system' is one 'where science gets to the heart of nature.' Their 'hair oil has coconut oil for intensive nourishment, almond oil for softening, vitamin E for protection and Vitamin F to replenish essential nutrients.' Even older, established porducts on the market like Bengal Chemicals' cantharidine hair oil 'brings long hair back to fashion' aided by 'Cleopatra's hair care secret, "cantharis" (after which the hair oil is named). Similarly, Dey's Medical with their traditional Keo Karpin hair oils have enlarged their range of hair care products to include vitalizers and nourishers. The latter, called 'Extra Hair nourisher' comprises 'five internationally proven proteins and vitamins of biotin, keratin, panthenol, nicotinic acid and resorcinol' in its composition and details the values of each for maintaining that lustrous mane.

Unsightly, unwanted body hair now has new and powerful enemies in Rowenta's Body Style Waxer which promises 'the easy way out' with which 'your skin has never looked better.' And felt better.' Anne French hair removing creams and lotions with their 'special baby oil gently dissolves all unwanted hair away, leaving you with satin smooth and silky skin.' The appeal to cosmopolitan lifestyles is clear in the marketing of the model from Satinelle from philips. Under the very caption 'Lifestylers,' it promises that 'using its internationally patented method of removing unwanted body hair swiftly, smoothly and cleanly,' It will result in 'satin smooth arms-n'-legs ... and a dazzling social life!'

THE BODY BEAUTIFUL

The one area where concessions are no longer made to older norms of Indian beauty is the body. Up until the 1980s, it was fine to be well-rounded and even voluptuous, and films and advertisements of those years reflect this. But come the 1990s, and Indian cinema and advertising reflect the arrival of the perfectly sculpted body to meet exacting international standards. It no longer matters that the international blueprint for beauty does not match the time-honoured, indigenous one: way taller than the average Indian woman with never-ending legs. If international beauty contests are anything to go by, then India is all set to replace Venezuela in producing international beauty queens: after Reita Faria won the Miss World crown in 1966, India produced no beauty contest winners till the '90s. But in the past six years alone, Sushmita Sen became the first Indian ever to be crowned Miss Universe in 1994 with model Aishwarya Rai grabbing the Miss World crown in the same year; followed by two more Miss Worlds, Diana Hayden in 1997 and Yukta Mookhey in 1999. Most recently Lara Dutta was crowned Miss Universe in the early part of 2000.

On fieldwork in India, I interviewed Pradeep Guha and Sathya Saran, part of *The Times of India* group which hosts the Miss India contest. The *Times* group are responsible for grooming the beauty pageant winners to perfection before dispatching them to compete with the best from the rest of the world. Both Guha and Saran averred that India is a huge market with enormous potential and that they are well-equipped to produce winners from such a huge crop of young hopefuls. The only two prerequisites were to be reasonable pretty and taller than average. The rest was 'positioning and packaging: two factors of utmost importance.' The formula which they described to me had been worked out to a pinnacle of perfection - after an initial screening, personalised food plans, fitness workouts to shape up and lose weight from 'trouble spots' like hips and thighs, plastic surgery if necessary, sartorial and physical grooming, etiquette, diction and general knowledge sessions, tossing difficult questions around and coming up with politically correct answers to be delivered while sashaying up that aisle victoriously'[5].

This 'tyranny of slenderness' as Kim Chernin (1981) calls it has now become an important feminine preoccupation. The beauty industry does not lag behind in what has become an eminently profit making venture and astute advertising now appeals to the 'modern' woman in urging her to invest in working out and getting fit which have been accorded status. The similarities for instance, in the Nike advertisement and the one for Hero Fitness apparatus are startling. The Nike ad depicts a small happy baby facing the camera with the accompanying text: 'One day you're strolling around ... and looking the world straight in the eye without so much as a blush. Then wallop! Puberty. Boys. Magazine images. Suddenly the mirror is no longer your friend ... Get real. Make your body the best it can be for one person. Yourself. Just do it.' The Hero ad in India is almost an echo of the Nike one. It pictures two small babies with their backs to the camera in this case, and it reads: 'Most bodies are born perfect ... a sweet tooth develops. Followed by the desire to curl up on couches and watch TV. And before you know it, you're embarrassed to attend your old school reunion ... exercise has never been more within your control. Nor has your shape. Get ready to get fit.' Both advertisements reflect infancy's untroubled state with one's own body, and how in later years, worries and anxieties about one's appearance develop. In both cases, exercise and physical fitness are clearly within one's control.

Physical exercise and working out, not just for women, as has been happening over the last decade, is something new in India. Indeed, well-fed bodies earlier were more testimony to the fact that the person came from a well-to-do family and ate well, rather than to bad dietary habits and lack of exercise. In this, India has fast caught up with the West. Today, the muscled, taut body has become something of a cultural icon: it flaunts to the world that one now cares for oneself and how one appears to others. Implicitly, one does not simply shape oneself, but one shapes one's life as it were.

This desirable and narcissistic body is on display not just on our beauty queens, but also on film stars, models and television celebrities. Not just that. Fitness centres and beauty parlours have mushroomed everywhere. Smaller Indian towns which used to have just a beauty parlour now find themselves neighbours of fitness and workout centres. Discourses of physical appearance and bodycare have shifted from the private to the public space now.

Academic writings are plentiful on the body as a socially and culturally powerful medium (see for instance, Douglas 1982, 1966; Bourdieu 1977; Foucault 1981; Brownmiller 1984; Jaggar and Bordo 1984; Bordo 1993). The point I wish to make in the contemporary Indian context is that today's urban, media-driven, consumer culture mirrors Western ideals of the perfect body - perfectly shaped, toned and exercised. In 1990s India, this has rightly been termed 'the arrival of the professional body; a body acquired, shaped and toned like any other professional skill' (Ghosh 1999:22). Nowhere is this more visible than in the case of the successful stars of Hindi cinema today who are all required to be dancers and action heroes/heroines in addition to being actors/actresses as well. Stars like Shah Rukh Khan, Hrithik Roshan, Salman Khan, Aamir Khan, Karishma Kapoor, Urmila Matondkar, Madhuri Dixit and others are ' ... all stars for whom the display of the body and the body-in-performance are integral to the spectacle' (ibid.). Beauty contest winners become Indian ambassadresses for international brands on the Indian market: Diana Hayden is the face of L'Oréal; Sushmita Sen for Seiko Epson computers; Rhea Pillai for Piaget; and Aishwarya Rai for Longines. On the Longines webpage in fact, Rai shares the honours with other international models (*Outlook India* 1999).

THE BEAUTY BUSINESS

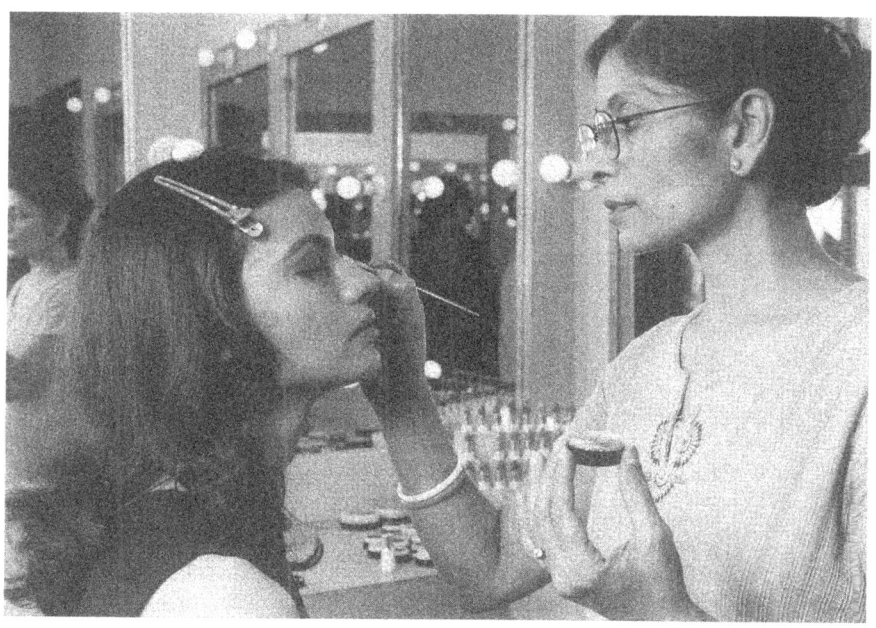

'A BEAUTY PARLOUR IN NEW DELHI'

While the beauty queens and media celebrities become the 'faces' and 'bodies' to launch a thousand fashion products, it is really the faceless urban Indian who is propelling the nation's beauty business which, 'worth Rs 1500 crores six years ago, has today grown to over Rs 3000 crores and can only spiral exponentially' (ibid.). As in any market driven scenario, it has to do with business and profits, the changing character of the consumer (especially women) and the shifting orientation of the market.

The old powder and cream routine, for long a staple in the search for looking good, is completely passé now. Between coloured contact lenses, smile enhancement surgery, liposuction and ever-increasing beauty parlours and weight reduction clinics, Indian women have realised that style is important. The sudden spurt of made-in-India international beauties has also done much to boost their self-esteem. Obviously the beauty business does not lag behind and are aware of the huge market. Leading global brands are sometimes priced at the top end of the spectrum, but they are aware that a market for their product exists. More affordable brands swamp the market place. Indeed, there is a war on now for cornering a segment of the nail enamel market which is being fought out between companies like Modi-Revlon, Lakme, Maybelline, Elle and others (*Business Standard* 2000). Nutritionist Anjali Mukherjee says ' a sizable percentage of my clients are women who want to get into shape post-pregnancy or post-lactation.' Cosmetic surgeon, Vijay Sharma, who sculpts faces and figures, is on record saying' 'my business has grown 600-fold since 1988 ... looking good has become an obsession with people.' Sharma terms this 'hyper-aesthetic tension' (*Times of India* 1999).

Such intensive investment in the outward physical appearance of the woman - hair shining and styled, nails painted, glossy lipsticked mouths, exercised taut bodies - makes media representations of such images a crucial area where discursive negotiation over the creation of meaning in portraying the 'modern' woman takes place. If 'representations of the "new woman" are ultimately bound up with the politics of identity' (Lee 1988:168), then media modes of address in India today recognise the intimate relation of appearance with identity in this portrayal.

BEAUTY GOES BEYOND THE MIRROR: CELEBRATING FEMININITY THE INDIAN WAY

So how do such media representations, particularly the beauty business, influenced as they are by global media flows and international standards of beauty, instill a sense of 'Indian-ness' and a pride in the image of India? As noted earlier in the paper, visual media in India now echoes post-liberalisation India with the youthful, westernised-yet-India-at-heart persona for whom London and New York are nearby but whose heart is in the right place, being unflinchingly Indian. The middle class urban Indian now comfortably straddles two worlds, and this is due, in large measure to how, in today's transnational world, 'questions of multiple citizenship and multicultural education have gained priority' and therefore 'hyphenated identities' (van der Veer 1999:7) or 'double coded identities' (Kellner 1995:242) have become the order of the day.

Two things then are happening in tandem with each other: both the producers of visual media and consumers/audiences feel that India has arrived on the 'global scene' - best exemplified by the victories at international beauty pageants - yet never forgetting one's Indian roots. Our beauty contest winners are the faces and bodies of the 'modern' Indian woman, connecting India as they do, to the outside world, and earning kudos for India on the global stage. Indians feel a great sense of pride at the victories of these young girls overseas. One only has to see the receptions they are accorded on their return to Indian shores, being fêted by the government, the media and the general public. They represent an 'international look' adhering to internationally accepted standards of physical beauty. At the same time, awareness of one's physical appearance, being fit, well-turned out sartorially has grown over the years, and the beauty business cashes in on this rapidly growing market eager for cosmetics and make up and fitness items.

How then is 'Indian-ness' signified? This is done through other means. Reams of print are given over to interviewing the beauty contest winners, their families, and those responsible for their success on the international arena. Over and over again, they all talk of how 'modern' the girls have become and can hold their own against the best from the rest of the world, yet how 'our girls' have not forgotten the importance of 'traditional Indian values.' Apart from the rigours of working out, training, physical fitness and beauty makeovers, those who prepare the contestants talk of the importance of 'a Vedic lifestyle, replete with yoga, mantras and meditation' (see for instance, *India Today* 1999). So prana shakti is skillfully juggled with Christian Dior, Estée Lauder and the 'Firm and Full' bust developer. All the contestants are on record saying how their parents are responsible for their mindset and how they have been 'driving forces in their rise to fame' (ibid.). The mother of Yukta Mookhey, Miss World 1999, in an interview with *The Times of India* (1999) says 'Indian women ... are modernising themselves without uprooting from traditional Indian values. The Indian woman of today represents a healthy blend of the modern and the traditional.'

Stereotypes of the 'modern' Indian woman are reinforced by other visual media representations as well. The 'face' of the music channel, Channel V,

Ruby Bhatia-Bali, a former Miss India who came from Toronto to work in the Indian media industry is a perfect example of this. Dressed in shorts and a T-shirt, with close cropped hair, she typifies a youthful westernised image. Yet in interviews, she says ' I had a nose ring for five years in Canada ... I was really attached to my culture, that's why I don't have a problem living in India, I love it. 'Cause I'm so Indian ... I'm vegetarian, I'm very religious, I can quote our ancient scriptures ... I was raised very Indian ... I wasn't allowed to date ...' (quoted in Butcher 1999:174). Furthermore, as Butcher notes, '... the Indianness of Ruby is signified (by placing) the body in context to remind the viewer that it is an Indian body: speaking Hindi, Hinglish[6], surrounded by Hindi pop and film music, and the station identification logos' (ibid.).

Popular Hindi cinema, or Bollywood films as they are called, and advertisements are also responsible in large measure for keeping this stereotype of the 'modern' Indian woman alive and well. Today's film stars and models dance and perform like on MTV, wear leather jackets and mini skirts as well as salwar kurtas and saris. They are practised in the ways of the West, and at the same time retain their Indian values. And media representations of them are that of straddling the cultural divide by appearing to have become global Indians who offer an appealing model of cultural coherence to Indians of all ages, whether within or outside the country. Karishma Kapoor has a perfectly sculpted body and wears designer togs, but tears up divorce papers in *Raja Hindustani* (King Indian); Mahima Kapoor may have reached Las Vegas but refuses to sleep with fiancé Apoorva Agnihotri till they are married in *Pardes* (Foreign Country); the Oxford-educated Rani Mukherjee returns in mini skirts and can pluck the strings of a guitar, but can equally well sing Om Jai Jagdeesh Hare (a devotional hymn) in *Kuch Kuch Hota Hai* (A Little Something Happens). Which is why in advertising discourses, the 'woman of substance' despite being 'worth it' and driving the Maruti 800 which 'helps her speed between two worlds,' regards 'a crèche, a ma-in-law and a good maid as the best support systems one can have' (*Femina* 1998). Which is why Subhash Ghai's *Taal* (Beat) which earned huge revenues in the overseas market, and which is reflective of today's genre of successful Bollywood films, takes the approach of appealing to all sections of opinion: it winks at a younger generation with skin tight lycra ensembles and a London-educated hero while at the same time, the heroine is Indian at heart despite her western clothes. *Taal*'s heroine is Aishwarya Rai, an earlier Miss World and supermodel, and 'Ash' as she is called in the media, mouths platitudinous dialogue like 'if an Indian girl wears western clothes, it does not mean that she ceases to have Indian values.'

It is the chicken-and-egg syndrome. Post-liberalisation India is a huge potential market and market research data shows how the 'modern' Indian woman has been growing dynamically, helped along in no small measure due to the success of made-in-India beauties on the international circuit. Correspondingly, the beauty industry is making the most of this profitable situation. But even economic imperatives have to pay attention to social and cultural standards to reap rewards. Which is why the 'marvellous me' persona wears the 'international' look on the outside, yet is a real 'home' girl at heart.

NOTES

1 I owe the title of this paper to Professor Jean Gelman-Taylor who told me about a primary school programme in America called 'Marvellous Me' for raising self-esteem in children.
2 Rs 1 crore is approximately equal to US$ 229,885, or a little less than a quarter of a million dollars which is US$ 250,000.
3 For studies on the televised epics, see for example, David Lutgendorf (1990) 'Ramayan: The Video,' *Drama Review* 34:2, pp. 127-76; and Purnima Mankekar (1993) 'Television Tales and a Woman's Rage: A Nationalist Recasting of Draupadi's "Disrobing" ,' *Public Culture*, 5:3, pp. 469-91.
4 Interview with advertising agencies on fieldwork in 1998-'99.
5 Personal interviews with Pradeep Guha and Sathya Saran, 1995-'96.
6 Hinglish refers to a mixture of Hindi and English. See Binod Agrawal 1997 for details.

REFERENCES

Agrawal, Binod C. (1997) 'The Meaning of Hinglishness: Liberalisation and Globalisation in Indian Broadcasting,' in: Kevin Robins (ed.) *Programming for People: From Cultural Rights to Cultural Responsibilities*. Italy: RAI, pp. 144-55.
Bordo, Susan (1993) *Unbearable Weight: Feminism, Western Culture and the Body*. Berkeley: University of California Press.
Bourdieu, Pierre (1977) *Outline of a Theory of Practice*. Cambridge: Cambridge University Press.
Brownmiller, Susan (1984) *Femininity*. New York: Ballantine.
Business Standard Weekend Section (2000), 1-7 April; 22-28 January.

Butcher, Melissa (1999) 'Parallel Texts: The Body and Television in India,' in: Christiane Brosius and Melissa Butcher (eds) *Image Journeys: Audio-Visual Media and Cultural Change in India*. New Delhi: Sage, pp. 165-96.

Chernin, Kim (1981) *The Obsession: Reflections on the Tyranny of Slenderness*. New York: Harper and Row.

Dash, Ruby (2000) 'Fusion or Confusion?,' *Business Standard Weekend Section*, 22-28 January.

Doordarshan (1997) *Audience Research Unit*. New Delhi: Directorate General Doordarshan.

Douglas, Mary (1982) *Natural Symbols*. New York: Pantheon.

--(1966) *Purity and Danger*. London: Routledge and Kegan Paul.

Dowling, R. (1993) 'Femininity, Place and Commodities: A Retail Case Study,' *Antipode* 25(4), pp. 295-319.

Femina (1998).

Foucault, Michel (1981) *The History of Sexuality: Volume One: An Introduction*. Harmondsworth: Penguin (first published 1976).

Ghosh, Shohini (1999) 'Local and Transnational Imaginary: Cultural Production in the Age of Satellite Broadcasting in India,' *IDPAD Newsletter* 6, pp. 19-23.

India Today (1999) 20 December.

Indian Market Research Bureau (IMRB) (1998) *Probe Qualitative Research on the Indian Woman*.

Internet (1999) *H-Asia Discussion List*, August.

Jaggar, Alison and Bordo, Susan (eds) (1984) *Gender/Body /Knowledge: Feminist Reconstructions of Being and Knowing*. New Brunswick: Rutgers University Press.

Kellner, Douglas (1995) *Media Culture: Cultural Studies, Identity and Politics between the Modern and the Postmodern*. London and New York: Routledge.

Lee, Janet (1988) 'Care to Join Me in an Upwardly Mobile Tango? Postmodernism and the "New Woman",' in: Lorraine Gamman and Margaret Marshment (eds) *The Female Gaze: Women as Viewers of Popular Culture*, pp. 166-72.

Lury, Celia (1996) *Consumer Culture*. Cambridge: Polity Press

Lutgendorf, David (1990) 'Ramayan: The Video,' *Drama Review* 34(2), pp. 127-76.

McRobbie, Angela (1991) *Feminism and Youth Culture: From 'Jackie' to 'Just Seventeen.'* London: Macmillan.

Macdonald, Myra (1995) *Representing Women: Myths of Femininity in the Popular Media*. London: Edward Arnold.

Mankekar, Purnima (1993) 'Television Tales and a Woman's Rage: A Nationalist Recasting of Draupadi's "Disrobing",' *Public Culture* 5(3), pp. 469-91.

Munshi, Shoma (1997) '"Women of Substance": Commodification and Fetishization in Contemporary Advertising within the Indian "Urbanscape",' *Social Semiotics* 7(1), pp. 37-53.

--(1998) 'Wife/Mother/Daughter-in-Law: Multiple Avatars of Homemaker in 1990s Indian Advertising,' *Media, Culture & Society* 20(4), pp. 573-91.

--(1999) '"Mera joota hai japani ... phir bhi dil hai hindustani": Visual Media, Consumer Culture and Identity Politics in India Today,' unpublished.

Outlook India (1999) 19 December.

Pathfinders India (1997) *P: SNAP Polls.*

The Times of India (1999) 12 December.

van der Veer, Peter (1999) 'ICTs: The Political Dimension,' unpublished.

Wilson, Elizabeth (1992) 'Fashion and the Postmodern Body' in: Juliet Ash and Elizabeth Wilson (eds) *Chic Thrills: A Fashion Reader.* London: Pandora, pp. 3-16.

Winship, Janice (1987) *Inside Women's Magazines.* London: Pandora

Wolf, Naomi (1991) *The Beauty Myth.* London: Vintage

Pathfinders: India (1997) *Youth P:SNAP Polls*

Zee (n.d.) Zee: *Always Better, Always Ahead.* Mumbai: Zee.

CHAPTER 6

SELLING THE 'MODERN WOMAN': CONSUMER CULTURE AND CHINESE GENDER POLITICS

PERRY JOHANSSON

The Chinese paradox of a Communist dictatorship with a fast developing capitalist economy has nourished an interesting discussion on the power of commercial culture. The arguments move between fear and hope. Those critical to the developing consumer culture feel that 'tradition has, to a certain extent, been replaced by the culture of consumerism,' with a risk of 'precious traditional values' being lost (Huang 1995); lamenting that the political is displaced with commercial (Dai 1999) asking 'what happens when the revolutionary hegemony is replaced by capitalist hegemony, namely, the commercial popular culture of today! (Liu 1997:119). Other voices in this discussion take the emancipatory view, believing that commercialisation and transnationalisation will bring about a 'detaching of Chinese subjectivity from the state' (Yang 1996:311) and that China will be transformed by the forces of 'soap operas, tabloids and bestsellers' (Zha 1995). Both among the pessimistic and the optimistic voices we find the same belief that the very nature of commercial culture works towards a depoliticisation and decollectivisation of the Chinese audience; and that capitalist popular culture by its very nature is intimate and individualising.

Culture has also been the focus of a related Chinese discourse. Ever since the brutal crackdown of the student demonstrations in 1989 Chinese leaders, intellectuals and others have pushed the idea of a specific 'Chinese,' 'Confucian,' 'East-Asian' or even Oriental culture (Barmé 1995). This culture is said to authoritative, patriarchal and family-oriented, and has been used to squelch calls for human rights and democracy, bashing the West for its lack of morals, family values and work ethic. As Anne McLaren points out there exists an implicit gender agenda in this Chinese 'cultural revivalism' where women become the bearers of essential national character (McLaren 1998:197).

Historically women around the world have been entrusted a double reproductive task in nationalism: as carriers of both - the nation's children and the nation's culture. Women have to deal with this double task - real and symbolic - in modern consumer cultures at two levels as well: one, being constructed by marketing as the main consumer segment for which the majority of products are advertised and two, as the most common represen-ation in advertising which sells goods and services. As the primary sign in modern consumer cultures, images of young 'beautiful' women are used to sell commodities not only to women, but also to men; and the image of the female body, clothed or nude, has in one sense come to represent both 'sale' and 'commodity.' The purpose of this chapter is to illuminate the gendered cross-workings of these two spheres by examining editorials and advertisements from two official women's magazines *Zhongguo funü* (*Chinese Women*) and *Hunyin yu jiating* (*Marriage and Family*); and look at how images of women and discourses on femininity from the first part of the 1990s are played out in a Chinese cultural politics of gender and identity.

Ever since the debates on cultural imperialism in the 1970s, capitalist culture and Western values and lifestyles have been conflated. Advertising is targeted as the main culprit in spreading consumerist Western, anti-traditional lifestyles where domestic values, like the importance of family and frugality are debunked. Capitalism thus automatically leads to homogenisation. Arjun Appadurai argues that globalisation actually does involve the use of a variety of instruments of homogenisation, like dress style, language, hegemonies and advertising techniques, but that these instruments are absorbed into local political and cultural economies and *repatriated* as heterogeneous dialogues of national sovereignty, free enterprise, etc. (Appadurai 1990: 307). He makes the important point that the state plays a delicate role as an arbitrator in this repatriation of difference, and as a result, an aggravation of internal politics of homogenisation is often played out in debates over heritage. The anthro-pologist Richard Wilk reaches a similar conclusion in an article about Belize beauty pageants. Female beauty in these pageants is made an important factor in the production, consumption and rejection of identities in a globalised context. These pageants, he writes, serve the state's interest in 'domesticating difference' by constructing a notion of a particular Belizean female beauty (Wilk 1996:218).

This chapter examines how images of women in two official Chinese women's magazines reveal a shared effort by the beauty industry and the Communist leadership to construct a 'modern Chinese woman' where 'modern' means investment in beauty and 'Chinese' entails an essentialised idea of an Oriental femininity. In unpacking the construction of a female 'Chinese beauty' in such a gender discourse, the chapter further suggests that the developing capitalist culture in China has moved from a wholesale acceptance of anything foreign in the 1980s to something like a 'repatriation' or 'domestication' of difference where, within the discourse of cultural identity, the values usually ascribed to Western consumer culture may remain only a surface phenomenon.

THE COMMERCIALISATION
OF CHINESE MEDIA

Advertising, which during the Cultural Revolution became a symbol of the decadence and waste of capitalism, reappeared together with the launch of the reform policy in 1979. Since then advertising has brought about a commercialisation of the media that has not only been accepted, but in fact propagated, by the leadership. State subsidies have been reduced for media closest to the ruling Communist Party. Even though Chinese media now has to rely on advertising revenues and sales, it is still expected to function as active organs of propaganda for the Communist Party. The media researcher Zhao Yuezhi has labeled this unique Chinese situation a 'propagandist/commercial' model of journalism (Zhao 1998 :98).

Newsstands in Chinese cities hold large numbers of titles geared towards female readers, and with few exceptions almost all of them are published by the official All China Women's Federation. Ironically, just as it was the media closest to the Communist Party, such as China's Central Television (CCTV) and the *People's Daily*, that were the most popular with advertisers in the 1980s, the official and authoritative magazines *Zhongguo funü* (*Chinese Women*) and *Hunyin yu jiating* (*Marriage and Family*) also proved popular with advertisers.

Ever since its inception in the 1930s, *Chinese Women* has been the Chinese leadership's most important media for constructing and carrying out politicised definitions of women and gender. The monthly *Marriage and Family* started only in 1984. It is published by the Association for Research on Marriage and Family (*Zhongguo Hunyin yu jiating yanjiuhui*) under the supervision of the All China Women's Federation and has its editorial office in the Women's Federation building in Beijing. Its function has been as a serious forum for discussing and carrying out ideas regarding women and family matters. In 1995 the monthly circulation of *Chinese Women* was 550 000 and for *Marriage and Family* 300,000, but since a large part of the subscribers are offices and workplaces these magazines reach a much larger number of readers (interview with editors at the two magazines in Beijing May 1996).

Up until the 1990s most Chinese magazines, including *Chinese Women* and *Marriage and Family* had only one lonely illustration in colour, the cover. And, just like most Chinese magazines at this time, the two magazines carried around fifty pages of text with a few black and white drawings printed on rough, darkish paper. When full-page multi-colour advertisements started to appear regularly in the early 1990s it changed the layout of the magazines. It also brought with it new sections and articles devoted to everyday life, love and relations, fashion, and beauty. In 1994, advertising space had increased to cover three of the four pages of cover spread, with an additional four pages of low-quality mail order advertisements without illustrations.

CONSUMER CULTURE AND IMAGES OF WOMEN

It has been popular over the last decade to talk about late modern societies as consumer cultures (Featherstone 1991; Slater 1997; Lury 1996). 'Consumer culture' then refers to economies built on mass consumption, as well as to a commodified symbolic universe where individual and collective identities are structured by products and advertising. Central to discussions on consumer culture lies the notion of the 'modern self' as reflexive, of a culture of performers where individual identity is no longer ruled by a hard core of integrity and character but is displayed in a masquerade of shifting appearances. With this growth of a culture of masquerade and appearance, it has been suggested that not only is woman at the core of modern consumer culture, but that consumer culture is in fact a result of femininity itself. In the words of British anthropologist Celia Lury, 'a specifically feminine subjectivity provides the basis for the emergence of an aestheticized mode of using objects and creating one's own identity. From this point of view, the gendered process of objectification and the associated relations of looking are not only a consequence of consumer culture, but also a causal factor in its development' (Lury 1996:152).

This idea of the feminisation of contemporary culture becomes interesting when we look at China. Here the focus on male and militant costumes and the de-feminising of women's clothing during the Mao-era has disappeared in favor of an intense interest in Chinese women's beauty and a re-feminisation of the dressing code in the 1990s. The Chinese female body, dressed and made-up has now come to stand for modernisation, progress and membership of the 'First World.' Li Xiaoping argues that since the early 1980s, the Chinese fashion industry has been a priority in national economic plans and that fashion 'is implicated in the state project of modernisation precisely because of its signification of change, and its identification with western fashion centers, high lifestyles, and most importantly, an exuberant modern society that China is striving to become' (Li 1998:87). Female fashion models are also made to represent the Chinese project of modernisation, both as representing Chinese essence and as 'sophisticated cosmopolitan citizen of the 'modern' world' (Brownell 1998:49). What we have here is the double foregrounding of the female icon: first, as representing a global 'modernity,' the primary sign, or rather the effect of which a modern consumer culture is the result; and second, as keepers who safeguard the Chinese way of life. This is the 'modern Chinese woman' we meet in the visual and verbal discourse of editorials and advertisements from the two magazines.

Chinese advertising, when it reappeared in the 1980s, was not sophisticated by Western standards. Although women were the predominantly targeted audience of the ads found in *Chinese Women* and *Marriage and Family*, these were pictures of what looked like casually dressed, ordinary young women. In the early 1990s, with the development of the Chinese advertising industry, the layout and atmosphere of ads were becoming more sophisticated and the photos as well The paper on which they were printed were also of a higher quality. The images of women also changed towards emphasising glamour, individualism, and hedonism. We can see an example in a cleansing cream ad where an Asian woman with jewelry, make-up and a fashionable haircut and with lips slightly parted points with, curved fingers and nails painted red, at a bottle in her left hand (fig. 1) (*Marriage and Family* November 1990). The woman stands in front of a fancy European-style hotel - an environment that evokes associations of the flashy lifestyle of the international jet set. From the hotel hang the French, British, Japanese, and American flags and city lights glimmer romantically in the night. The accompanying Chinese caption 'Longfeng Cleansing Cream OK' (*Longfeng xiye OK!*), with 'OK' in Latin letters, accentuates the foreign atmosphere.

The tentative sensuality and cautious display of the body seen during the 1980s is replaced by more nudity and by a more daring approach in the first years of the 1990s. This is particularly the case with ads featuring Caucasian models, where we can see wet women in swimsuits or almost nude after taking a bath (fig. 2) (*Chinese Women* January 1993). One thing that ads from early 1990s featuring Caucasians and Asians share is the way the models look directly into the camera. Although the ads with Caucasian models definitely show a lot more bare skin, ads with Asian women also begin to employ nudity and sex appeal.

As Ellen McCracken reminds us the main function of the covers of women's and fashion magazines is as advertisement for the product - the magazine itself (McCracken 1993:14-18). In the Mao-era, covers of *Chinese Women* from the 1980s were mainly propaganda images featuring serious-looking working class heroines in dirty overalls, old Party women in blue Mao jackets or young female soldiers in aggressive poses. From its first issue in 1985 *Marriage and Family's* covers were also dominated by images with a political message. They frequently showed mothers and happy couples with a single child, or young childless couples holding hands. These covers promulgated the family planning ideology of the government in the early 1980s. In the late 1980s however, two things happened that changed the look of the magazines. First the dull cover paper with its bleak colours was replaced by thicker glossier paper; and then the images used for covers changed from the revolutionary representations of the Mao-era giving way to enticing, beautified and fashionable young women. Louisa Schein has commented on how eroticised images of the white woman was used in the 1980s as a way of mediating a shift in Chinese values on sex and women, but how in the 1990s Chinese women recuperate this symbolic space of desire (Schein 1994:152).

On the changing magazine covers of the two magazines discussed in this paper, we can see an indication of this as more seductive sexualised Asian models are featured on these otherwise prude and 'correct' pages. The covers now displayed new desirable careers such as Air China stewardesses in sky-blue dresses, young secretaries in front of computers; as well as leisure scenes with women in revealing party dresses, seductive night gowns, conspicuous fashion clothes and expensive jewelry. Some illustrations go quite far in breaking with conventional role models for women, for example showing a young woman in a sleeveless silky evening dress and high-heel pumps sitting by a bar table with a glass of wine raised to her mouth looking right into the camera with a faint smile (fig. 3) (*Marriage and Family* July 1990). Such representations strike one as quite emancipated in a society where women in general do not drink or smoke and where going to bars has been a pleasure reserved for men only. Through ads and covers, the state and the market in concert present an image of the post-Mao woman as a seductive hedonist.

Such images of women seem to reflect a post-Mao re-feminisation which fits well into the idea of globalisation leading to a universal consumer culture, propagating (allegedly) Western ideals and values such as individualism and hedonism. In a superficial way there are similarities in the Chinese development and changes in the understanding of the self that took place in the developing consumer culture of the United States that Warren Susman has written about (Susman 1984: 282). During the nineteenth century, books and manuals on how to lead a successful life talked mainly of people's character and were full of words like citizenship, duty, work, golden deeds, conquest, honour, reputation, manhood and morals. That changed in the first decade of the twentieth century when individuality and charisma became more important for a successful life. The vision of self-sacrifice then began to yield to that of self-realisation, and it was no longer important to follow the advice and directions of others. Individuality and the ability to stand out from the crowd began to matter more. Susman talks about a 'culture of performers' thereby stressing how the exterior and the visible by then had replaced the focus on intrinsic moral qualities (Susman 1984:280).

Susman's description of a 'culture of performers' is helpful in describing the emerging Chinese urban middle-class culture in post-Mao China. No longer was a revolutionary or sacrificing character seen as something to strive for. Instead people wanted to stand out from the crowd, to act and express themselves individually. One ad for a Chinese joint venture featuring a row of good-looking Asian models, illustrates well how individuality and difference replaces collectivity and sameness (fig. 4) (*Chinese Women* March 1993). Some of the women are dressed up in different professional suits: a business dress, a construction worker's jeans, and helmet, the white dress of a nurse. Others are dressed in sports and leisure wear: one in a swim suit, another poses as a painter with an easel, while a third is dressed in shorts standing with a football. Smiling and holding on to each other they all look happy and satisfied with themselves. The ad is for sanitary towels and the idea is of course that women, regardless of what activities they are engaged in, whether at work, leisure, or sport, can use Anle's towels. But the ad can also be read as an illustration of the changing times. The caption runs, 'The choice of modern women' (*Xiandai nüxingde xuanze*) and, unlike their mother's 'choice' of dressing uniformly and being politically correct, these women have chosen to express their individuality through their looks and dresses. Instead of pursuing socialism or the latest Party guidelines, they are pursuing individual careers and lifestyles. None of the women in this ad don the Mao-uniform but instead express their individual tastes in dress, whether at work or leisure.

To sum up, the first years of advertising in the two official Chinese women's magazines *Chinese Women* and *Marriage and Family* articulate values that are not only usually associated with advertising in general, but also with Western consumer culture in particular, like individualism, luxury, pleasure, joy, fun, happiness, youth, beauty, play, sexuality, modernity, movement and vitality. Resembling the West of the early twentieth century, mass-consumption and image culture seems to contribute towards modelling a new project of the self where appearance and image become more important than character and collective morality. Furthermore the changing images of women underwrite the thesis that the revolutionary discourse is being challenged by a capitalist commercial culture. But, as we shall see, the Chinese relation between politics, market, and culture is more complex than this.

FEMININITY AFTER MAO

In Mao Zedong's China, gender categories were superseded by revolutionary role models based on class. In the belligerent Cultural Revolution, feminine beautification through cosmetics and fashion was practically outlawed. With the partial dismantling of the Maoist ideology in the 1980s, people were again allowed a certain degree of individual freedom, including the right to choose how to dress, what hairstyle to wear and whether or not to use make-up. The repressed gender categories resurfaced together with a great interest in the body and in sex: interests that carried with them the reappearance of ideas that saw gender differences as grounded in biology. These were ideas that were rooted in medical discourses from the Republican period when Chinese medical science tried to ground gender in biology by referring to hormonology: Scientists then argued that male hormones created the 'air of a man' while female glandular secretions transformed pre-pubertile androgynous girls into adult women (Dikötter 1995:151). In young women, physical characteristics like breasts and the broadening of the pelvis were thought to be followed by distinct psychological features that made them 'gentle and soft,' 'bashful' and 'sentimental.' (Dikötter 1995:151).

In the early 1980s, similar biological explanations of gender differences resurfaced in the popular press. Quasi-medical articles talked about a difference in brain functions between boys and girls that predestined them for different work activities (Honig and Hershatter 1988:15). Women for example, were said to fall behind men in adolescent intelligence tests. Subdermal fat and finer bone structure made them slower and weaker than men and therefore less suitable for certain kinds of jobs (Honig and Hershatter 1988:17). Simultaneously, critical voices denounced the 'Iron Girl Brigade' as role models for women and newspaper and magazine articles articulated a rejection of the idea of gender equality, scornfully admonishing women to stop act like 'imitation boys' and 'iron women' (Honig and Hershatter 1988:25). Chinese women should no longer strive to compete with men in the workplace. When girls grew up, it was argued, love, marriage and childbearing put such a heavy burden on them that it became hard for them to pursue a career (Honig and Hershatter 1988:17).

The dismantling of the revolutionary practice in the 1980s meant that gender once again assumed its former importance as a social category. But as a legacy of the Mao period, and due to changes in the economy, gender categories became unstable. The question of what a woman really was became an important issue. By the early 1990s this had become so pressing that it triggered a series of articles in the authoritative *Chinese Women*.

Under the heading 'What is the Beauty of Modern Women?' (*Shenme shi iandai nüixing mei?*) a lengthy discussion continued in 1991 and 1992. The discussion opened rhetorically by an editorial referring to what the American-resident scholar Zhao Haosheng had said while visiting China: 'There are no real women in Mainland China (*dalu mei you zhenzhengde nüxing*) ... in everything from attitudes to looks they do not even resemble women' (*Shenme shi xiandai nüxing mei?*, *Chinese Women* August 1991:4). According to this scholar, Chinese women had lost their 'female charac-teristics' (*nüxingde tedian*) as well as their 'proper charm' (*yingyoude meili*). Chinese women, he claims, fail to understand that their true power lies in their 'femaleness' (*nürenwei*). It is interesting to note that the criticism of Chinese women is voiced via a Chinese living in the US, supposedly familiar with both cultures. The editor (a lady) expressed full sympathy for the scholar's feelings. He 'enlightened' her, she writes, to the realisation that: Modern Chinese women have to once again examine what their sexual characteristics (*xingbie tese*) consist of and become aware of sexual differences (*xingbie yishi*). Modern Chinese women ought to fully express their own female beauty (*nüxing mei*). (*'Shenme shi xiandai nüxing mei?'* *Chinese Women* August 1991:4).

The response from the readers was reportedly immense, and every subsequent issue of *Chinese Women* in 1991 and several issues from 1992 published letters and articles summing up the views of the readers. Good looks and beauty seemed important qualities for 'modern' women, and many readers expressed the view that a good, 'modern' Chinese woman must be beautiful and well-dressed. But even if the letters seemed sympathetic to women that dressed up and beautified themselves, there were some readers who called for moderation. One reader wrote that she grew up in a time when 'the individual and 'looks' did not exist' (*wuwo wuxingde shidai*). She supported the strive for personal beauty, but with the condition that 'women should not, as many now do, blindly follow fashion, paint their lips all red and only wear famous brand-name clothes' (Xiao 1991:22). The readers seem unanimously to agree on one thing: contemporary Chinese women are too strong and coarse, acting too much like men (*jia xiaozi*). 'Strong women' (*nü qiangren*) - an expression signifying women with careers and positions of their own - were definitely not feminine. A woman should not, because of work or studies, forget that after all she is a woman, a wife, and a mother. Chinese women needed to be more concerned with their husbands and families.

The discussion started by the criticism of a scholar based in the US the West did not provide the ideal and many readers pointed out the differences between Western and Asian women. Sun Wanqun from Jiangsu, for example, favoured the traditional Chinese ideals of femininity, writing that

'Chinese women should preserve their Chinese characteristics and, compared to Western women, be more reserved and shy (*hanxu*) (Sun 1992:18).' Respondents repeatedly pointed to the qualities of 'reserved and shy' as constitutive characteristics of a Chinese woman. Many letters talked about similar qualities that modern Chinese women should possess: she needs to be 'soft and gentle' (*wenrou*). One female reader wrote that 'gentleness indicates the soft and lovable, it is a fine quality for a woman, and not at all a shortcoming '(*'Xinde nüxing yu xinde shidai' Chinese Women* December 1991). It was by not being soft, shy, reserved, with a gentle sensuality that Western women were said to differ and fall short of Chinese women. In short, post-Mao Chinese women should stop acting so assertively. Women were allowed to be good looking and intelligent, but should downplay and not flaunt these qualities. They should instead pay more attention to serving their husbands and children.

Articles in *Marriage and Family* also talked about the softness of women. One went quite far in describing how a gentle woman should treat her husband. If he is in a bad mood, shouting and throwing things about, she should tolerate this and try to comfort him. She should then rub his forehead and beseech him, saying: 'Tell me, what's bothering you?' (*Gaosu wo, nar you bu shufu?*) (Yao 1993: 22). She is then advised to take him out to a karaoke bar and let him have some fun. The author describes an exemplary woman she knows, a woman not pretty but 'soft as water' (*wenrou ru shui*) (Yao 1993: 22). Every morning this friend of her rises from bed earlier than her husband, boils water and prepares his breakfast. With a gentle and quiet voice she then asks him to get up and eat. The author concludes that these qualities give great charm to a woman and will be of much help in finding a husband.

In another article some years later in *Marriage and Family* under the section 'Men Speaking From Their Hearts' (*Nanren zhen xinhua*), we return to the 1991-'92 discussion reported above. It takes up where the earlier debate in *Chinese Women* left off. The article, 'China Has No Women,' clearly refers to what the US-based Chinese scholar had said when visiting China. The article repeats that a woman should not only be 'soft' (*wenrou*) but also 'natural and naive' (*tianzhen*) (Liu 1995:40-1). Modern men do like women who are educated and intelligent, but they disapprove if women flaunt these qualities. Women must be 'reserved' (*hanxu*), and not show off their knowledge and intelligence. 'Nowadays men seldom look for a woman that is stupid, but neither does he like one that takes pride in being clever.' Similarly, men do like women who are 'pretty and coquettish' (*yaoyan*) but a woman does not have to be beautiful: 'a sweet, happy woman can gratify a man because most men love women who, now and then, cleverly say 'thank you.' What really moves a man, the article continues, is a woman who listens respectfully and with full attention to a man's opinion. Men in general also like a woman to show him how much she appreciates and worships him. The author says he has never in his lifetime met a man who likes a fearless and brave woman, a woman who speaks in a loud and clear voice, or a woman who likes to tell dirty jokes, gamble, and swear (ibid). The author obviously feels threatened by the intelligent, assertive, and good-looking women of contemporary China.

In a typical move, this article defines women's good qualities from a man's point of view. A 'good modern woman' is someone who immediately relates to a man's well-being. A self-sufficient and strong woman is unattractive. She can only become a 'real' woman when she makes herself soft, reserved, and submissive. The lack of femininity in contemporary Chinese women is blamed on the Mao period when 'looks and the individual did not exist.' But, although the discussion was started by a critique from a US-based scholar, the West does not provide the ideal. Rather, femininity is exemplified by the traditional, soft-spoken and submissive woman, a set of distinctly Chinese values imagined to have existed in pre-Communist China.

THE 'ORIENTALISATION' OF CHINESE WOMEN

If Western women ever since early 20th century have been represented as the ideal strong body that a Chinese biopolitics should strive to achieve (Brownell 1996:229), we now see how a 'Chinese' femininity is called for. A self-orientalising attempt that seeks the ideal 'modern woman' in someone who does not 'flaunt her qualities.' That the Women's Federation actively propagates for distinctive Chinese or Oriental feminine qualities which Chinese women should possess is seen by its sponsorship of a magazine called *Dongfang nüxing* (Oriental woman) where Chinese female role models are promoted together with articles about Chinese fashion and traditional dresses. Official discourse thus portrays the Chinese woman as someone who serves the family, is attentive to her husband and devoted to her child. This feminine ideal is constructed against its 'Other,' the stereotype of the individualistic and hedonistic Western woman. But what about the emerging Chinese consumer culture? Does not the beauty industry promote an alternative image of women? Let us take a look at the leading cosmetic company in China of the 1990s, Yue-sai Cosmetics.

Yue-sai Cosmetics
When the American cosmetic group Coty opened a plant in Shanghai 1998 it had to go into a joint venture with a local company as all non-Chinese

companies do. But while this usually means partnership with a Chinese counterpart, Coty joined with the American Yue-sai Cosmetics Incorporated. The Chinese-American Kan Yue-sai (or Jin Yuxi as she is known in China) was invited from the US to run a television show on China's Central Television Network (CCTN) in the early 1980s. Presenting stories from around the world in a country that had just recently broken its isolationist policy, Kan Yue-sai soon became a household name among the Chinese audience.

Kan Yue-sai has ever since the start created an image of her business as being in the interest of China and its women. She willingly gives interviews in all sorts of popular magazines and also contributes regularly to a weekly feminist television show called 'Half of the Sky.' Furthermore, during the International Women's Conference in Beijing Yue-sai cosmetics was advertised as 'the appointed product of the '95 Women's World Conference.' Kan Yue-sai says she is driven by two things. First, she wants to make Chinese women as beautiful as other women around the world, by teaching them how to dress and put on a make-up. Kan Yue-sai is discontented with the way Westerners perceive Asian women's looks: 'They think we are exotic, but not beautiful. In a lot of advertisements, they make us look weird. I want to set a standard' (Seno 1998). Kan Yue-sai argues that Asian women have a different skin complexion and facial features than Western women; and her products, she claims, are the only ones that are produced exclusively for Chinese-Asian skins.

Kan Yue-sai accomplishes the transformation of a beauty esthetics into a beauty politics, where the goal of female beautification lies not on a heterosexual or narcissistic level, but in making China an accepted member of the First World by the beauty labour of its women. In this process she also manages to fortify the notion of a particular Asian 'yellow' skin in ways that resemble how Western ideas of a 'yellow' race was adopted by nationalist thinkers in the early 20th century to create a stronger Chinese identity (Dikötter 1992:124). Furthermore, she perceives this cultural/national identity to be something one does not change: 'whether you wear Armani or Valentino you are still at the bottom a Chinese or Egyptian' (*'Haiwai jiechu ...'* 1989:19).

Orientalist advertising representations
Kan Yue-sai's marketing blend of aesthetics and politics is perhaps most elegantly expressed in a campaign for cologne from 1994. Here we see the back of an Asian woman with a pageboy haircut that reveals a smooth, naked neck with a pearl necklace (fig. 5) (*Chinese Women* June 1994). The woman is dressed in what resembles a white embroidered wedding gown. The picture is taken with a soft lens producing a mellow, romantic flavour

intensified by the warm soft colours of yellow and cream-white. The caption reads 'How can you ever forget your first love?'(*ni zen neng wangji di yici ai*) The body language of the woman expresses softness, modesty, and a certain elusive charm that stands in sharp contrast to how women were portrayed in earlier ads. This woman seems too bashful and reserved to even meet the gaze of the beholder. She turns her head away from the camera so as not to reveal her face. This ad illustrates well the notion of a particular Chinese beauty but in a new cultural economy of desire. The woman is portrayed as bashful, modest, reserved, but only in a staged way as we realize as soon as our attention turns to the unzipped zipper of her dress.

A similar construction of this shy-acting Oriental woman is made in a series of five only slightly different ads that appeared in five consecutive issues of *Chinese Women* (figures 6-10) (January to June 1994). In the first ad we see a woman's head and shoulders covered with a pink cloth. In a representation of a traditional Chinese wedding we see the bride preparing to show her face to the bridegroom. She has started to gently lift the veil with her well-manicured, red-nailed fingers and only one part of her face is visible - her red luscious lips. The caption promises to 'reveal to you the secret of the women from the south (*jiangnan nüzi*).' In the following month's issue she has raised the veil a bit further and now her left eye meets that of the reader/groom. In the third ad her whole face is unveiled and she is smiling shyly. Her head is slightly tilted forward in what looks like the beginning of a respectful bow. By way of the elegant device of a veil, the woman is revealed to us piece by piece. First her bright red lips, then her lips together with her left eye, and in the last ad her eyes and her hands with their perfect long red-nailed fingers. In an image governed by the male gaze she presents the reader (the male gaze of an imagined groom) her attractive femininity bit by bit, fetishizing each part of her face as a separate desirable object. In the fourth ad the woman tries to cover her face again, this time by putting her well-manicured hands across her mouth. In his book on gendered body display in ads Erving Goffman calls this gesture 'licensed withdrawal,' a move to conceal face or mouth when under the influence of emotions that might risk losing control over one's expression (Goffman 1987:57). Is it fear or joyous laughter at meeting the groom's gaze that causes the bride's response? Her eyes are still seductively fixed directly on the one who is admiring her, indicating that any shyness is simply acted. In the fifth and last ad she lets go her hands and with a faint smile reveals that she was just playing a game of seduction. Accompanying the five different pictures a short text urges the reader to 'Listen for a while, to the legend of silk.' The text weaves a smooth rhetorical rope consisting of the 'southern woman's' beautiful character, her sleek skin, pure silk, and finally, the skincare products of Simisi asking 'Why is it that so many women from the south have skin like packed snow, together with an inborn beautiful character?'

The young woman is presented to the reader as if to a presumed husband waiting for the consummation of their marriage. She is beautiful but bashful enough to hide this. The woman is portrayed giving herself away to the groom, unwrapping herself with acted shyness. Read against the social context of contemporary China, the Simisi representation of a traditional wedding becomes a bit disturbing. The arranged weddings of pre-modern China were managed by parents often against the will of the young brides.

In another Simisi ad the caption boldly spells out that 'Simisi's women are very Chinese' (*Chinese Women*, November 1994). Here we see a woman in a traditional embroidered dress with wide sleeves and high collar. With hair artfully arranged she tilts her head looking down playing serenely on a flute (fig. 11). The pictorial assertion of the cosmetic company's resuscitation of old gender ideals in a modern society is followed by the prophetic promise 'from this moment starts the transformation of beauty. Retrace the tactful gentleness, the smoothness and the clear spirit ... Make a very Chinese woman (*zuo yige hen zhongguode nüren*).'

These advertisements all express a refined and gentle sensuality that is different from earlier advertisements. First, they read like inverted mirror images of the advertising stereotypes of bold Western women. A dichotomy is made between East and West. This also came through in my discussions with Chinese editors and creative departments of advertising agencies: when the 'inner beauty' (*neizaide mei*) of Chinese woman often was positioned against the 'outer beauty' (*waizaide mei*) of Western woman (Johansson 1999). The Chinese models construct an image of femininity (read 'beauty') that resembles stereotypical, Orientalist representations of a woman equipped with refined, sensual and submissive desire. However, here the Oriental stereotype is not the representation of alien issues, rather a consumerist construction that fortifies a Chinese self-identity. Second, the advertising images are clearly ruled by a male gaze. But instead of a visual language focusing on the display of the body and face, indicating a project of the self, ruled by outer qualities such as looks and appearance, the women in these Chinese ads make themselves invisible. The covering up of the 'outer beauty' is made to express the 'inner beauty' of an essentialised Chinese femininity. The Chinese models in these ads turn their heads away shyly so we don't see their full faces, or they cover their faces with their hands or by using a veil. It is as if by 'acting shyly' they can resolve the contradiction of simultaneously living up to the narcissistic female exhibitionism of the new consumer culture, while symbolically also succumbing to an ideal of a submissive Chinese woman.

纯正含丝化妆品

倾听，关于丝的传奇

为什么江南女子多肌如凝雪，天生丽质？
为什么缫丝女工的手特别细腻润滑？
为什么真丝衣裙特别体贴滑爽？
为什么纯丝蛋白特别滋润肌肤？
为什么丝密斯被誉为"美容圣品"？
…………

轻轻撩开丝的面纱
丝密斯
向您缓缓道来丝的传奇，和
江南女子的秘密

详见内文7页

江南女系列广告之一

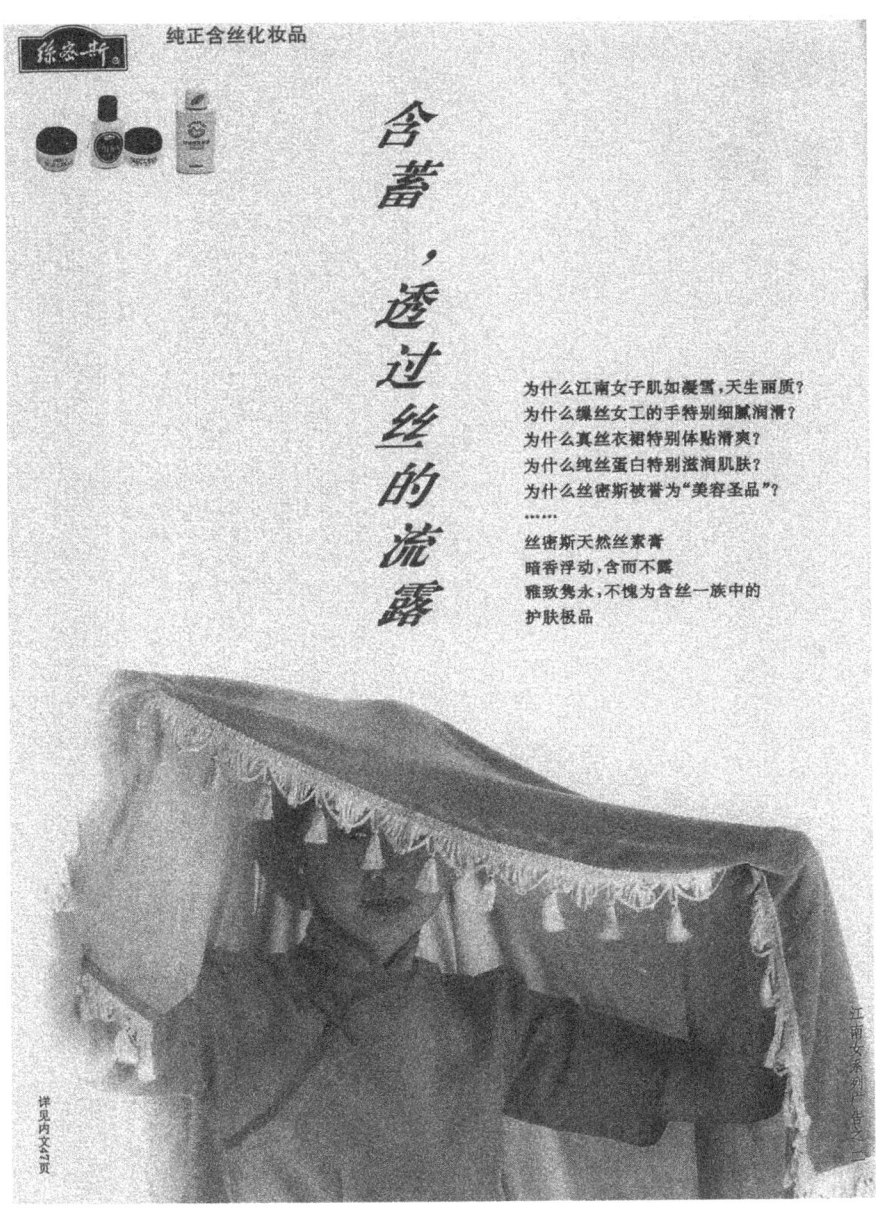

纯正含丝化妆品

含蓄，透过丝的流露

为什么江南女子肌如凝雪，天生丽质？
为什么缫丝女工的手特别细腻润滑？
为什么真丝衣裙特别体贴滑爽？
为什么纯丝蛋白特别滋润肌肤？
为什么丝密斯被誉为"美容圣品"？
⋯⋯
丝密斯天然丝素菁
暗香浮动，含而不露
雅致隽永，不愧为含丝一族中的
护肤极品

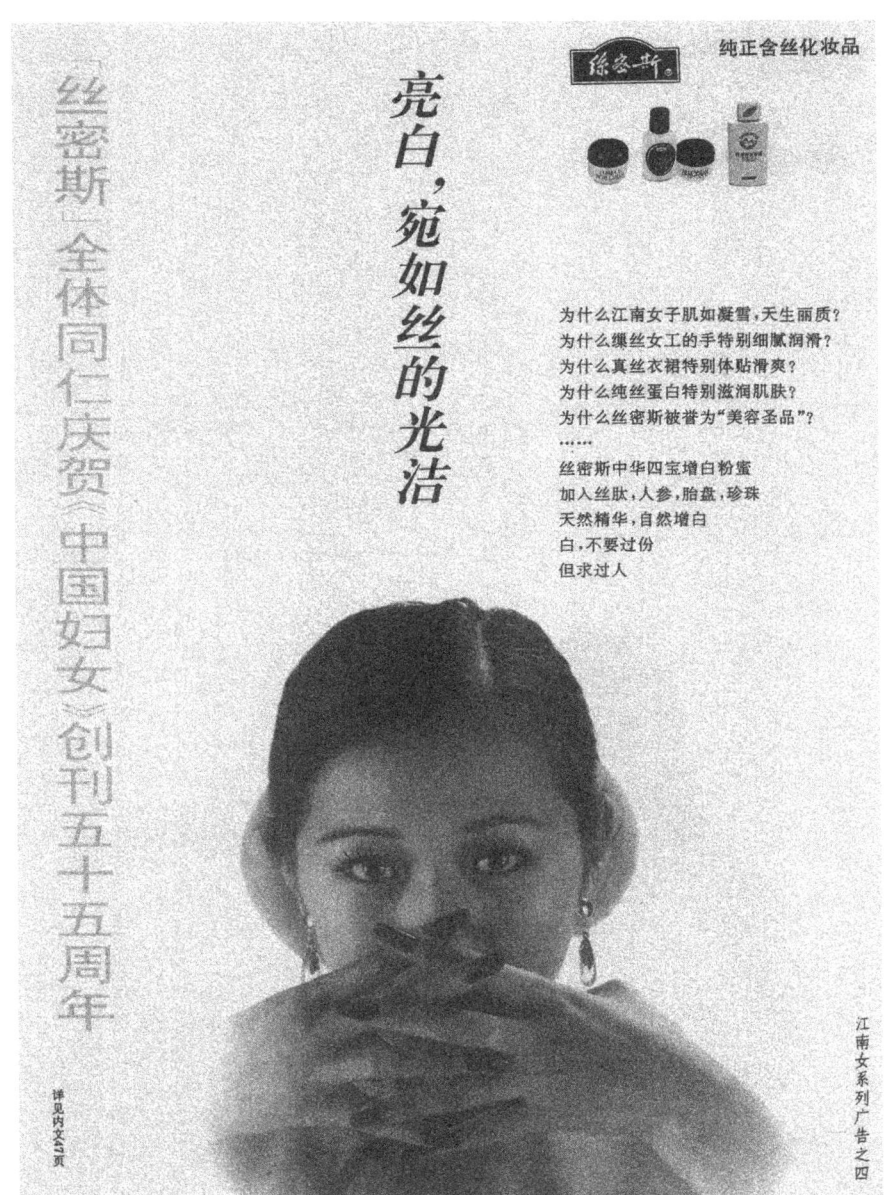

亮白，宛如丝的光洁

纯正含丝化妆品

为什么江南女子肌如凝雪，天生丽质？
为什么缫丝女工的手特别细腻润滑？
为什么真丝衣裙特别体贴滑爽？
为什么纯丝蛋白特别滋润肌肤？
为什么丝密斯被誉为"美容圣品"？
⋯⋯

丝密斯中华四宝增白粉蜜
加入丝肤，人参，胎盘，珍珠
天然精华，自然增白
白，不要过份
但求过人

「丝密斯」全体同仁庆贺《中国妇女》创刊五十五周年

详见内文41页

江南女系列广告之四

116

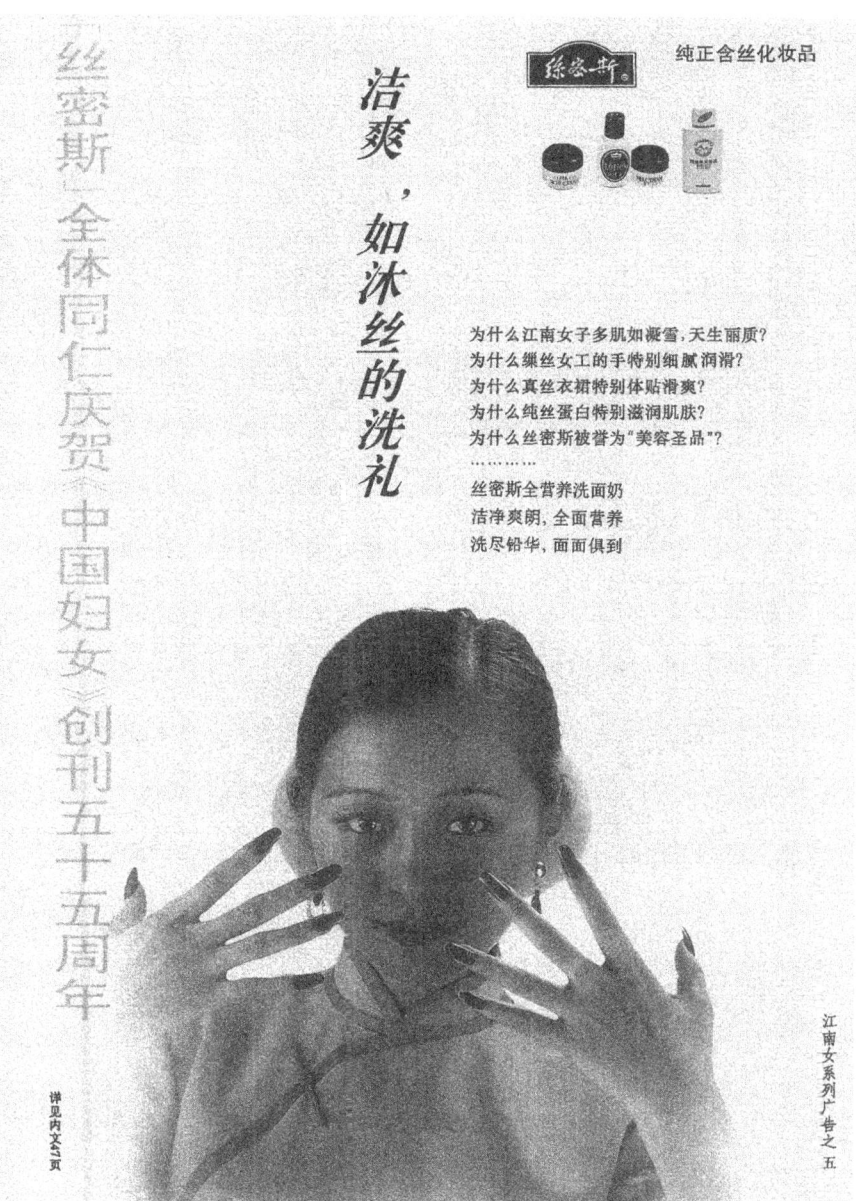

美麗的蛻變，
從這一刻開始

找回溫婉、細膩、清靈……
做一個很中國的女人

絲密斯純真含絲化妝品
專為中國女士而配制

滋潤在膚
清明在心

The Chinese women are in many aspects losers in the economic reforms In the countryside women have been left to run the farms while men go to the cities to find work. The daughters likewise often stay at home so their brothers can go to school. In the cities women stand a risk of losing their jobs simply because employers do not want to put up with the inconvenience of child-rearing workers. The harsh population policies have meant that some women have been tricked, pressurised by economic incentives, or even forced, into undergoing sterilisation and abortions. Simultaneously, young rural women and girls are kidnapped to be sold as brides or prostitutes. Prostitution has reappeared on a large scale and continues to flourish despite yearly crackdowns. Women are now working as entertainers at karaoke bars, expensive restaurants and hotels and the practice of polygamy has also reappeared as businessmen from Taiwan and Hong Kong keep second wives at their postings on the Mainland. In the light of this Chinese backlash, it is disturbing to see how the official endorsement for the re-domestication of woman is fortified by the beauty industry which actively propagates a return to a pre-Communist image of women. Anthropologist Elizabeth Croll has described the attempt to evolve a 'feminism with Chinese characteristics as a continuing official attempt to separate the import of Western goods from Western culture' (Croll 1995:178). But the construction of a distinct Chinese femininity goes longer than just a separation of Western goods from Western culture. The 'difference' of an emerging consumer culture is safely repatriated into a discourse of 'traditional' Chinese gender roles.

CONCLUSION

When advertising reappeared in China with the new reform policy, pictures of shy-looking, amateurish Asian models soon changed into something like a celebration of Western consumer culture where more professionally created advertisements showed images of pleasure, beauty, and individualism, including large numbers of scantily-dressed, enticing Caucasian models. In the two official women's magazines, *Chinese Women* and *Marriage and Family* these ads were followed by new editorial sections on beauty and consumption and with cover girls portrayed in settings of desirable professional careers, leisure and entertainment. In a discussion of 'modern Chinese women's beauty' in *Chinese Women* , 'woman' was made into a sign without a referrent. The beauty industry was fast in filling in this empty sign with advertising representations of women which referred to the same specific 'Chinese' femininity discussed in the editorial discussion, using images of a 'traditional' Chinese woman as a submissive and shy housewife.

Consumer culture as a global phenomenon, incorporating and spreading ideas and images of a 'modern,' Western, hedonistic, and individualistic lifestyle is evidently capable of resolving, at least symbolically, the seemingly contradictory relationship between 'traditional' and 'modern' lifestyles. In this case it seems that the idea of consumer culture leading to homogenisation does not hold true. On the contrary, the consumerist discourse of advertising partakes in the construction of indigenous identities. Chinese cultural and national identity is fabricated and fortified all along: whether it is when a US-based Chinese scholar talks about Oriental women; or when the Simisi cosmetic company conjures up traditional Chinese culture; or a former Chinese-American TV-personality employs nationalist rhetoric in marketing beauty products.

This conflation of official and commercial images of women undercuts the potential of consumer culture as presenting an alternative symbolic space for Chinese women. Instead of a 'detaching of Chinese subjectivity from the state,' these images of women in advertisements and official media articulate a metaphorical identification of the subject with the state, the private with the public, and the past with the present (Wang 1991:29). The seemingly disparate discourses of the Communist Party and that of modern consumer culture converge into a shared notion of what a contemporary 'modern' Chinese woman should be like: an obedient traditionally minded housewife but also a consumer who cares about her looks.

REFERENCES

Appadurai, Arjun (1990) 'Disjuncture and Difference in the Global Cultural Economy,' in: Mike Featherstone (ed.) *Global Cultures*. London: Sage.

Barmé, Geremie R. (1995) 'To Screw Foreigners is Patriotic: China's Avant-garde Nationalists,' *The China Journal*, No 34, July .

Brownell, Susan (1998) 'The Body and the Beautiful in Chinese Nationalism: Sportswomen and Fashion Models in the Reform Era,' *China Information*, Vol. XII, Nos. 2/3, Autumn/Winter, pp. 36-59.

Brownell, Susan (1996) 'Representing Gender in the Chinese nation: Chinese Sportswomen and Beijing's Bid for the 2000 Olympics', *Identities*.

Croll, Elisabeth (1995) *Changing Identities of Chinese Women*. Hong Kong: Hong Kong University Press.

Dai Jinhua (1999) 'Invisible Writing: The Politics of Chinese Mass Culture in the 1990s',' in: *Modern Chinese Literature and Culture*, vol 11, No. 1, Spring 1999, pp. 31-48.

Dikötter, Frank (1995) *Sex, Culture and Modernity in China: Medical Science and the Construction of Sexual Identities in the Early Republican Period*. Hong Kong: Hong Kong University Press.

Dikötter, Frank (1992) *The Discourse of Race in Modern China*. Hong Kong University Press: Hong Kong.

Featherstone, Mike (1991) *Consumer Culture and Postmodernism*. London: Sage.

Featherstone, Mike (1982) 'The Body in Consumer Culture.' *Theory, Culture and Society*.

Goffman, Erving (1987) *Gender Advertisements*. New York: Harper and Row.

'Haiwai jiechu nü huaren yingping tianshi Jin Yuxi' (An outstanding Chinese abroad, the angel on television: Kan Yue-sai) (1989) *Shijie shizhuang zhiyuan* (A garden of world fashion), Spring.

Hooper, Beverley (1994) 'Women, Consumerism and the State in Post Mao China,' *Asian Studies Review* Vol. 17, No. 3, pp. 73-83.

Honig, Emily and Gail Hershatter (1988) *Personal Voices: Chinese Women in the 1980s*. Stanford: Stanford University Press.

Huang Fing (1995) 'New Dilemmas About Consumerism,' *China Daily*, October 12.

Johansson, Perry (1999) 'Consuming the Other: The Fetish of the Western Woman in Chinese Advertising and Popular Culture,' *Postcolonial Studies*, Winter 1999.

Johansson, Perry (1998) 'White Skin, Large Breasts: Chinese Beauty Product Advertising as Cultural Discourse,' *China Information*, Vol. XII, Nos. 2/3, Autumn/Winter, pp. 59-84.

Li Xiaoping (1998) 'Fashioning the Body in Post-Mao China' in: *Consuming Fashion: Adoring the Transnational Body*. Berg: New York.

Liu Kang (1997), 'Popular Culture and the Culture of the Masses in Contemporary China,' *Boundary* , 2, 24:3, pp. 99-122.

Liu Xiaoou, (1995) 'Zhongguo wu nüren' (China has no women), *Hunyin yu jiating* March 1995 pp. 40-41.

Lury, Celia (1996) *Consumer Culture*. Cambridge: Polity Press.

McCracken, Ellen (1993) *Decoding Women's Magazines: From Mademoiselle to Ms*. MacMillan: Houndsville.

McLaren, Anne (1998) 'Chinese Cultural Revivalism,' in: Krishna Sen and Maila Stevens (eds) *Gender and Power in Affluent Asia*. London: Routledge.

Schein, Louisa (1994) 'The Consumption of Color and the Politics of White Skin in Post-Mao China,' Social Text, 41, pp. 141-64.

Seno, Alexandra A. (1998) 'When Weird Does Not Work,' *Asiaweek*, July 31.

'Shenme shi xiandai nüxing mei?' (What is the beauty of modern women?) August 1991, *Zhongguo funü* .

Slater, Don (1997) *Consumer Culture and Modernity*. Cambrigde: Polity Press.

Sun Wanqun (1992)'Chongsu nüxingmei de kanke zhi lu' (The rough and bumpy road towards a remolding of female beauty), *Zhongguo funü* February.

Susman, Warren (1984) *Culture as History: The Transformation of American Society in the Twentieth Century*. New York: Pantheon.

Wang Jing (1991) '*Heshang* and the Paradoxes of Chinese Enlightenment,' *Bulletin of Concerned Asian Scholars* 23.

Wilk, Richard (1996) 'Connections and Contradictions: From the Crooked Tree Cashew Queen to Miss World Belize', in: Colleen Ballerino et al. (eds) *Beauty Queens on the Global Stage: Gender Contests and Power*. Routledge: New York.

Xiao Ping, (1991)'Xiandai nüxing mei zhi wo jian' (My views on the good qualities of modern women), *Zhongguo funü* , September .

'Xinde nüxing yu xinde shidai' (New women, new times), (1991) *Zhongguo funü*, December .

Yang, Mayfair Mei-hui (1996) 'Mass Media and Transnational Subjectivity in Shanghai: Notes on (Re)cosmopolitanism in a Chinese Metropolis,' in: Aihwa Ong and Donald Noninim (eds) *Underground Empires: The Cultural Politics of Modern Chinese Transnationalism*. New York: Routledge.

Yao Fuyou, (1993) 'Nürende rou' (The softness of women), *Hunyin yu jiating* October.

Zha Jianying (1995) *China Pop: How Soap Operas, Tabloids and Bestsellers are Transforming a Culture*. New York: The New Press.

Zhao, Yuezhi (1998) *Media, Market and Democracy in China: Between the Party Line and the Bottom Line*. Chicago: University of Illinois Press.

CHAPTER 7

MULAN ILLUSTRATION?
AMBIGUOUS WOMEN IN CONTEMPORARY CHINESE CINEMA

STEPHANIE HEMELRYK DONALD AND CHRISTINA LEE

Young women, especially, feel themselves to be hovering within a plurality of expectations originating from a variety of sources including state, family and male, so that the identification of 'proper' or 'appropriate' female behaviour and priorities seems difficult in the absence of a single rhetoric defining proper female needs and interests appropriate to the 'modern' woman (Croll 1995:171).

In her mid-decade analysis of the *Changing Identities of Chinese Women*, Croll describes these young women as in confusion, tense and ambiguous. To develop her point, she uses contemporary women's fiction and letters to the press to explore the confusions generated in a rapidly changing society. The analysis is timely and sensitive to the unkindness of a male dominated world, where women are generally expected to maintain socially convenient responsibilities and identities (home-making, child-rearing, political invisibility) whilst engaging with the demands of a different financial and political order of priorities. Revolutionary women had to be revolutionary, devoted to the Party *and* domestically effective (or live with the tension between the two) (Croll 1995:27; Evans, 1999:63; Fan Hong 1997:22, Wolf 1985:81). Contemporary women have to be market-able, flexible and, still, domestically pliant (Jacka 1997:22; Johnson 1983:167). In the latter case, Croll notes that fictional accounts dwell on the conflicting criteria of a good professional and a good mother, and the personal crises caused by social, political and industrial blindness to these conflicts.(Croll 1995:172). The crises of modernity have not, it seems, changed in the transitions between revolutionary culture and the socialist market. Many 'modern' women in China continue to be over-burdened with workplace responsibilities and gendered social demands. The formations of the 'modern' female condition in the People's Republic are, however, particular to variants of culture, class, generation, and ethnicity. In this project we do not venture far into those variations except in so far as they are evident in filmic culture. However, we contest that our theoretical claims offer a starting point for nuanced readings of many different women's political potential. In order to complement Croll's and Evans' accounts, we make an argument here about film and 'modern' feminine experience. We investigate the ambiguity of the filmic woman, praising it as a condition of self-recognition, which adult women can use as a means of 'coming home' to their bodies, as a collective, although diverse, population.

The tensions and contradictions of modernity are painful - and sometimes insurmountable - obstacles in the pursuit of female autonomy and the female general good. Nevertheless, we argue that the ambiguity engendered in these difficulties is a commodity of self-acknowledgment. The condition of ambiguity can, as a marker of female subjectivity, be a political motivation (Creed 1989:63-89; Kristeva 1982:4). It is an experienced constant, which refuses assimilation into the mores of female-dependent societies and economies (Honig and Hershatter 1988:3, 141). As the cultural manifestation of ambiguity in film is our main interest here, we accept that the bounded text of a film can avoid the multiple contradictions of female daily life. However, the ambiguous women in these texts embody the recognition of difficulty, which is essential to political visibility and audibility for the 'modern' collective subject.

The emergence of the international Chinese film in the 1980s has produced a currency of cinematic femininity, which fascinates in both new and familiar ways (Chow 1995:24; Dai 1995:298; Yau 1989:6-21) Women always seemed to be dying (or going crazy) in the Mainland films of the 1980s' Fifth Generation (*Yellow Earth, Red Sorghum, Raise the Red Lantern, Ju Dou, The Good Woman*). This was perhaps partly a reaction to the previous paradigms of revolutionary strength and indomitable courage. It also followed directly on from the plucky melodramatic heroines of popular post-Mao films (*Hibiscus Town, The Legend of Tianyun Mountain*). In these films women suffered through particular political causes, and not always to the point of death (Pickowicz 1993:296). However, where the Fifth Generation constructed tragic and hopeless ends for women, these popular melodramas recouped female suffering into an optimistic sacrifice for future generations.

Towards the end of the 1990s, the figuring of womanhood appears to be in the process of re-invention in cinemas across Asia and the United States of America. For one thing, the scope and ambiguity of recent characters render contemporary heroines less susceptible to early death. One explanation for this lies in the commercialisation of the domestic mainland industry, where studios have had to compete for funding since 1995. Chinese women on screen are also therefore competing for international and domestic visibility (Donald 1998:91-3). The eighties' version of modern China, couched - as in Zhang Yimou's films - in pre-Liberation sexual dramas has now been superceded by the hybridised appeal of greater China. The glamour and enigma of Asian femininity has gone diasporic and tough.

From Maggie Cheung's role as the French silent cinema vamp *Irma Vep* (Assayas, 1996) to the misappropriation of Gong Li in *Chinese Box* (Wayne Wang 1998), the figure of the Chinese woman is transcending her categories. Cheung's performance was a star turn, in a film that knew her status. Gong Li was used as a foil for White self-obsession with the enigmatic Chinese object of desire. Despite the differing levels of self-awareness in each film, in both cases the actress's performance left her star quality intact. We argue here that the main characteristic of these stars, and therefore the strength of the cinematic figure which they embody, is the sense of ambiguity which they bear. Filmic narratives are developing a space in which the experience of womanhood is played through as difficult, frustrating, but not necessarily negative in prospect. Without pretending that the condition of the ambiguous is in itself liberatory, cultural texts suggest that the *necessary ambiguity* of femininity and female subjects in the symbolic and experienced world is evidence of the instability of current codes of gender identity. The immediate and material negative effects of these codes fall on women, but their instability is a potential fulcrum for progress towards political identification and action. We draw a distinction between the *contradictions* at play in the expectations and experience of women in society and the *ambiguities* which these produce in the subject. As we have noted, the contradictions are narrativised as painful and infuriating (Croll 1995:171-6), but the ambiguity which is formed and understood through contradiction is a held experience. Once embedded in cultural practice it may translate into a shared and public comprehension of women's contemporary conditions (Donald 2000). Furthermore, in the political realm disjunctures between *rhetoric* and lived experience in revolutionary and modern China are only recognisable by women *because of* the ambiguous nature of their citizenship and agency (Croll 1995:84-7). In making this argument we move between the films of early modern cinema in China through the films of Liberation, the Fifth Generation new wave, and films of the 1990s, paying particular attention to the warrior's (loosely conceived) and prostitute's roles in narratives of national development.

MULAN JOINS THE ARMY (AGAIN)

In 1998 Mulan joined the army in a big way. She is, as far as we can ascertain, the first Disney heroine of Chinese ethnicity, and a cross-dresser at that. Teamed up with an African American dragon (Eddie Murphy) and a bunch of low life comrades, she defeats the 'Huns' and saves the Emperor from assassination in his own palace. Based on a 5th century poem which tells of the filial courage of a young girl, Fa Mulan, the film uses the story of daughterly devotion to weave a tale of girlhood amongst dragons, cranky ancestor demons, an ageing emperor, a gloriously handsome warrior-captain and ghastly barbarians. Mulan's Disney incarnation deals with all this rather well, as she is spunky, cool and deeply Asian American.[1] She wears her traditional *qipao* with the awkward grace of a teenager in a best dress, and her military fatigues with the energetic ease of a teenager in a shopping mall. Even the supposedly awkward transition to a masculine mode of walk and speech reads more as a question of urban style than a description of temporary gender performance. Her gender status is however hurriedly re-inscribed by the pretty- pink romance scene at the end of the film, as the Grandmother asks the Captain to stay for a meal, 'stay forever?' This ending is a Disney pre-requisite for the domestic market, and it strays far from the filial emphasis of the original poem, in which Mulan returns to her natal family after twelve years of hard fighting. It is still arguable that *Mulan*'s impact lies not so much in a pretence to authenticity as in the very fact of the film's making, and in the momentum of distribution - this is a version of Chinese heroism that was screened on the Mainland as well as in the general US international film market.[2] Commentators have noted however that, whilst the film is true to the story if not its moral emphases, the marketing of the film was detrimental to the Chineseness of the subject, and therefore to the possible multicultural benefits of its distribution:

> While Disney's *Mulan* stays true to the story (without emphasising those virtues though [filial piety, preservation of family honor, devotion to one's country, enormous personal sacrifice]), most of the media coverage was not. Most coverage praised the movie's beautiful artwork and successful marketing, [only] a few remembered to mention the heroic nature of *Mulan*, the character (Berggreen 1998:12).

Berggreen's critique is interested in the ways in which the film addresses a pre-school audience. Her comments point to the market's avoidance of Chinese values over American values, and thus to an unease at the heart of the story-telling. There is a double ambiguity in play here. Mulan's heroism is undercut by her re-submission to the handsome captain (whom she outclassed in battle strategy), but her *Chinese national* status is also undermined by the final third of the film, where the comedy of the penultimate fight scene, followed by her return to domesticity and barbie-pink romance, reduce personal sacrifice to adolescent spunk. If we turn to that adolescent audience, there is another dynamic to be taken into account. For the over 10's *Mulan* is a cross-cultural event which is strongly inflected by the diasporic aspirations of young people of Chinese ethnicity outside the geographic scope of the traditions of Fa Mulan. It was enjoyed in the theatres and on video by the 5-8 age-groups, but it also has an after-life on teenage websites. These veer between discussion of the film as a role model (or not) for Asian-Americans, and a visual icon of 'cool' for Asian American teenage girls. It is both an introductory lesson in hybridity and a brief on the international and technological scope of children's culture.

Disney's *Mulan* is also a re-make. In 1939, *Mulan Joins the Army* (*Mulan cong jun*), Pu Wencang's live action version of the legend, also recounted the story of a young girl who went to war in place of her father, who crossed the Yellow River and made for the Black Mountains of the barbarian hordes, and who returned home to live once again a girl-woman of 'cloud-like hair.'[3] This film, shot in black and white for the Hua Cheng studios, describes Mulan's story with a strong focus on filial duty, but also an emphasis on the new woman of new China (Liu 1994:161). The nationalist overtones are strong in this version as it was intended to play to a Chinese domestic audience in a time of war (with the Japanese). The nationalism in the 1990s *Mulan* is somewhat obscure as the animated characters exist in a post-historical world of anachronism and generality (moreover, some audiences confused Hun with Han and decided that the Disney Studios had failed in their homework). What the two characterisations share is their necessary ambiguity. Who is Mulan? Does her performance of masculinity define her femininity as the classic masquerade of psychoanalytic theory? Does her return to society and womanhood deny or complete her performance? To what extent does she complement or contradict the women of contemporary Mainland film? Is she a mere trope of the Orientalist, or a lucky inflection of the dissonance at the centre of womanliness in societies in and out of China? Mulan's transformation from girl to man, and from man to woman, takes her into the realms of learned behaviour and performance. It takes the audience into a world of political contingency: 1939, one legendary woman stands for the national body in *Mulan Joins the Army*, and in 1999 one girl-woman-barbie doll becomes a virtual-body bridge of genre, diasporic ethnicity and gendered expectations[4]. In the final fight scenes, after Mulan has been exposed and shamed as a female, Mulan's comrades also cross dress - as women - in order to infiltrate the Emperor's palace and save him from the very masculine villain, Shan Yü. The men's masquerade is pure drag, very much in the Hollywood musical vein of comic drag sequences, compare for instance the sailors as Arabian dancing girls in *On the Town* (Donen and Kelly 1949). The sequence does not threaten Chinese masculinity so much as confirm its impermeable character, it is as impossible for these soldiers to pretend to the feminine as it was for Frank Sinatra and Gene Kelly in late 1940s America. The ambiguity of cross-dressing is denied in the performance of drag in both these films. The masculinity of the characters never gives way to a plausible performance of the other gender. Mulan's successful performance is a signal of her ambiguity, lying at the centre of feminine adeptness at masquerade. *Mulan* shows us that in cultural texts women are at their most convincing when they are pretending to the masculine.

Two decades after Mulan joined the Army as a national heroine of pre-Liberation Shanghai, other warrior girls took to the screen. In 1957 the young Xie Jin made *Woman Basketball Player No 5*. The 'warriors' are national grade sportswomen who strive to represent China's national body as unambiguously strong. The drama of the film lies in the internal conflicts which the coach has to overcome through an emphasis on collectivity and the general good. The film ends as the girls board a plane, smilingly united and devoted to the cause of the national image, which rests on their expected performance overseas. The girls' *explicit* strength is in their talent at basketball, combined with team spirit. They are sports women and the film is concerned with the disciplining of their bodies into a performative emphasis on competitive physicality. In particular, one girl has to learn to 'renounce' the performance of femininity - considered as excessively and inappropriately engaged with clothes and personal appearance. Despite the rhetoric that drives the film, the contradictions are close to the surface of the text. The militaristic body language of fists striking young breasts in a fervour of team spirit reads rather oddly when a young woman makes the gesture to show her worthiness to an only slightly older man. The *inexplicit* nature of the relationship between the coach and the girls, and the male Party Secretaries and the team captain informs the film with a hierarchy of the national body. The girls' bodies as sports warriors are in the service of the nation, and of the men who oversee its progress. But necessarily these girls' bodies are not tucked away inside baggy Mao suits, they are crisply taut underneath starched shirts. Their sexual potential is unavoidably inscribed into their athleticism. It is, simply, very difficult to make a film about strong young women without acknowledging the shape of strong young bodies. This is again a necessary ambiguity which is engendered by the contradictions inherent in the rhetoric of bodies as metonyms of the nation, but which leaves the meaning of the film open to other performative readings and other biographies of desire, abuse and frustration. There is a similar narrative of bodily subjection to the performance of revolution in another 'warrior' film, *Girl Pilots* (Cheng Ying and Teng Kena 1966). The film charts and lauds the women's dedication to the socialist cause and to their profession, seen as especially arduous because of their gender. Despite low levels of education, physical disability and an annoying boyfriend (in one case) they achieve competence. The competence transcends gender, but the tension in the very title of the film is a reminder of the social ambiguity at the core of the film's narrative. It betrays a deeply felt belief that women can *not* do what they are expected to do in any particular society. Their competence is a singular performative event, which must be played out in cultural spaces again and again, but never believed at the level of social common sense or cultural naming. More recently, in women's magazines the dual images of the new Chinese woman: *jianqi liangmu* (virtuous wife and mother) and *xiandai huaping* (modern flower vase woman), have been extended by the superwoman (Jaschok 1995:123; Evans 2000). China's first female body-building champion, Zhang Ping, features as an excessive version of this in an article in *Women of China* which describes her husband's slow acceptance of her sport. Once he recognises its importance he takes on the duties of balancing family and work duties so she can train in the evenings (Zhu Fushi 1991:37-8). Hers is an excessive performance of the strong body, again trained in the cause of a national championship, and again described as the extraordinary event of male belief in female competency.

THE PERFORMANCE OF AMBIGUITY

Ambiguity emerges in cultural texts as a formation of equivocation and obscurity, which both challenges and confirms social and sexual order. The notation of the ambiguous can only be through a recognition of its inexplicit (in)articulacy - the way in which the threat of change is coded as present on-screen and in the working-out of a particular character. Its performance on screen relies on two pillars of support for its legibility: the use of known stars in familiar roles and the symbolic but profound narrative abuse of the actor's body. With these strategies in place the film constructs a space for the contingent readings of social norms to work their duty of confirmation. The abuse occurs where these are absent, or in some degree untrusted as is generally the case, in which case the ambiguous body is made an *explicit* victim of society. In such cases it is as though the ambiguity posed in the performance of a certain situation may only be answered with the inarticulate certainty of destruction. In the context of our positive argument here, this marks the articulacy of the 'modern' woman as opposed to the inchoate structures of social control which she suffers. An early evocation of cinematic ambiguity is central to Wu Yonggang's silent drama, *Goddess/ Prostitute* (*Shen nü*) (1934). The central female character, played by Ruan Ling-yu, is a prostitute in Shanghai. She is struggling to raise and educate her infant son, against the vicissitudes of her trade and the cruelties of social opinion. The film is important as a text of the Left Wing cinema movement, as a paean to the star quality of Ruan, and as an early classic in the Shanghai city genre which continues to this day. Without discounting these qualities, we focus on one sequence in which the ambiguous status of the feminine is uncompromisingly described, but is eventually inexplicit in the formation of its female subject. In the first half of the sequence Ruan rocks her young son to sleep in her arms, and then puts him to bed. A cut to the clock indicates late evening, and she crosses to the mirror to start transforming herself from mother to whore. The preparation is a banal process. She changes her dress, puts up her hair, puts on earrings, applies make up and slips on evening shoes. She then leaves the house and walks down the street, soon to be joined by an unidentified male escort. What makes this sequence of banal events extraordinary is the shift in the camera's treatment of her body. As she leaves the house neighbours whisper, and the camera adopts their disapproving and prurient point of view. Shots of the head and torso are replaced in the process of transformation by fetishized close ups of smaller parts of the whole (her ears, her legs, her ankles). The maternal wholeness (and wholesomeness) in the scene with the child is thereby carefully and surely fragmented. Finally, the memory of her closeness to the child is replaced by a sudden intimacy with the adult male companion., and the sequence closes. The ambiguity carried in the *Goddess* may seem at first to be simply that of the opposite poles of the social female: the maternal and the sexually active. Yet there is of course no essential opposition that can be placed between the mother and the whore, whatever assumptions of maternal purity or erotic infecundity may haunt masculinist appropriations of the female body in symbolic practice. Ruan's body plays both roles in quick succession, with the acknowledgment that her performances are discretely determined by the social eye of the camera but with the expectation that each performative incarnation is interdependent on the other. Her maternity is made tragically sweet by the impossibility of happiness signified in the sexual core of her trade. Her sexual availability is both charged and invalidated by the audience's knowledge of her maternity. Her ambiguity lies not in any necessary difference between her two major narrative functions, but rather in the social necessity of refusing to accommodate their coherence.

Goddess intensifies the experience of necessary ambiguity by placing the burden of co-existence on one character. Other films of the period are more conservative in their delineation of social order amidst feminine chaos. In *Street Angel* (*Malu tianshi*) (Yuan Muzhi, 1937) the character is literally divided. Xiaohong is the good girl whose love triumphs. Xiaoyun is her elder sister, already working as a prostitute, and she remains a social outcast. The easy division of roles in *Street Angel* is nonetheless an acknowledgment of ambiguity. The women are in a *sisterly* relationship. Their screen space is likewise coded in relation one to another: by darkness and light, by proximity to windows or to shady corners, and by the amount of dark shadows on their bodies. These codes only work in a discourse of mutually constructed danger and salvation. These children of urban China look backwards and forwards in a simultaneous and infantile disavowal of the impossibility of their separation. They give the lie to the revolutionary family (*Geming jiating*) (1960, Shui Hua) that was a staple of post Liberation film. Whereas the revolutionary family is bounded by the integrity of its members as well as, or in place of, blood relations, here the ambiguous intimacy of sisterhood suggests that family connections can never quite rid the future of the past imperfect.

The circular passage from the virtuous to the lost soul in early cinema is re-visited in films of the 1990s. Again, the figure of the prostitute is used to both enjoy and disfigure the female condition. Here too the socially supposed dissonance between maternity and overt sexuality is made *inexplicit*. Li Shaohong is a female director of the fifth generation, or 'new wave' of Mainland film-makers. Her films include *Bloody Morning, Family Portrait,* and *Blush. Blush (Hong fen,* 1995) explores the condition of the feminine through a series of related tropes: sisterhood, beauty, maternal instinct, national appropriateness, and sexual jealousy. The story revolves around two women, Zhou Qiuyi and Xiao E, both prostitutes in the old society (pre-1949). Forced by the social and political revolutions of Liberation to abandon their trade and re-train as useful citizens, the women discover that their performative certainties are no longer legible. In the opening scene the women leave the brothel on Green Cloud Street and walk towards the canal, where boats wait to take them off to the rehabilitation centre. As they move into the sunlight their make-up and silk clothes appear garish and, against the plain green of the soldiers' uniforms, unexpectedly meaningless. The scene is shot in documentary mid-length with no extreme close-ups. The featured characters are denied cinematic privacy in keeping with this most public humiliation. Then, the over-determined masquerade of prostitution spills into an agonising performance of feminine grace as Qiuyi extends an arm to a young soldier, that he might help her onto the boat. He refuses the gesture. The misfit of her particular beauty with this particular moment renders her inexplicit. She no longer functions as a prostitute, but in losing her explicit description she becomes ambiguous and powerful - cinematically - in the performance of her beauty. Qiu Yi escapes rehabilitation and goes to live with an ex-client from Green Cloud Street, Xiao E is too timid to run away and, finally, fits rather well into the revolutionary and institutionalised family of the centre (after all, she was a daughter of the institutional family of the brothel). In contrast to the binary distinctions between the sisters in *Street Angel,* however, Qiu Yi refuses political reconstruction but is nonetheless reborn into New China, whereas

Xiao E's character is not so much 'good' as devoutly opportunistic. There is a binary structure in place in the film but it is not fixed around either character. Rather, each woman moves across and between the new and the old, discovering and inhabiting the inconsistencies of change and liberation. Sisterhood is established in the brothel, lost in the process of rehabilitation, regained briefly as friends, and then lost again when Xiao E marries Qiu Yi's lover, Lao Pu. The women eventually deal with the problematic of a sisterhood without trust by the exchange of the child, born to Xiao E in her marriage to Lao Pu. This maternal exchange symbolises the return of Qiu Yi's sexual legitimacy and also, as she renames the boy Xin Hua (New China), confirms her national appropriateness as mother of the future. Her rehabilitation is completed. Xiao E's opportunism, which once allowed her to survive rehabilitation, takes her away from her child and back into the mires of sexual freedom and inappropriate behaviour. These life stories return us to the opening scene where the personal beauty of Qiu Yi marks her out in the sunlight against the tawdry prettiness of the younger woman. The original refusal of beauty has become, by the end of the film, a return to the redemptive power of beauty in adversity. It is not entirely unexpected. There are parallel events of 'haircutting,' in which the women are re-described in a sisterly relation of redemption and loss. In traditional Chinese practice, 'the shaving of the head is a ritual performed upon the newborn. The 'female (biological) birth' is regarded as polluted and wild. So the infant has a ceremonial 'social birth' to allow its cleanly passage into the social.' (Emily Martin 1988:165-7). In *Blush*, the symbolic cutting of hair is used as a parallel narrative event to institute the connection between the two women and the new society, and a new bundle of sexual mores. The form and context of the haircutting is in each case highly redolent of the commitment to the social they each experience. Qiu Yi's is a self-administered close crop, at which her lover recoils when they next meet. Xiao E's is a standard style, which she adapts immediately to her own sexual advantage. Xiao E's hair is cut in a bob at the Rehab Centre. She and Lao Pu use the new style as a fulcrum for their treacherous flirtation. In the wake of Lao Pu's betrayals Qiu Yi tries to enter a convent. As a signal of her intent, her hair must be shorn to the scalp. It is her most glorious feature, and she cuts it herself, weeping, as the camera prowls around in a 360 degree description of her despair. In these sequences the women are disfigured in different way, one by an internal betrayal, the other by the ravage of her physical beauty. These disfigurements are also performances of each woman's traumatic relationship with the new China. For Xiao E, the haircut initiates a new strategy of dependency on men, using marriage as an advanced form of permanent, socialist prostitution. Qiu Yi's professionalism still distinguishes between the client and the lover, and for her haircutting is a recognition and a refusal of the new formations of sexual dependency.

The greatest irony to emerge from these shifts in performance and suitability is this discrepancy between passion and politically appropriate behaviour. Qiu Yi's lover, Lao Pu, share the one erotic sequence in the film. They make love in daylight in a richly appointed bourgeois bedroom. This is not taking place in the sleaze of the call-girl's boudoir (see for instance in the love-making scenes in Stanley Kwan's 1989 film *Rouge*), but nonetheless the frank meditation on the quality of their passion is undermined by Lao Pu's pre-Liberation status, which recasts Qiu Yi as desirable (in contrast to the opening scene) but always the whore. As Qiu Yi stands before a full length mirror, Lao Pu undresses her. The sequence is cut with close ups of their faces rubbing, of her dress falling around her thighs, and of their legs close together. It is now private and intimate, but this performance of romantic love proves as impossible in new China as it was in the sludge of bought sex. The love-making is an embodiment of loss and of the necessary ambiguities of survival. Qiu Yi is constantly reborn into the knowledge of such moments and of their passing. As the camera keeps her in medium shot, encircles her shorn head or, as here, pans in close up on her naked flesh, we are reminded of the multiple performances necessary to being female in this society, now, and then. She is open to denial, to desire, and to humiliation, and these performances filter finally into her role as adoptive mother - and daughter - of New China.

HOME, BODY, AND VISIBILITY: 'MODERN' WOMEN

The cinematic image of the 'modern' woman in China is not, we are arguing, entirely discrete from older images of Chinese femininity. Women on screen have encapsulated the possibility of modernity since the great era of Shanghai film-making in the 1930s and 1940s (Zhang 1996:185-231). Revolutionary screen women have been active on their own accounts, as well as on behalf of the nation, since Liberation. The tensions between social expectations and the performed female body are visible in examples of cinema before the advent of modernisation through capitalisation, and the associated international engagement with China. Contemporary cinema, both Chinese and diasporic, builds on this twin repertoire of the national feminine and the constrained sexualised female. Moral outcomes continue for women in uncomfortable social circumstances: warriors and prostitutes being prime exemplars in the medium. Warrior women are submerged in romantic or filial return *or* their bodies are sublimated to national ends at the expense of the personal. Prostitutes (or sexually active women in general) are killed, incorporated into maternal chastity, or returned as ghosts to an anachronistic past life (Chow 1998:134-7).

Perversely, we contend that, despite these endings, the condition of ambiguity continues as a positive marker in cinematic treatments of the 'modern' woman. It is not the case that *images* of women are especially radical. Rather, we need to look to the *performative* and *corporeally experienced* aspects of film to understand how women on screen are helpful to the spectator. Vivian Sobchack argues for an approach to images that acknowledge the gravity and depth of the body:

> ... we recognise vision as embodied and representable not only in its objective dimensions as the visible skin of things, but also in those subjective dimensions that give visual gravity to us. That is, we must remember *in our seeing* that we transcend and subtend the images we produce and allow ourselves to be produced by. At home, and regrounded in our bodies, we have dimension, gravity, and the enabling power to regain our sense of balance and to comport ourselves differently - first, perhaps, *before*, our images, and then, one hopes, *within* them (Sobchack 1999:60).

In relation to films and to women on film, such an approach expects the spectator to *recognise and acknowledge* the absences and contradictions inherent in the figuration of women's lives on screen. Film form involves closure, yet women's social lives are denied closure. The experience of being female in contemporary conditions is neither coherent in principle nor adequately named and resourced in daily cultural and political practice. But the memories carried in the woman's body produce the knowledge of her difference from the social. In film, this knowledge is carried also in the performance of the actress, and understood by the female spectator and experienced in the cultural discomfort of the political imaginary. Every time a woman's image appears on screen, the explicit function of the feminine also carries the inexplicit meaning of the female. The play between the explicit and inexplicit dimensions, both in seeing and in being seen, maintains a constant performance of ambiguity in cinema.

Sobchack advises us all to come home to our bodies and thereby 'regain our sense of balance.' We argue that, in coming home, we are where we have always been, but with an important advantage. The woman's image is never finally dis-incorporated. The *social* requirements and *political* status of the body in narrative time and place are, however, dis-articulated, or 'out of sync.' In 'coming home' our project is finally to re-articulate through political action . In the more immediate future, 'coming home' allows women to savour ambiguity as a collective sign of visibility in contemporary film.

NOTES

1 Her hybridity confirmed by the joint casting (voice / vocals) of Ming-na Wen / Lea Salonga. (Lea Salonga is from the Phillipines). Comments from a webzine:

'The poem of Hua Mu'Lan 's not like this. Disney mess it up, but anyway movie is movie. I still love this awesome animation. All of characters's movement looked real and the picture, characters design, coloring,etc. About the voice of Mulan, Disney production should use Lea Salonga voice of both path of conversation and singing' -Thomas Chen -Age:16 Sex: Male Date Reviewed: Wednesday, April 7, 1999. Website address: http://www.meekosmulanpage.com/.

2 Released in China February 29th 1999.

3 This version is itself a borrowing from the silent Mingxing Studio film of the same name from 1928.

4 Mulan's Barbie version has not yet been included in the Anglo/Hispanic/ Black webpage versions of the doll (www.barbie.com) - unless you go through the 'ivory skin colour' route and pretend hard - as in this design-a-doll extravaganza made by my Anglo-Australian four year old: Presenting Mulan, specially made for Morag by the makers of Barbie® doll!

Mulan has sparkling brown eyes and long wavy black hair. She is wearing her new Cool Jeans Outfit with extra City Shopper accessories. Her birthday is in January. She lives in a big city and spends a lot of time building things. She's interested in history, loves to design clothes and enjoys being with her cousin. Mulan is a special friend of Barbie, personalized by you, Morag!

OR: She is still a 'niche' market item tied to the single character.

REFERENCES

Berggreen, Shu-ling (1998), 'Playground Lost: television, Video and Chinese-American Children's Imaginative Play,' *Asia Pacific Media Educator*, Issue 5, July-December 1998, pp. 7-30.

Chow, Rey (1995) *Primitive Passions: Visuality, Sexuality, Ethnography, and Contemporary Chinese Cinema*. New York: Columbia University Press.

--(1998) *Ethics After Idealism: Theory-Culture-Ethnicity-Reading*. Bloomington: Indiana University Press.

Creed, Barbara (1989) 'Horror and the monstrous-feminine: an imaginary abjection,' in: James Donald (ed.) *Fantasy and the Cinema*. London: British Film Institute, pp. 63-89.

Croll, Elisabeth (1995) *Changing Identities of Chinese Women: Rhetoric, Experience and Self-Perception in Twentieth-Century China*. Hong Kong: Hong Kong University Press.

Dai Jinhua (1995) 'Invisible women: contemporary Chinese cinema and women's film,' *Positions* 3(1), pp. 255-80.

Donald, Stephanie (1998) 'Symptoms of alienation: the female body in recent Chinese film,' *Continuum* 12(1), pp. 91-103.

--(2000 forthcoming) *Public Secrets, Public Spaces: Cinema and Civility in China*. Lanham: Rowman and Littlefield.

Evans, Harriet (1999) 'Comrades sisters: gendered bodies and spaces,' in: Harriet Evans & Stephanie Donald (eds) *Picturing Power in the People's Republic of China: Posters of the Cultural Revolution*. Lanham: Rowman & Littlefield, pp. 63-78.

--(forthcoming 2000) 'Fashioning identities: consumer passions,' in: Stephanie Donald & Harriet Evans (eds) *New Formations* 41, pp. 1-20.

Fan Hong (1997) *Footbinding, Feminism and Freedom: The Liberation of Women's Bodies in Modern China*. Great Britain: Frank Cass & Co.

Honig, Emily & Hershatter, Gail (1988) *Personal Voices: Chinese Women in the 1980s*. Stanford: Stanford University Press.

Jacka, Tamara (1997) *Women's Work in Rural China: Change and Continuity in an Era of Reform*. Cambridge: Cambridge University Press.

Jaschok, Maria (1995) 'On the construction of desire and anxiety: contestations over female nature and identity in China's modern market society,' in: Barbara Einhorn & Eileen Janes Yeo (eds) *Women and Market Societies: Crisis and Opportunity*. Aldershot: Edward Elgar Publishing Company, pp. 114-28.

Johnson, Kay Ann (1983) *Women, the Family and Peasant Revolution in China*. Chicago: The University of Chicago Press.

Kristeva, Julia (1982) *Powers of Horror: An Essay on Abjection*. New York: Columbia University Press.

Liu, Lydia H. (1994) 'The female body and nationalist discourse: Manchuria in Xiao Hong's *Field of Life and Death*,' in: Angela Zito & Tani E. Barlow (eds), *Body, Subject and Power in China*. Chicago: The University of Chicago Press, pp. 157-77.

Martin, Emily (1988) 'Gender and ideological differences in representations of life and death,' in: James L. Watson & Evelyn S. Rawski (eds) *Death*

Ritual in Late Imperial and Modern China. Berkeley: University of California Press, pp. 164-79.

Pickowicz, Paul G. (1993) 'Melodrama representation and the "May Fourth" tradition of Chinese cinema,' in: Ellen Widmer & David Der-wei Wong (eds) *From May Fourth to June Fourth: Fiction and Film in Twentieth-Century China*. Cambridge: Harvard University Press, pp. 295-326.

Sobcahack, Vivian (1999) '"is anybody home?": embodied imagination and visible evictions,' in: Hamid Naficy (ed) *Home, Exile, Homeland: Film, Media, and the Politics of Place*. London: Routledge, 45-61.

Wolf, Margery (1985) *Revolution Postponed: Women in Contemporary China*. Stanford: Stanford University Press.

Yau, Esther C.M. (1989) 'Cultural and economic dislocations: filmic phantasies of Chinese women in the 1980s,' *Wide Angle* 11(2), pp. 6-21.

Zhang, Yingjin (1996) *The City in Modern Chinese Literature and Film: Configurations of Space, Time and Gender*. Stanford: Stanford University Press.

Zhu Fushi (1991) 'China's first female body-building champion. trans. Lin Guanxing,' *Women of China* 11, pp. 34-5.

CHAPTER 8

PROSTITUTION, POLITICS AND POWER: ISSUES OF THE 'FOREIGN' IN WESTERN TELEVISION DOCUMENTARIES OF FEMALE SEX WORKERS IN THAILAND[*]

RACHEL HARRISON

> Always in our dreams we hear the turn of the key that shall close the door of the last brothel; the clink of the last coin that pays for the body and soul of a woman; the falling of the last wall that encloses artificially the activity of woman and divides her from man; always we picture the love of the sexes as once a dull, slow-creeping worm; then a torpid, earthy chrysalis; at last the full-winged insect, glorious in the sunshine of the future (Schreiner 1911).

Since the days of the Vietnam War Thailand, formerly known as Siam, has made an indelible imprint on the popular imagination of the West as home to a widespread and unrestrained sex industry. It was during that era that American G.I.s sought sexual pleasures in the towns around their Thai airbases and in the cities and beach resorts where they took their 'Rest and Recreation' ('R & R'). As a result, in addition to its common tourist-brochure appellation as 'The Land of Smiles,' Thailand has become less flatteringly known as 'The Brothel of Asia,' its capital Bangkok earning the definition in the Longman Dictionary of English Language and Culture as 'a place where there are a lot of PROSTITUTES' (1992:79, emphasis in original). What I argue is that this dominant Western perception of Thailand is both reflected in and stimulates a particular flavour of media coverage of the country which in turn perpetuates pre-existing views: the attention of Western television documentaries on Thailand is more often than not turned to the theme of prostitution.

As religion is to Belfast, racism to Johannesburg and street crime to New York, so prostitution is to Bangkok, or so claims one Thai journalist writing in the English language daily, *The Bangkok Post*. In the same article s/he elaborates, however, that, 'You can hear about it from upstanding members of old families. You can hear about it from taxi drivers, newspaper columnists, doctors, businessmen, businesswomen; everyone, it seems, but the prostitutes themselves' (BP 1990:31). The journalist's point is a vitally important one, for it highlights the fact that the significant degree of public interest and media attention leant to the Thai sex industry - both at the local and global level - is more often than not constructed over the silence of those who work within it.

This chapter argues that the representation of this industry is a highly complex one, involving numerous players, each satisfying their own sets of motivations and desires; and rather than clarify it, the position of the Thai sex worker tends to be obfuscated by the perspectives which such parties have to offer, with their greater power, voice and access to modes of representation. As a result, discussion of Thai female sex workers seems inexorably destined to silence their own voice rather than to offer them a venue for self-expression. This is broadly true at the national level but is particularly pertinent to the Western media coverage of prostitution in Thailand which forms the focus of this paper.

As an extension of this silencing of the Thai female experience, media representation of prostitution - perhaps somewhat ironically - serves to perpetuate a certain censorship of female sexuality which has taken its grip via the long-standing Thai cultural division of women into 'good' and 'bad' - the 'Madonnas' and the 'Whores.'[1] In a society in which female sexuality is morally acceptable only within marriage and monogamy, sexual contact outside this context tends to be equated with prostitution, regardless of whether there is an exchange of money or not. Local media coverage serves largely to reflect this view together with that, widely held by Thai society, of the prostitute as a woman lacking moral fibre, more or less regardless of the circumstances which may have drawn her into this profession. As a result, even those newspaper and journal articles which discuss the cases of individual prostitutes from a quasi-sympathetic angle, nevertheless tend to speak from a position of moral superiority, of the 'good' relating the mishaps of those who have fallen from grace.[2]

Although the sexual mobility of young, urban Thai women appears to have increased in recent years, this remains a subject for the private rather than the public domain. Local media depicts the 'modern' Thai woman as youthful, outgoing, gregarious, fun-loving and often rather 'girlishly' cute, yet avoids any suggestion of her sexual agency or availability. Underlying this construction of 'modern' Thai womanhood is a much older tradition of the feminine, with its emphasis on grace, beauty, neatness and good manners; and it is these traditional features that nationalist sentiment accentuates in its presentation of the image of the Thai woman, both at home and abroad.

Yet despite the relative clarity of division in Thai society between the 'good' woman and the 'bad,' documentary footage produced by the West on female prostitution in Thailand has found it either irrelevant or impossible to acknowledge this important stratification, thus creating and/or contributing to the false impression among its audiences that 'ALL Thai 'girls' are *easy*'!

In addition, the coincidental accordance between local and global media in their overemphasis on the role of the 'foreign' with regard to the issue of prostitution has further contributed to a misreading of the Thai sex industry and those who work within it. The frequent arguments made, for example, for the Vietnam War as the cause and origin of the industry overlook a much longer history of prostitution in Thailand, one serving a largely local clientele. In so doing they instead validate a somewhat spurious association between female promiscuity and the 'foreign,' one which holds its separate appeal for Thai and Western audiences alike: for the former it opens up a crucial space for locating the socially unacceptable in the realm of the 'other'; and for the latter it perpetuates an eroticisation of the East that took root in the colonial era. Western film and media have also played their part in constructing an image of Thailand in the popular imagination as a haven of sensual pleasures and sexual abandon. As a result of this conveniently titillating fabrication, a wide disparity can be seen to exist between local constructions of 'modern' Thai womanhood and global understandings of both Thai women and the society in which they function.

THE ORIGINS OF THE CONSTRUCTION OF THAILAND AS A SITE OF SENSUAL PLEASURE IN WESTERN FILM

With regard to the medium of film, the association between Thailand and prostitution/concubinage was first made in the Western imagination with the production in 1946 of the Rodgers and Hammerstein musical *Anna and the King of Siam*. Based on the novel and play of the same name by Margaret Landon (written in 1944), the tale was in turn adapted from the allegedly autobiographical writings of Anna Leonowens, English governess at the Siamese court of King Mongkut (Rama IV, r. 1851-68).[3] It portrays the experiences Anna has when she arrives in Bangkok - described by the captain of the ship on which she travels as a dreadful place, in which a widower such as herself had better not set foot - to teach the Thai King's wives and children. A decade later the film was remade as the seemingly interminably popular classic *The King and I*, starring Yul Brynner as an irascible, barbaric and yet still oddly lovable King Rama and Deborah Kerr as the patronizing English governess who deems it her Christian duty to correct him in his ways.[4] While Leonowens undoubtedly saw herself as a moral crusader bringing a combination of education and charm to the

Siamese Palace, the widely held Thai view of her is an entirely contrary one, of a stern-faced, low-class widow with a fanciful imagination that brought great embarrassment to the Thai nation (Schloss 1998). As a result, *The King and I* remains banned in Thailand to this day for its disrespectful depiction of the Thai monarch.[5]

Much of Leonowens' Christian moral line as depicted in the film is represented by her views on King Mongkut's attitude to Thai women, reflected by his extensive harem and his treatment of its members.[6] The concubine Tap Tim epitomizes their plight, portrayed early in the film as a gift from the ruler of Burma (Myanmar) and hence deprived on the opportunity to marry her long-standing lover: when Tap Tim and her lover elope together, both are caught, and much to the governess' horror, the former is severely beaten and the latter executed.[7]

This central theme of *The King and I* denotes one of the earliest steps in foreign film depictions of Thailand of its culture of concubinage. It consequently establishes a link in the viewer's imagination between Thai female sexuality and power and it is this agenda, one still not condoned by most Thai themselves, that continues to be played out in Western film and media representations of the country in the latter half of the twentieth century.

Despite the negative portrayal in *The King and I* of the promiscuity of the powerful Thai male and the inequality of the sexes, the film effectively serves to sow the seed of what later becomes a less negative and indeed rather titillating Western perception of Thailand as a site of unrestrained eroticism and sexual license.

The exotic-cum-erotic labeling of Thailand (though this time of the country rather than its people), took a further step with the release in 1974 of one of the West's best-known soft-porn films, *Emmanuelle*, in which Thailand forms an outré and enigmatic backdrop to the exploration of Western sexual desire. *Emmanuelle* was marketed as the 'scandalous' story of a nineteen year old French woman who, as wife to a diplomat posted to Bangkok, 'learns to throw away the pleasures of love and realize her wildest fantasies' in a Thailand of giggling, teenage masseuses, chicken-slaying children, leprous beggars and silk-clad maidservants, the latter shown to take quiet yet unmistakable pleasure in the experience of rape. The pinnacle of Emmanuelle's sexual abandon is marked by her visit to a Thai boxing ring, where, to a traditional Thai musical accompaniment, she makes love with the champion Thai boxer before an audience of fellow fighters.

Although Thai women and men are not the central focus of the *Emmanuelle* narrative, the film is nevertheless responsible for establishing Thailand as an appropriate setting for and encouragement to Western erotic fantasy and as a site of the sexually exotic, liberated and unrestrained. This it achieved at a time when the United States' war with Vietnam was drawing to a close, a war in which numerous American troops had been based in Thailand and/or had travelled to Bangkok for regular 'R & R' periods.

PROSTITUTION AND WESTERNISATION:
OVER-EMPHASISING THE 'FOREIGN' IN THAILAND'S
SEX INDUSTRY

Commentators on prostitution in Thailand, from journalists, academics and NGOs to government and tourist industry spokespeople - Thai and Western alike - have invariably argued that the Vietnam War era was almost wholly responsible for the emergence of a large scale Thai sex industry from the late 1960s onwards. In doing so they draw a link between female promiscuity and the 'foreign' which is constantly reiterated in both national and international media representations of the Thai sex industry.

In reality, although the withdrawal of the American GIs after 1975 certainly left Thailand with a legacy of go-go bars and massage parlours that catered to their particular sexual tastes, it is misleading to suggest that there was not also a larger industry catering to the indigenous market which existed alongside and largely separately from it. The extent of the industry for local clientele is difficult to pinpoint precisely, though some sense of its size is offered by Cohen's assessment that only approximately 0.5-2 per cent of his estimate of the total number of Thai sex workers (viz. approximately two million) are engaged in tourism-related services (Cohen 1986). In relation to this Cohen argues that,

> the precise share of tourism-related prostitution in the total prostitution scene in Thailand is unknown; it appears that the great majority of prostitutes still serve a local Thai and Chinese clientele ... while only a minority works with European, Australian, American, or Japanese tourists. These, however, may well constitute a majority of the clients of the higher quality establishments (Cohen 1982:406).

While the go-go bars and massage parlours inherited from the Vietnam War were, in its aftermath, undoubtedly re-marketed as attractions to male tourists, Cohen's comments place in perspective the degree to which widespread prostitution in Thailand can be linked to international tourism.[8]

Despite the division to which Cohen alludes however, there has been a disproportionate emphasis in both the Thai and Western media on the association between the Thai sex industry and its foreign clientele. A survey of the coverage of prostitution in the Thai (English language) press, for example, reveals a significantly unequal allocation of space to stories concerning Thai women lured into prostitution in Japan, Germany, the Middle East, Greece, Hong Kong and Singapore - almost everywhere, it seems, but for Thailand itself.

Such newspaper reports reflect the tendency to associate the socially unpleasant with the 'foreign,' similarly characteristic of some academic texts tracing the history of prostitution in Thailand. Writing in the decade before the onset of the Vietnam War, Somsamai Srisudravarna, for example, retains the emphasis on the presence of the foreigner as the significant source of demand for commercial sex. In his comments on the taxation of commercial sex in the former Siamese capital of Ayutthaya (1350-1767), Somsamai clearly links its existence to the presence of European traders - people whose 'free-spending habits induced an even larger number of women [...] to take up this occupation. 'He goes on to write, 'at the end of the Ayutthaya period, it was notorious that increasing numbers of unfortunate women were being forced to grit their teeth, shut their eyes, and sell themselves to foreigners' (Somsamai [1957] in Reynolds 1987:134).[9] Somsamai goes on to point out that a Royal Edict was issued in 1763, stating that, 'Henceforth, Thai, Mon and Lao are forbidden to have sexual intercourse in secret with Indians, French, English ... and Malays - who are heathens (i.e. not Buddhists) - in order to protect the people from misfortune' (ibid.:134). As he wryly comments, 'This meant that it was perfectly all right for prostitutes to have sexual intercourse with Thais who, because they were Buddhists, were not heathens violating the principles of the Religion!' (ibid:134).

Maintaining the existence of a 'close association between prostitution, migrant communities and economic development throughout Thai history.' Wathinee and Guest also link the growth of prostitution in the subsequent Bangkok period (1782-present) with a community of outsiders (Wathinee and Guest 1994). Their work explores an area of Bangkok's Chinatown following the influx of largely male Chinese migrants to Thailand in the reign of King Rama I (1782-1809) which became known as *Sampeng*, from the Khmer word for prostitute. According to Wathinee and Guest, most of the prostitutes working in *Sampeng* (which remained a notorious red-light district until the reign of King Rama IV) were Chinese and even those who were ethnically Thai, adopted Chinese pseudonyms (ibid. 1994:2-3), presumably either to distance themselves from their real ethnic and cultural origins or to hold greater appeal for their Chinese clientele.

Wathinee and Guest's assessment of the demand for prostitution being a largely foreign one is not limited to the Chinese, as they go on to quote the following:

Sampeng was both a commercial and residential centre in Bangkok for the Chinese. As the Thai economy developed and new communities of foreigners were established, prostitution also expanded with prostitutes adapting to the characteristics of their new customers. For example, as Bang-rak developed as a community of mainly Europeans, it attracted prostitutes who often adopted foreign names in order to identify with their clients. (IPSR 1991, quoted in ibid:3)

Wathinee and Guest do however, acknowledge that prostitution was not confined to serving foreign communities alone and that there was in addition 'a well-documented sex industry operating in regional centres' (ibid.:2). Thus they raise the important point that prostitution in Thailand is not entirely or even largely a 'foreign' issue; and this is backed by a broader body of academic work from Thai and non-Thai scholars alike (for example Pasuk 1982; Sukanya 1983 and 1988; Thitsa 1990; Truong 1990; and Harrison 1995, 1997 and forthcoming b).

THAI CONSTRUCTIONS OF FEMALE SEXUALITY AND THE INDIGENOUS SEX INDUSTRY IN THAILAND

The assertion by Thai academic Sukanya Hantrakul (1983 and 1988) that institutionalized prostitution existed in Siam prior to the arrival of the first foreigners is also supported by Thanh-Dam Truong's valuable research on the topic (1990). Truong notes, for example, the observations of an English commentator, Mr Salmon who visited Siam in 1725 that, 'If a Person of Quality's Daughter goes astray, she is sold to an Officer who has a Patent from the King for liberty to prostitute Young Women; and he has not less than Five or Six Hundred of these ladies under his care' (quoted in Truong 1990:148). Salmon similarly acknowledges that the crime of adultery among the royal concubines was punishable by condemnation to a house of prostitution for noblemen (ibid.:148).

The institutions of concubinage and polygamy among the ethnic Thais are widely thought to date back to a royal decree of 1361, which was later endorsed by the Law of the Three Seals (*kotmaai traa saam duang*) of 1805. This perpetuated the three existing wives category: viz. primary wives (*mia klaang meuang*), minor wives (*mia klaang nork*) and slave wives (*mia klaang thaasi*) (ibid.:146). In its section on the husband and wife, the Three Seals Law also provided what appears to be the first official usage of the word prostitute in Thai - *ying nakhorn sopenii* (Sukanya 1983).[10] Moreover, the fact that the Law of the Three Seals also granted women fewer property rights and gave husbands the permission to sell their wives or to use them as collateral, meant that women became vulnerable to sale and resale (Truong

1990:147). The provisions of the Three Seals Law can therefore be seen to have created the legal basis under which prostitution could thrive. At the same time they also contributed to a cultural possibility of female prostitution by their implicit division of women into 'good' or 'bad,' according to their sexual availability.

As Sukanya testifies, the effects of this division are still felt in Thailand today, where the assertion of the Three Seals Law that 'A good woman should not let more than one man gain access to her body' still rings on in the ears of most middle class Thai women, despite its official repeal in 1908 (Sukanya 1988:116-17). As a result, 'good' Thai women remain, broadly speaking, those who perform their roles as dutiful daughters and faithful wives and whose concern with sexuality focuses on their aspirations of motherhood and their fulfillment of their husband's desires; while the 'bad' are those whose sexual contacts outside the institution of marriage are automatically equated with prostitution (Sukanya 1988:118). At the same time, the institution of polygamy for Thai men condoned by the Law of the Three Seals, created a parallel social structure which actively encouraged them in their role as sexual adventurers.[11]

Pasuk Phongpaichit adds to this the observation that it was the Sinicisation of Thailand in the late nineteenth century which further condoned 'a culture of polygamy and concubinage which ... legitimates the commoditisation of women' (Pasuk 1982:6). It can be argued that consequently, Thai and Sino-Thai males received a certain legal and cultural encouragement to have extra-marital affairs, whereby their sexual encounters were deemed as an admirable complement to ordinary family life (Suntaree 1991:41). Moreover, the historically created culture of male sexual license has held fast long after the official repeal of the Law of the Three Seals in 1908, the emancipation of female slave labour in 1909 and the legal ban on polygamy in 1935. For, as Truong argues, the trade of female sexual labour and the accumulation of wives as a symbol of social prestige and sexual prowess continued beyond these dates (Truong 1990:153) and female slaves newly freed after 1909 turned instead to prostitution (Sukanya 1983:6).

While the details of Thai social and judicial history are important for their revelations of the development of male sexual license, an examination of the national religion of Buddhism is also essential for the light it sheds on the institutionalisation of gender inequality in Thailand. Van Esterik (1982, 1989), Kirsch (1982), Sukanya (1983, 1988), Truong (1990), Mills (1995), and Harrison (1997) have all contributed to the analysis of the mechanisms by which Buddhism serves to undermine women. Van Esterik, for example, discusses the broad notion that religious ideology provides and reinforces for key images of masculinity and femininity (1989:82). Sukanya argues more pointedly that Buddhism contains within it daily reminders of women's religious inferiority. This manifests itself in the value placed on masculine asceticism (with all its implications for detachment, otherworldliness and avoidance of lust) over feminine sensuality, embodiment, fertility and nurture. Because of the close association between women and the world of embodiment, they are forbidden access to the monkhood and cannot be ordained, so denying them the opportunity to make sufficient religious merit in order to achieve Enlightenment. As a result, whereas male children repay their debt to their mothers for bringing them into the world by ordaining as Buddhist monks and transferring merit to them, female offspring repay their filial debt by working and contributing to the family income.[12] In areas where employment opportunities are low, such as the north and north east of Thailand, finding work usually means migrating to the city, often to join its thriving and relatively lucrative sex industry (see for example, Pasuk 1982).

An investigation of legal, cultural and religious practices in Thailand offers sufficient evidence that sexual inequality, concubinage and female prostitution share a lengthy history, contributing to the basis of the contemporary Thai sex industry, independent of the Vietnam War and of subsequent international tourism. Despite this reality, Western media representations of Thailand are invariably drawn to discussions of its sex industry as a phenomenon of international tourism, in an implicit statement that it is prostitution which forms both the focus and the limits of Western interest in Thailand. As discussed earlier, this interest has its roots in a previous trend established in Western film to eroticise and sexualize Thailand in the popular imagination. What it further serves to do is to act as a metaphor for Western (mis)readings and (mis)representations of the East, and of Asian women in particular.

DOCUMENTARY COVERAGE OF THE THAI SEX INDUSTRY SCREENED IN BRITAIN: THE CASE OF *FOREIGN BODIES*.

In the two decades following the release of the erotic adventures of *Emmanuelle*, television audiences in the United Kingdom have viewed a number of documentaries confirming the popular Western perception of Thailand as a world centre of promiscuity. In 1981 the BBC screened *One Way Ticket to Hualampong*, a harrowing account of how young female migrants from north and north east Thailand are unwittingly lured into prostitution upon disembarkation at Bangkok's main Hualampong railway station.

146

Some years later, in a series of programmes on Southeast Asia entitled *Slow Boats to Surabaya*, presenter Jack Pizzey's episode on Thailand included the obligatory reference to Bangkok's notorious red-light district of Patpong, three side-streets catering primarily to European, American and Japanese sexual tastes, the nature of its services openly visible to the public. (This contrasts with the massage parlours, brothels, tea-houses, karaoke bars, coffee shops, barbers, member clubs and discotheques, all of which offer sexual services to a largely Thai/Chinese clientele but which are less obviously recognizable as places of prostitution and therefore less 'photogenic.') Against a backdrop of scantily-clad go-go dancers gyrating their way round neon-lit metal poles, Pizzey interviewed one of the working girls who consented to take him back to her village in rural Thailand. The interview with her continued, via interpreter, on the local bus back home, with questions dealing with how and why she had chosen to become a prostitute, conducted with surprising insensitivity within earshot of all fellow passengers. In this way, the programme indicated either its total lack of consideration for the sensitivities regarding work in the sex industry in Thailand, or its unawareness of their existence.

The BBC's *Rough Guide to Bangkok* took a similar, mandatory step down Patpong, as its presenter, Magenta Divine pushed her way through the crowds of onlookers - sex-tourists, pimps and hookers alike. While expressing her horror and the scale and magnitude of the Thai sex industry, used, she acknowledged, by foreigners and tourists alike, Magenta conducted the majority of her interviews and commentary-to-camera clad in a tight-fitting, bust-revealing mini-dress that Thai viewers would ironically have associated with easy sexual availability and prostitution.

A documentary film by Australian producer Dennis O'Rourke entitled *A Good Woman of Bangkok* was first screened in UK at the London Film Festival in 1991 and was subsequently released on British television.[13] O'Rourke's eighty-minute documentary broke with tradition by focusing specifically on the life of one twenty five-year-old Bangkok call-girl, named Aoi, of whom O'Rourke was also a client. The single mother of a child conceived before Aoi's husband left her, O'Rourke's 'Good Woman' was also blind in one eye. The film makes passing reference to her semi-blindness. It is only in a further investigation of the film by Thai academic Kaanjanaa Kaewtep that one learns this to have resulted from the poignant tragedy of a failed abortion attempt by Aoi's own mother during pregnancy (Kaanjanaa 1994:119). O'Rourke's footage comprised extracts of Aoi's daily life together with extensive interviews with her and monologues to camera. He filmed her waking, naked, in a short-time hotel where, upon realizing the presence of the camera, she coyly hurried to cover herself with the sheets. No explanation was attempted as to why a woman who was

147

sexually available to anyone who could afford the modest fee for her services, might be concerned about being revealed naked to the public eye. But a growing sense of Aoi's irritation with the camera's invasion of her every privacy was captured as O'Rourke recorded her lunching on noodles at a roadside food stall. Without the details of Thai cultural norms regarding restraint of expression of anger, the intensity of Aoi's irritation was lost on the viewer and rendered unimportant in the context of the wider narrative. Although this film, more than any other, revealed the harrowing despair of life on the streets and the psychological damage inflicted by such work, the exploitative invasion of the 'Good Woman's' privacy by the camera served primarily to reiterate the objectification of her as a prostitute. O'Rourke, who, the film announces somewhat self-pitifully in its prologue, had gone to Bangkok to discover 'the meaning of love' in the aftermath of his divorce, ended his voyeuristic portrayal of Aoi with the damning acknowledgement that she had returned to prostitution less than a year after he had 'bought her out' with payment for her participation in his documentary.

With growing awareness of the extent of HIV infection and child prostitution in Thailand, Granada television screened *Other People's Children* in 1993, with its emphasis on the role Western governments might play in convicting tourists guilty of sex crimes committed while holidaying abroad. Only weeks later, a BBC documentary team covered almost identical issues in its shocking report *Dying for Sex*, differing from all its predecessors, however, in one important aspect, conveyed in its opening statement:

Thailand's sex industry is legendary. It attracts men the world over. *But the carnal cabarets playing to foreigners are only a tiny part of it. There's a much larger local flesh trade, in which many of the prostitutes are children.* Now the Thai government has ordered a crackdown in a desperate bid to stop one of the fastest spreading AIDS epidemics the world has ever seen (emphasis mine).

Dying for Sex was the first of all the television documentaries investigating Thailand's sex industry to make the significant point that the majority of its clients were Thai men rather than Western tourists. The Thai press appreciatively acknowledged that, 'the explicit documentary really hit the nail on the head, ramming home the message about cultural nationwide practices that will almost certainly leave millions dead by the end of the decade' (*Nation* 1993c:A13).

It seemed that now AIDS had established a firm foothold in Thailand, prostitution was sufficiently sensational to be presented to Western audiences in its own right, no longer requiring the focus of Western sex tourism to stimulate foreign interest. Moreover, it might be argued, that just as Thailand was anxious to pin the blame for the rapid spread of AIDS on

Western sexual involvement in their country, so too were Western television audiences relieved to learn that the 'brothel of Asia' was not one into which they alone, or even primarily, had dipped.

Although *Other People's Children* and *Dying for Sex* provided the most up-to-date coverage of the AIDS crisis in Thailand, Channel Four's earlier documentary *Foreign Bodies* had been among the first to raise the issue of AIDS. Produced by freelance film-makers Alison Poteous and Tim Cooper, *Foreign Bodies* examined the dangers posed to Western sex tourists by the disease and, in particular, by the Thai government's lack of commitment to tackling the problems both of widespread prostitution and its related potential for widespread HIV infection. The year of filming was 1987, nominated by the Tourism Authority of Thailand as 'Visit Thailand Year' and three years after the country's first reported AIDS case.

Foreign Bodies opened with the image of a fifteen year old northern Thai girl called Bee making a traditional offering of incense before a Buddhist shrine. Bee, the programme explained, was sold into prostitution by her father at the age of thirteen, and although no longer a bonded-sex worker, had remained irrevocably captive to Thailand's extensive sex industry. Shifting to scenes of Western tourists and then to naked go-go dancers in the seaside tourist resort of Pattaya, *Foreign Bodies* informed its audience that in 1987 almost three million tourists visited the country, many to use the services of its 700,000 prostitutes.[14] This, narrator Tim Cooper misleadingly explained, was due to a 'demand for sex on this scale created by European, American and Japanese men.'

Although Pattaya, where much of *Foreign Bodies* was filmed, is undoubtedly a magnet for Western sex tourists and US marines on 'liberty,' its places of sexual entertainment are highly segregated along racial lines, with separate massage parlours catering to Western, Middle Eastern, Singaporean/Malaysian and Thai tastes. Similarly, the documentary's secretly filmed footage of a transaction between the programme makers and a Patpong pimp for the purchase of two fourteen year old virgins from northern Thailand, inaccurately implies that such girls are primarily initiated into sexual experience by foreigners. While some foreign tourists in Thailand undoubtedly seek teenage virgins, the majority of their customers are the wealthy Sino-Thais. As government advisor, Dr Saisuree Chutikul acknowledged that, 'Chinese men have an idea that sleeping with young girls will keep them young, so they will seek out young girls. This was happening long before the tourists came' (*Nation* c. 1990).[15]

Similarly, while *Foreign Bodies* did not make explicit how the film-makers found Bee or where she was working at the time of filming, it broadly implied that Bee was sold to a brothel with the same clientele as that of the Pattaya beaches and the Patpong sex shows. Yet when Bee related in an interview the circumstances in which she had lost her virginity and her resignation to the fact that she had become a 'fallen woman' whose reputation is indelibly blackened by having slept with so many different men, this was unlikely to have had much connection with international sex tourism in Thailand.[16]

The obfuscation of these issues in *Foreign Bodies* was perpetuated by the change in scene made in the documentary from its interview with Bee to the shores of Pattaya beach and the disembarkation of US marines at 'liberty' for the first time following over two months of military exercises in the Philippines. Cooper's narration provided the clichéd explanation of the association between the US military and the growth of prostitution in Thailand during the 'Rest and Recreation' days of the Vietnam War, the legacy of which the World Bank advised Thailand to use in developing its tourist industry. Thus his programme contributed to the perpetuation of a myth that has effectively served to conceal the complex reality and extent of Thailand's sex industry both before and since the 1960s.

By comparison, very little was said in the Cooper documentary of Thailand's own cultural relationships with sexuality or with prostitution. Filmed footage of a spirit shrine adorned with numerous phallic images was not investigated as a site of animist worship associated with the Indian Sivaite influence on early Thai religious culture that it undoubtedly was; but was instead (mis)taken as a shrine to the worship of the modern-day penis, and a representation of the economic aspirations associated with Pattaya's sex-tourist trade. Lip service was similarly paid to the influence of the national religion of Buddhism in the creation of Thai women's low social status, the link between Buddhism and prostitution in Thailand being largely lost in the brevity of Cooper's statement, made as he himself sat at the centre of a host of silent, smiling Thai masseuses. With the camera centred firmly on this Western male narrator, the Thai women around him formed nothing other than a silent, decorous and totally anonymous support-group for his sensationalized narration to follow:

> You see, Thailand's a Buddhist country and women are considered to be inferior to men. If they lead a blameless life and are very lucky then they might just make it back as a man in the next life. So, with the odds stacked against you like that, then it's not surprising that a woman's at the beck and call of a man. And in the case of these girls, that might mean up to five men a night.

The impact of this criticism made by Cooper was, however, considerably lessened by the perspective of his own narration, in its overt claim for a greater human value for men than for women - switching from his passing references of the position of women in Thailand, Cooper quickly proceeded to what was presented in his film as 'unquestionably the most shocking part' of Thailand's sex industry: for in Cooper's view 'the most tragic characters in Pattaya,' were not the women at all, but 'the boy prostitutes'!

THE REPERCUSSIONS OF FILMING: POLITICAL AND ECONOMIC AGENDAS

Several days after the *Foreign Bodies* team left Thailand following the completion of six weeks filming, headline news in one of the country's two leading English-language newspapers reported that:

> Thai authorities were enraged by a group of British documentary makers who completed a 60-minute TV documentary on police corruption, prostitution and the AIDS problem in Thailand without soliciting views from government officials (*Nation* 1987c).

Deputy government spokesman Montri Chenvidyakarn complained that the crew had not only entered Thailand without stating the real purpose of their visit, but that the subject matter of their documentary implied serious criticism of the Thai government's tourism policy (ibid.). *The Nation's* claim, however, that the views of government officials were not solicited, was strictly inaccurate - what angered the government was that the film crew's request for official comment on their findings came at what it saw as too short notice. According to Thai officials, they were occupied at the time with preparations for the Thai premier to pay a visit to neighbouring Malaysia. The timing of the request thus became an issue to be used to the political advantage of both parties: by the *Foreign Bodies* team, who no longer ran the risk of Thai government comments confusing the often superficial arguments presented in its footage; and by the Thai authorities, who were subsequently able to avoid the embarrassment of having to comment on what were, and remain, clearly sensitive issues.

Similarly, the British authorities sought political gain from a situation with potentially embarrassing repercussions at the diplomatic level. Against the important background of the rapid economic growth Thailand experienced from the beginning of the 1980s and the increased opportunities for international trade which that entailed, the British Embassy in Bangkok saw fit to stand by the Thai government in its complaints against Mr Cooper. In a statement of accord, the British Embassy also concluded that 'the British film crew did not have the real intention to interview the Thai government officials for their opinions' (ibid.). In addition, the Embassy released to the Thai press their intention that the British Foreign Office try to urge the Independent Broadcasting Authority (IBA) to advise Channel Four to reject the documentary film unless its producers sent a representative back to Thailand to seek the response of the Thai government (ibid.). Thai deputy government spokesman Montri consequently expressed his gratitude to the British Embassy, purposely stating that its action 'would strengthen the friendship between the two countries' (ibid.).[17]

The resulting compromise was that pressure was brought to bear on film-makers to solicit comments from the Royal Thai Embassy in London. In consequence, the UK screening of *Foreign Bodies*, originally scheduled for November 1987, was delayed until 9 June of the following year.[18] Despite this, the final version of the documentary still maintained that the Embassy had refused to provide comments and written answers to three simple questions on tourism, prostitution and AIDS. Nevertheless, the resulting delay in screening had served a valuable political purpose. It had allowed the Tourism Authority of Thailand's high profile international campaign to attract tourists to the country under the promotional banner of 'Visit Thailand Year - 1987' to reach an uncontroversial close.

In the year of filming *Foreign Bodies*, 'Visit Thailand Year' attracted a record number of visitors to the country, approximately 73 per cent of which were male (Truong 1990). While not all came to Thailand as sex tourists, the country's tourist industry still operated on the basis that prostitution was a major attraction to overseas visitors. This at a time when the issue of AIDS was becoming increasingly important on the international agenda, with pressure being placed on Thailand to reveal the extent of its rates of HIV infection. The speculations of AIDS nursing specialist, Summatra Troy, (interviewed in *Foreign Bodies*) that the very low figures for HIV infection provided by the Thai government in 1987 were virtually impossible and that sero-positive cases were, in actuality, likely to run into five figures, have since proved correct[19]. As Cohen argues, 'Under the circumstances, the principal concern of the authorities and the tourist industry was to prevent any untoward impact from the emergence of AIDS on the image of the country abroad or on tourist arrivals' (1988:468).[20] The then Permanent Secretary of the Ministry of Public Health, Dr Pairote Ningsanonda, admitted as much in his comments that 'inappropriate AIDS coverage will affect the tourist industry, Thailand's major source of income' (ibid.:469). 'To talk repeatedly about AIDS,' he said 'will cause the public to panic. And if there is panic, tourism will certainly be affected' (quoted in *The Nation* 1987b:17).

To suppress the reality of Thailand as a 'potentially explosive breeding ground for AIDS' (Troy, quoted in *The Nation* 1987a:17), the issue of the 'foreign' was highlighted in local discussions of the disease. The first reported cases of AIDS in Thailand were significantly all among either Thais who had lived abroad or Westerners based in the country and suggestions were even made that Asians may genetically immune to HIV.[21] The authorities consequently adopted a somewhat conflicting stance with regard to HIV infection, on the one hand distancing it from the local population as 'foreign' while on the other hand keen to maintain the high rate of visitors to Thailand from abroad. The short-lived campaign in 1987 to have all foreigners entering Thailand tested for AIDS provides a clear example of such tensions.[22]

Part of the controversy surrounding *Foreign Bodies* can therefore be understood in terms of both national and international political and economic concerns, in particular with regard to Thailand's dependency on tourism, the country's major earner of foreign currency from the mid-1980s onwards. Linked to this is Thailand's continued campaign for a clean international image, one which inevitably privileges the role of the 'good' Thai woman - the all-giving mother, the faithful wife and the devoted daughter - and downplays the existence of the 'bad.' Consequently, the plight of those Thai women working in the sex industry, is disregarded by the government, the realities of their existence silenced. As Thai journalist and prominent anti-sex tourism campaigner, Ing Kaanjanaawaanit (pseud. Ing K.) pointedly explains, the focus of the government is on 'the creation of an image of Thailand the Newly Rich, a country in which industry comes before agriculture, international before domestic, businessmen before farmers, and sex tourists before the farmers' daughters' (Ing K. 1988:23).

NATIONALIST SENTIMENTS AND THAI IMAGE CONSCIOUSNESS

Thailand's need for a clean international image, although undoubtedly linked with economic and political concerns, additionally derives from a strong cultural tendency to bring only the morally acceptable into the public domain. Predictably then, when *Foreign Bodies* was eventually screened in the UK, it provoked largely indignant responses from the Thai community there: 'But how dare they!' wrote one London-based Thai journalist. 'Who do these white men think they are, making such a fuss about Thailand while they have plenty of problems of their own back home? And why pick on Thailand when the world outside its borders is anything but prostitute-free?' (Wattana, 1988).

Offence is caused in Thai eyes by the fact that *Foreign Bodies* and the many other documentaries like it are wholly critical of Thailand and fail to show what Thais (and most Westerners) rightly see as the many positive aspects of the kingdom and its people. Understandably, as with all nations, there is also a greater sensitivity towards criticism that hails from outside rather than within.[23] Moreover, Thai defensiveness in the face of overt criticism, both at home and from abroad, has its cultural basis in a deep-rooted tradition of the avoidance of conflict and dominant interpretation of criticism as negative rather than constructive. As a result, the cultural norm has been to 'save face' (*raksaa naa*) and to 'turn a blind eye' (*tham pen mai ruu mai chii*). Children's rights activist and lawyer, Associate Professor Vitit Munthabhorn of Bangkok's Chulalongkorn University, himself an interviewee in *Foreign Bodies*, is fond of referring to this attitude as that of the well-known ancient symbol of the Three Monkeys - one refusing to hear, one refusing to see, one refusing to speak. For many Thai activists like him, bent on implementing social change, they frequently find themselves caught in cultural conflict, disliked by those nationalists who see them as 'unpatriotic' in their views. Since the analysis of sensitive issues is commonly construed by Thais as negative and inappropriate, the screening of television documentaries on the topics of prostitution and AIDS always constitutes an act of deep and embarrassingly public humiliation. This is compounded by the particular trajectory that Thailand's relationships with the outside world have followed since the nineteenth century in the sense that the country, formerly Siam, derives an understandable amount of national pride from having avoided colonization. As Britain and France swept up its immediate neighbours in the grip of colonial rule, Siam remained steadfastly independent as a result of a combination of artful diplomacy on the parts of both Rama IV and Rama V (r. 1868-1910) and the fact that Britain and France recognized the advantage of retaining Siam as a neutral buffer state. A strong sense of pride in the independence of Thailand's culture therefore runs high, albeit despite the country's superficial propensity to absorb influences from the West.[24] The legacy of Thailand's non-colonial past, however, has had a specific effect upon its subsequent relationship with the outside world and, in particular, on the nature of its cultural integration with it.

Nowhere are these sensitivities better illustrated than in the case of the Longman dictionary which the Thai Foreign Ministry banned in Thailand on account of its reference to Bangkok as a city of many prostitutes. Thai voices in support of the book were few and far between: they included the children's rights activist, Sapphasit Khumpraphan, who broke the traditional cultural mould with his opinion that arguments over Thailand's image merely wasted time. In interview to the press, he expressed the view that, 'These publications are just reporting what they know. If you take off your clothes and walk down the street and then someone shouts, 'Look! A naked guy!,' are you going to be angry with that person or are you going to hurry up and get some clothes on?' (Nithinand and Jones 1993:C1). Similarly, veteran Thai columnist, Kanjana Spindler wrote of the dictionary; 'No, I don't think it's biased... True, prostitutes exist all over the world, but not in this abundance. In most cities it's not something that hits you in your face every day, every hour.' Kanjana went on to say that,

Perhaps the authorities should be aware that the overwhelming dominant media coverage of Thailand around the world, day by day, week by week, focuses on AIDS and the sex industry here. And it will continue as long as the reality of the situation here does not change. We can protest all we like, but the world will laugh at our dishonesty and self-deception (Kanjana 1993).

Nevertheless, the commonest Thai response to the Longman entry was one of patriotic outrage, sparking protests by Thai university students outside the British Embassy, in a public denunciation of Longman for creating a poor moral image of their country. The then government spokesman, Abhisit Vejjajiva championed their cause by suggesting that a future Thai dictionary may seek revenge on Britain by describing it as a former colony-hunter that currently had terrorist groups such as the Irish Republican Army (BP. 1993a:1). Refusing to be placated by the fact that Longman also described London's Soho and King's Cross as areas of prostitution, the Ministry of Foreign Affairs maintained their argument that prostitution existed not only in Bangkok but also in London and elsewhere (*Nation* 1993a:A1); and despite Longman's subsequent agreements to redefine Bangkok in keeping with Thai sensitivities (*Nation* 1993b:A4), the then Foreign Minister, Prasong Soonsiri retorted that, 'Although they [Longman] have apologised, we have to keep watching their attitude,' (BP. 1993b:3). While all copies of the offending edition were withdrawn from the Thai market, diplomatic tensions later returned when a Thai visitor to a Singapore book fair unearthed an original version of the dictionary on sale several months later.[25]

Ironically, though not surprisingly, the prostitutes of Bangkok were themselves unaware of their place at the centre of an international dispute. Those interviewed by *The Nation* newspaper did not even know what a dictionary was. One could not even pronounce the word, although it has long been adopted into the Thai language; and another learned of the controversy while waiting for customers behind the one-way mirror of a Bangkok massage parlour (Paisal 1993:A8).

In its efforts to diminish the significance of the sex worker in the popular Western perception of the Thai woman, nationalist sentiment and image-consciousness has instead focused on her reverse image - that of the morally and sexually 'good.' While Thailand undoubtedly draws important revenue from sex tourism, rather than remember its raunchy go-go dancers, most Thais would prefer that international visitors recall the beautiful, graceful, polite, softly-spoken and neatly-dressed women employed in the tourist industry as waitresses, hotel staff and air hostesses. This image of womanhood, deeply embedded in Thai cultural tradition, instead privileges elegance of body and serenity of mind, having its roots in such prescriptive texts as the *Suphaasit sorn ying* ('Maxim for the Conduct of Ladies') by the renowned (male) poet Sunthorn Phu (1786-1855). Sunthorn Phu's advice to women covers many aspects of female manners, from tending to ones husband to 'correct' modes of eating, speaking and walking, as illustrated by the following stanzas:

On the subject of walking:
Take small, graceful steps when walking outside.
Forbidden is it to swing your arms back and forth
Hence you will attain serenity and good manners.

Do not allow your breasts to swing or raise your shawl as you go.
Do not run your hands through your hair while you walk.
Do not talk nonsense
And do not linger outside once your business is done.
(Cheuacheun and Nol 1971:8)

And in a later verse:

With whomever you choose to speak
Do not raise your voice or rasp.
Do not use common language or phrase
Or people will deny you respect. (Prakaaitham 1996:168)

The tradition prescribed by Sunthorn Phu is one which primarily sees the place of the woman in the home, performing her duties as faithful wife, all-loving mother and dutiful daughter, whose free moments may be those of making intricate handicrafts (weaving, basket-making and so forth) and carving decorative vegetables and fruits;[26] and although the 'modern,' middle class Thai woman now pays scant attention to these verses, they nevertheless hold a place in the relatively recent development of 'good' Thai female behaviour, having been composed by one of Thailand's most revered poets, less than two hundred years ago.[27] Most importantly, despite its archaic qualities, Sunthorn Phu's work upholds the clear distinctions that still pertain between the 'good' Thai woman and the 'bad,' exemplified in the following stanza:

Do not associate with women of ill repute
Who dress in unfortunate ways
wandering aimlessly in the late afternoon
with their seductive and tricky airs (Prakaaitham 1996:172).

BEYOND GOOD AND EVIL:
THE RESPONSE OF THAI FEMINISTS

While the Western media has largely focused on those 'women of ill repute' whom Sunthorn Phu implores his 'good' women to shun, nationalist sentiment would instead have the beautiful and well-mannered as the ideal image of Thai womanhood to present to the outside world. In contrast to this, however, women's rights activists understandably favour a far more complex picture of the 'modern' Thai woman and, rather than conceal the presence of prostitution in Thai society, would prefer an open discussion of what they themselves see as a much worse picture of the sex industry than that that shown by such documentaries as *Foreign Bodies*. Their criticisms of the film *Foreign Bodies* concerns not what the programme has said, but the many things it left unsaid: 'What appears in *Foreign Bodies* does not seem so foreign at all when compared to the existing reality' wrote *Bangkok Post* journalist, Supapohn Kanwerayotin, in her aptly named report on the programme - 'Activists: Reality worse than film' (Supapohn 1988a). Her comment that most activists 'have seen things far worse than those that have been brought to light in media exposés' is supported by Sukanya Hantrakul in her remarks on *Foreign Bodies* that:

I don't think there is any scene in the production that exaggerates what really goes on here. In fact, a lot of seedy brothels exist that house abused prostitutes being tortured and taken advantage of to a far greater extent than what is shown here. It surprises me that people have gotten so worked up over such an understatement of the situation as *Foreign Bodies* (quoted in ibid.).

If Thai feminists saw *Foreign Bodies* as a tame underestimation of the grim reality of Thai sex workers' lives, they nevertheless thanked the film for raising the profile of a problem sorely in need of discussion and solution: 'Most people agreed that *Foreign Bodies* wasn't so much a good movie - many have disparaging comments - as a *good thing*, that gets people talking...' (Usher 1988). Vitit Munthabhorn echoed this sentiment, in his statement that,

> this kind of airing is extremely healthy. We don't have to believe it all, but we can talk about it and look at the real root causes - the laws, the people concerned, the lack of implementation of the laws, the strategies we need to develop. I think the press has an important role to play in this regard. It's a sad fact that this violation of a basic human right in our society is not talked about at the classroom level, or discussed in the home, as that kind of exposure can help change attitudes before children and other people concerned accept prostitution as a coffee-table norm (quoted in Wipawee 1990:28).

Siriporn Skrobanek, head of the Thai Foundation for Women (*Munithi phuuying*), also felt that the concern provoked by *Foreign Bodies* should be used to the advantage of the activists in drawing public attention to their cause (Supapohn, 1988a). Having obtained its own copy of the video, the Foundation chose to use *Foreign Bodies* as an educational tool, showing it to rural girls at risk of being lured into prostitution, to members of non-government organizations working in the field and to women already employed in the Thai sex industry (Supapohn 1988b).[28]

It was in this context that the bargirls of Pattaya, whom *Foreign Bodies* featured in part, gained an opportunity to see the film. Supapohn reported their immediate responses as a mixture of 'cynical acceptance,' 'frustration' and 'extreme embarrassment' (ibid.). Frustration and cynical acceptance because of their lack of control over how their lives could be represented by the film-makers, extreme embarrassment as a result of the manipulation of footage: two of the women recognized themselves in the programme in what, according to Supapohn, appears to have been 'something of a set up' (ibid) - film of the girls' swaying bottoms, inscribed with the message 'F*** ME USA' in a greeting to American servicemen.[29]

This example of the abuse of Thai sex workers 'caught on camera' in Western television documentaries that profess to discuss their plight is merely one among many. For what the Western media tends to achieve in its production of such programmes is an extension of the process of the objectification of the prostitute, one that is already set in motion by the very nature of the profession of the sex worker itself. Thai sex workers are subjected in these programmes and films to the all-powerful gaze of the film-makers and their audiences - poignantly illustrated in the case of *The Good Woman of Bangkok*. And while this gaze is not a singularly male one, it is essentially masculine in character because of the power of interpretation that it has over those who remain oddly *silenced* by it. Both film-maker and audience collude in a pre-conceived agenda, planned in the studio before filming on location even takes place and to which material is moulded to fit. Moreover, it is an agenda heavily influenced by factors which have no connection with the Thai prostitutes themselves, their backgrounds, their experiences or their emotions. Such factors include the long-standing construction, through film and the media, of Thailand as a site of erotic delights and sexual promiscuity in the popular imagination of the West. They include the contribution made to this image by the Vietnam War and by the subsequent rise in sex tourism to the country. They also include the erroneous focus on the association between tourism and prostitution in Thailand, with little or no acknowledgement of the cultural factors influencing certain patterns of gender relations between Thais themselves. The preoccupation of the Western media with prostitution in Thailand as a product of the West (at least until the advent of AIDS) suits not only the purposes of its media, who appear only to be able to capture the interest of a television audience providing that the subject matter is of direct relevance to them. Furthermore, it suits the political and economic agendas of the Thai government and the nationalistic sentiments of the population at large, anxious to portray their country's extensive sex industry as a 'foreign' problem. This in turn permits the otherwise uneasy combination of continued revenue from sex tourism and the simultaneous preservation of the good moral image that Thailand demands of itself, and specifically of its women.

CONCLUSION

The price for these misconstructions, misrepresentations and misleading emphases is paid by Thai women in general and female prostitutes in particular. In the midst of the battle between the powerful voices of the media, the audience and the politicians, the subject of their discussions - the Thai female sex worker - remains silenced and disempowered. The overridingly important issue, of comprehending the reality of the lives of prostitutes in Thailand, is therefore obfuscated. By implication, so too is that of understanding the wider complexities of the construction of the 'modern' Thai woman and the imagery surrounding her sexuality. The perpetuation of a thriving sex industry in Thailand, whether through tourism or a home market, results not only, as social scientists repeatedly argue, from the economic hardships that drive poorly-educated, rural women to prostitution due to lack of alternative employment. It also has a little-explored cultural dimension, one which disadvantages women and which demands that they are clearly segregated into the 'pure' and the 'impure,' according to their sexual availability. These subtleties being apparently either too complex for Western documentary makers to articulate on screen or for their audiences to care to comprehend has allowed for an unchallenged media construction of Thailand as a nation of 'prostitutes-en-masse,' willing to service any passing foreign tourist. And it is this image of the 'modern' Thai woman which the world beyond Thailand's borders unfortunately takes with it into the twenty first century.

NOTES

* The necessary research for this paper was made possible by the support of the Southeast Asia Committee of the British Academy in 1996-7. I also owe great thanks Nicola Liscutin for her valuable comments on earlier verisons of this paper. There are several different ways of transliterating Thai into English, none of which are entirely satisfactory or accessible. The method I have chosen to use here preserves the distinction between the long and short 'a' and 'i' vowels. Thai words are written as they would be pronounced in Thai rather than transcribing the letters with which they are written. I have, however, retained the spelling of Thai names as they appear on publications by those authors in English; hence Sukanya Hantrakul rather than Sukanyaa Haantrakun, Vitit Munthabhorn rather than Witit Mantaporn and Abhisit Vejjajiva as opposed to Apisit Wechaachiiwa. It is also Thai convention to quote authors by their first, rather than their surnames in academic references, thus Sukanya, 1983 and not Hantrakul, 1983. This convention is similarly reflected in the layout of the bibliography at the end of this paper.

1 For further details of the way in which this division manifests itself see Harrison 1997 and forthcoming a and b.

2 The same outlook pertains in the depiction of the prostitute in much modern Thai fiction. See Harrison, forthcoming b.

3 Landon's work draws on two novels by Leonowens, namely *The English Governess at the Court of Siam* (1870) and *Romance of the Harem* (1973), which Kepner has covincingly shown to have spurious claims on the reality of the times and to be largely the product of fantasy on the part of their author (see Kepner, 1996:). The film version of *Anna and the King of Siam* was directed by John Cromwell and starred Irene Dunne as Anna and Rex Harrison as the Thai King.

4 Brynner was awarded an Oscar for his performance. In Leonowens' own words, King Mongkut was 'a living human being - erratic, formidable, generous, penurius, brilliant, irascible, devout, lascivious, cruel and kind' (quoted in Kepner 1996: 16).

5 This in a country where the monarchy is much revered and beyond criticism and where the charge of *lese majesté* can still be applied, leading to jail sentences of up to fifteen years. After the release of *The King and I,* Margaret Landon, author of the novel on which the film was based, never returned to Thailand and, according to her children, she received death threats for her association with the production. Moreover, when Twentieth Century Fox approached the Thai authorities in October 1998 for permission to film a remake of *The King and I* in Thailand (under the title of *Anna and the King*) their request was pointedly refused. In fact, the reality of the original Anna Leonowens and her relationship with the Siamese court was very much more complex than the film and fictional versions of her life betray. This is brought to light in Kepner's detailed research paper on Leonowens.

6 While no indication of the actual number of women comprising the royal harem is provided in the film, Truong, in her astoundingly thorough and insightful *Sex, money and morality: prostitution and tourism in Southeast Asia* quotes Craig Reynolds in stating that King Mongkut had six hundred wives and concubines (Truong 1990: 150). Moffat notes that the King fathered a total of eighty two children, the first being born in 1823, the last in the year of his death in 1868. This was a considerable achievement, considering that he spent twenty-six of his adult years as a celibate Buddhist monk (Moffat, quoted in Kepner 1996: 23).

7 In Leonowens' novel, *The English Governess at the Court of Siam,* as in the film *Anna and the King of Siam,* Tap Tim suffers a worse fate than this - she is burned at the stake for her treachery (Kepner 1996: 18).

8 As Truong notes, the inflow of US aid, loans and military support went into steep decline following the US withdrawal from Indochina in the mid 1970s. At the same time, Thailand faced unfavourable world market conditions for its major foreign exchange earners of rice, rubber and tin. Therefore, with the support and involvement of the Thai military, tourism policies were implemented to increase national revenue (Truong 1990: 160).

9 Somsamai Srisudravarna is the pseudonymn of Jit Puumisak, a radical Thai intellectual who was shot dead by government forces in 1966, following his affiliation with the outlawed Communist Party of Thailand. Despite the progressiveness of his political views, Jit was rather more the traditionalist with regard to women. Mettarikanond also provides information regarding the legal existence and taxation of prostitution during the Ayutthaya period (Mettarikanond 1983).

10 The term *ying nakhorn sopenii* is an antiquated one, literally translatable as 'a lady of the town.' In modern usage it is contracted to simply *sopenii*, derived from the Khmer word for prostitute.

11 The institution of polygamy received further support from King Rama IV in the arguments he expounded in his *Kitchanukit* ('A Book Explaining Various Issues'), written in 1867. In it he 'set out differences between male and female nature and sexuality and concluded that polygamy in Thailand was functional to male sexual convenience and the male need for merit-making. Polygamy enabled a man to alternate among his wives so as not to force himself to anyone against her will, and thereby lose merit' (Truong 1990: 150).

12 As Van Esterik argues, in the Buddhist belief system, women are confined to making religious merit through their attachment to the world of the senses, namely as providers of sons who can become ordained and as providers of food for the monkhood. Van Esterik illustrates this with reference to a fifty five year old woman from Central Thailand who stated that by breastfeeding her thirteen children she created a close enough bond with them for her sons to repay their indebtedness by becoming ordained and for her daughters to attend Buddhist sermons and care for her in her old age (Van Esterik 1982: 77).

13 The film was first screened in 1991 at the Sydney Film Festival.

14 Estimates of the number of prostitutes working in Thailand vary widely, from 80,000 (the Thai Public Welfare Department, 1993) to 500,000 (DaGrossa, 1989; Sanitsuda, 1991) and 2 million (Prawase, 1991). The figure of 2 million is also supported by Sapphasit Khumpraphan, head of the Bangkok-based Centre for the Protection of Children's Rights (private interview, 3 December 1996).

15 Dr Saisuree was speaking in her capacity as inspector general on women, youth and education of the Office of the Permanent Secretary, the Prime Minister's Office. For the purposes of this article, the term Chinese refers to Chinese-Thais. Following the mass immigration of mainland Chinese to Thailand from the end of the nineteenth century onwards the Chinese community has become well integrated in Thailand, with many Thais being at least of part Chinese ancestry.

16 A woman who commits this cultural 'offence' is pejoratively known in Thai as *phuuying thii mii phua laai khon*, a 'woman with many husbands.' For further details see Harrison 1997.

17 By contrast, the United States showed far less concern for courting the friendship of the Thais when a fifteen minute report on prostitution and tourism in Thailand was broadcast on ABC's *Prime Time* television show only days before an official visit by the then Prime Minister, Chatichai Choonhavan, in June 1990. Characteristically unruffled by the furor, retired army General Chatichai jovially commented, during an interview given from Bangkok's military-owned golf course, that tourists came to Thailand because Thai women were beautiful (*Nation*

1990). His defence that prostitution exists throughout the world included the observation that many people went to Paris and Tokyo for the same reason (ibid.). On a more serious note, government spokesman Suvit Yodmani recognized the damage which the ABC documentary had done to Thailand's international reputation and seized the political opportunity to turn the issue of prostitution to the Thai government's avantage by pleading with the US to help Thailand eradicate the poverty said to provoke commerical sex by operating a less protectionist trading policy.

18 The documentary was also screened across Scandinavia. It may also have been shown in other parts of Europe.

19 At the time of filming *Foreign Bodies*, the Thai government reported a total number of 150 AIDS cases in the country. On 25 June 1987 the Department for the Control of Communicable Diseases reported eleven cases of AIDS and thirty HIV carriers. Its Director General was reported to comment that 'The situation is not serious' (*Nation* 1987b: 17). By contrast, figures published by the Ministry of Public Health in Thailand for World AIDS Day (1 December) 1998 indicated a total of 27,279 deaths from AIDS since the first case was discovered in Thailand in 1983. As of 31 October 1998, 99,555 people were reported have developed the full-blown phase of the disease, while a further million are estimated to be HIV-positive.

20 Cohen refers here to an article in the Bangkok Post entitled 'When openness is the best policy,' 28 July 1987.

21 Although the exact origins of AIDS in Thailand cannot be ascertained, the likelihood is that it was imported from the West.

22 For further details of the campaign see *Bangkok Post* 1987a: 2.

23 By contrast, criticism from within is relatively vociferous, exemplified by the high degree of freedom of the press in Thailand itself, especially in comparison its Southeast Asian neighbours - Malaysia, Myanmar, Vietnam and Indonesia.

24 Thai culture is often argued to be highly eclectic, with a marked tendency to accept and accommodate outside influences. Nevertheless, there remains, in my opinion, a resistant core belief in what is non-negotiably Thai, the very existence of which allows for surface cultural imports.

25 A similar response as that to the Longman dictionary had earlier been solicited by an article in the *Far Eastern Economic Review* entitled 'The Lust Frontier' (Handley 1989). Attacking Thailand's reluctance to confront the problem of its widespread sex industry, journalist Paul Handley argued that the industry thrived as a result of the financial gains it offered a triumvirate of brothel owners, police and politicians.As a

result of his descriptions of scenes at a Patpong sex show in which 'one of the hostesses punctures large balloons with darts from a small blow gun ... [put] between her thighs' and where 'a gleaming motorcycle descends from the ceiling and on it two young Thais, with considerable difficulty, copulate,' the Tourism Authority of Thailand (TAT) made the telling accusation that Handley's piece was 'written with bias and intention to destroy Thailand's image' (Sumontha Nakornthab, director of TAT's public relations division, in a press release quoted in *The Nation*, 11 November, 1989). TAT proceeded to request a ban on the sale of the Hong Kong-based journal in Thailand and made representations to the Ministry of Foreign Affairs to deny Handley an extension of visa (*Nation* 1989), although neither request was actually granted.

26 The relationship between women and the creation of intricate handicrafts still pertains, symbolized by the Queen of Thailand in her presiding of the Thai national handicrafts centre. Interestingly, certain 'rehabilitation' programmes for 'rescued' female sex workers, such as that piloted by Khunying Kanittha Wichiancharoen in Dorn Meuang, north Bangkok, have concentrated on teaching women new skills such as weaving and basket-making. In terms of Thai cultural tradition, this can be read as an attempt to convert the 'bad' woman into the 'good.'

27 Prakaaitham's text, from which some of Sunthorn Phu's verses are drawn, refers to him in its title both as 'one of the most renowned poets in the world' (*kawii ek khorng lok*) and as 'the eternal poet' *(nak kawii omata mahaa nirandornkaan).*

28 The Foundation later went on to produce its own educational video in 1990 which opened with a discussion of *Foreign Bodies* by Thai social workers and was designed to be shown to school teachers in rural areas (Mayuree 1990: 27).

29 According to the Foundation for Women, the two women featured in this way had asked if it was possible to delete their pictures from the film, their European boyfriends having recognised them in the programme and having written to say how upset they were to have seen the girls going off with somebody else (Supapohn 1988b). This results from the fact that it is not uncommon for Thai women working with primarily Western clients in Patpong and Pattaya to have aspirations of marrying a foreigner and moving to live abroad. This, they often hope, will be a route which may lead them to a better life, one in which, because of the higher economic status of the West, they would still be able to send money back to their families. The nature of such Thai-*farang* relationships is best investigated in two papers by Cohen, viz. 'Thai Girls and *Farang* Men. The Edge of Ambiguity' (1982) and

'Lovelorn *Farangs*: The Correspondance Between Foreign Men and Thai Girls' (1986). The word *farang* refers to a white caucasian.

REFERENCES

Bangkok Post (1987) 'Asian-Pacific nations won't require AIDS testing for tourists,' 23 July, p. 2.

--(1990) 'From Khon Kaen to Patpong,' 15 October, pp. 31-2.

--(1993a) 'Abhisit swipes at UK publisher,' 4 July, pp. 1 and 3.

--(1993b) 'Longman issues apology for Bangkok dictionary entry,' 6 July, pp. 1 and 3.

Berry, Chris, Annette Hamilton and Laleen Jayamanne (eds) (1997) *The Film-maker and the Prostitute. Dennis O' Rourke's 'The Good Woman of Bangkok,'* Sydney: Power Publications.

Cheuacheun Siiyaaphai and Non Noraakorn (eds) (1971) *'Sunthorn Phu' sorn ying. Sawadiraksa lae saalaakawii* (Sunthorn Phu Teaches Women. Sawadiraksa and Salakawi), Bangkok: Samnak phim Khlang witthayaa.

Cohen, Erik (1982) 'Thai Girls and *Farang* Men. The Edge of Ambiguity,' *Annals of Tourism Research* 9, pp. 403-28.

--(1986) 'Lovelorn *Farangs*: The Correspondance Between Foreign Men and Thai Girls,' *Anthropological Quarterly* 59(3), pp. 114-27.

--(1988) 'Tourism and AIDS in Thailand,' *Annals of Tourism Research* 15, pp. 467-86.

DaGrossa, Pamela (1989) 'Kampaeng Din: a study of prostitution in the all-Thai brothels of Chiang Mai city,' *Crossroads* 4(2), pp. 1-7.

Handley, Paul (1989) 'The Lust Frontier,' *Far Eastern Economic Review*, 2 November.

Harrison, Rachel (1995) 'The writer, the horseshoe crab, his "golden blossom" and her clients: tales of prostitution in contemporary Thai short stories,' *South East Asia Research* 3, September, pp. 125-52.

--(1997) 'The Good, the Bad and the Pregnant. Why the Thai prostitute as literary heroine cannot be seen to give birth,' in: Virada Somsawasdi and Sally Theobald (eds) *Women, Gender Relations and Development in Thai Society*. Chiangmai: Women's Studies Centre, Faculty of Social Sciences, Chiangmai University Press, pp. 323-48.

--(forthcoming a) 'The Disruption of Female Desire and the Thai Literary Tradition of Eroticism, Religion and Aesthetics' in: *Tenggara*.

--(forthcoming b) 'The Madonna and the Whore: Self/Other tensions in the characterization of the prostitute by Thai female authors,' in: Peter Jackson and Nerida Cook (eds) *Genders and Sexualities in Modern Thailand*. Chiangmai: Silkworm.

Ing, K. (1988) 'Of foreign bodies, false shame and becoming a NIC,' *The Nation*, 23 July, p. 23.

IPSR (Institute for Population and Social Research) (1991) *NIC: Free Zone of Prostitution.* Bangkok: Mahidol University, ISPR Publication No. 148.

Kaanjanaa Kaewtep (1994) *Wijaan nang thatsana mai (New Perspectives on Film Analysis),* Bangkok: Gender Press.

Kepner, Susan (1996) 'Anna (and Margaret) and the King of Siam,' *Crossroads*10(2), pp. 1-32.

Kirsch, Thomas (1982) 'Buddhism, sex-roles and the Thai economy,' in Van Esterik, Penny (ed.) *Women of Southeast Asia.* Occasional Paper No. 9: Northern Illinois University, Centre for Southeast Asian Studies.

Mayuree Rattanawannatip (1990) 'Video tackles prostitution,' *The Nation*, 11 January, p. 27.

Mettarikanond, D. (1983) *Prostitution and Policies of Thai Government during 1868-1960.* Thesis submitted to the Graduate School, Chulalongkorn University, Bangkok.

Mills, Mary Beth (1995) 'Attack of the widow ghosts: Gender, death, and modernity in Northeast Thailand,' in: Aihwa Ong and Michael G. Peletz (eds) *Bewitching women, pious men. Gender and body politics in Southeast Asia.* Berkeley, Los Angeles and London: University of California Press.

Moffat, Abbot Low (1961) *Mongkut the King of Siam.* Ithaca: Cornell Paperbacks, Cornell University Press.

The Nation (1987a) 'AIDS. The right to know the truth,' 13 September, p. 17.

--(1987b) 'Government cover-up or just ignorance?,' 13 September, p. 17.

--(1987c) 'British TV Crew Stirs Controversy,' 30 September.

--(1989) 'TAT calls on police to impose ban on FEER,' 11 November.

--(1990) 'PM plays down American TV programme,' 10 June.

--(1993a) 'Police review Longman dictionary,' 4 July, p. A1.

--(1993b) 'Pressure mounts on Longman,' 8 July, p. A4.

--(1993c) 'BBC shows how to do it,' 18 July, p. A13.

Nithinand Yorsaengrat and Jones, Dylan (1993) 'Up against the ropes,' *The Nation,* 5 August, p. C1.

Paisal Chuenprasaeng (1993) 'Ignored in the fracas, prostitutes define their feelings,' *The Nation*, 18 July, p. A8.

Pasuk Phongpaichit (1982) *From peasant girls to Bangkok masseuses.* Geneva: International Labour Office.

Prakaaitham (1996) *Khom waathii kawii ek khorng lok. Sunthorn Phu - nak kawii omata mahaa nirandornkaan* (Sharp words from one of the most renowned poets in the world. Sunthorn Phu - the eternal poet). Bangkok: Thammasaphaa.

Prawase Wasi (1991) 'Tourism and child prostitution in Thailand' in: Koson Srisang (ed.) *Caught in modern slavery: tourism and child prostitution in Asia*. Bangkok: Ecumenical Coalition on Third World Tourism, pp. 37-46.

Reynolds, Craig (1977) 'A Nineteenth Century Thai Buddhist Defense of Polygamy and Some Remarks on the Social History of Women in Thailand,' Paper prepared for the Seventh Conference of the International Association of Historians of Asia, Chulalongkorn University, Bangkok, 22-6 August.

Sanitsuda Ekachai (1991) 'How did we get to this state of affairs,' *Bangkok Post,* 11 February.

Schloss, Glen (1998) 'Hollywood's Tale of Thailand Tossed,' *Asia Pacific Front Page*, 28 October.

Schreiner, Olive (1911) *Woman and Labour*. London: T.F. Unwin.

Somsamai Srisudravarna ([1957]1987) 'The Real Face of Thai Saktina Today,' in: Craig Reynolds (ed.) *Thai Radical Discourse. The Real Face of Thai Feudalism Today*. Ithaca and New York: Cornell University Press.

Spindler, Kanjana (1993) 'The Lady doth protest too much methinks,' *Bangkok Post*, 7 July.

Sukanya Hantrakul (1983) 'Prostitution in Thailand.' Paper presented to the Women in Asia workshop at Monash University, Melbourne, 22-4 July .

--(1988) 'Prostitution in Thailand,' in: Glen Chandler, Norma Sullivan and Jan Branson (eds) *Development and Displacement in Southeast Asia*. Monash University: Centre of Southeast Asian Studies.

Suntaree Komin (1991) *Psychology of the Thai people: Values and behavioural patterns*. Bangkok: The National Institute of Development Administration.

Supapohn Kanwerayotin (1988a) 'Activists: Reality worse than film,' *Bangkok Post*, 14 July.

--(1988b) 'Child prostitution in Thailand. Where do we go from here?,' *Bangkok Post,* 24 July.

Thitsa, Khin (1990) *Providence and Prostitution: Women in Buddhist Thailand*. Women in Society, Series no. 2. London: Change International.

Truong, Thanh-Dam (1990) *Sex money and morality: prostitution and tourism in Southeast Asia*. London: Zed Books.

Usher, Ann Danaiya (1988) 'Foreign bodies on Foreign Bodies,' *The Nation*, 2 September.

Van Esterik, Penny (1982) 'Laywomen in Theravada Buddhism,' in: Penny Van Esterik (ed.) *Women of Southeast Asia.* Occasional Paper 9. Northern Illinois University, Centre for Southeast Asian Studies.

--(1989) *Motherpower and infant feeding.* London: Zed Books.

Wathinee Boonchalaksi and Guest, Philip (1994) *Prositution in Thailand.* Salaya, Nakorn Pathom: Institute for Population and Social Research, Mahidol University.

Wattana Manaviboon (1988) 'Report from London. Facing the reality: the ugly side of the tourism industry in Thailand,' *Bangkok Post*, 22 June.

Wipawee Otaganonta (1990) 'Child Prostitution in Thailand. Turning a blind eye,' *Bangkok Post,* 1 August, pp. 27-8.

CHAPTER 9

A SUITABLE ROMANCE?
TRAJECTORIES OF COURTSHIP
IN INDIAN POPULAR FICTION*

PATRICIA UBEROI

This paper analyses the narrative structures and substantive characteristics of a small set of romantic short stories published in the fortnightly English-language women's magazine, *Woman's Era* (*WE*), over the period from March 1994 to October 1995.[1] Identifying several contrasting trajectories of narrative development in these stories, the paper seeks to understand, in particular: (i) why and how romantic courtship is constituted as so problematic in contemporary Indian society; (ii) the criteria of a suitable 'match' that the stories construct and endorse; and (iii) the set of circumstances that are expected to lead to a happy conclusion to a romantic encounter - that is, obviously, the marriage of the chief protagonists.

These fantasized accounts of romantic relationships are used in conjunction with other materials published at this time in the same magazine - editorials, non-fiction instructional articles, and the several medical and personal advice columns. The magazine's section of matrimonial advertisements, very often on behalf of rather over-age or otherwise matrimonially defective parties, are of corroborative interest, too. As with *WE*'s self-promotional advertisements, these disclose the uncertain balance between politically conservative positions and the supposedly 'progressive' social values that characterise this magazine and its several sister publications, in English and in some Indian vernaculars.[2]

Symbolic of its stance on social and political issues, *WE* announces prominently that it does not accept advertisements for government-run gambling (lotteries); cigarettes and tobacco; alcoholic drinks; vim, vigour and sex-strengthening drugs and treatments; and home made educational degrees and courses. It also refuses to publish astrological forecasts, though such features are invariably popular in the mass media, and it offers 50 per cent concessional rates for matrimonial advertisements that refrain from mentioning the caste or religion of the advertisers or desired respondents.[3] Though dedicated to the self-improvement of Indian women, *WE* has a marked horror of the independent women's movement, deeming 'women's lib,' so-called, a dangerous and foreign-inspired fad that will surely corrupt Indian womanhood and cut at the heart of Indian family life. An editorial of the period we are concerned with summed up the magazine's opinion of 'women's liberation':

There is no doubt that women have traditionally been an oppressed lot. Religion, scriptures, social systems and man-made institutions all gave women a lower place in society. Naturally, the fight for sexual equality has been a long drawn-out war.

In India, the freedom movement also contained the seeds of women's liberation. Most of our national leaders and prominent writers, though males, were champions of women's causes. Naturally, free India's Constitution guaranteed equality of opportunity to women and prohibited any discrimination on grounds of sex.

However, women's liberation cannot be brought about by mere law or constitutional provisions. Centuries-old attitudes have to be changed through education, social work and, above all, removing poverty to ensure the well-being of the family. The process of reform has been going on, though slowly.

But then a section of the urban elite women was not satisfied with the reforms: it wanted revolution. They looked towards the West for inspiration where the women leaders had given a new meaning to liberation. Women's lib for them meant what they wanted it to mean. *And what they want amounts to domination over men. Creating problems in the family and rifts between husband and wife were the results of this aggressive women's lib.*[4]

Like most other women's magazines, *WE* focuses generally on home-making. It contains articles on cookery, housekeeping, family relationships, health, child-care, fashion, etiquette and consumer education, to which have recently been added sections for film reviews and Bollywood gossip, instructional articles on investment and financial management (apparently a unique feature in women's magazines [Bajpai 1997]), and regular features on domestic and foreign travel. The magazine has several write-in advice columns on personal, medical and child-care problems, including the 'Teenache' 'agony column,' on which we will draw extensively in this paper. Like its very popular sister publication, the Hindi language *Sarita* (see Kumar 1997), *WE* is widely known and appreciated for its short stories and serialised novellettes, carrying about five short stories in each issue.

Though *WE* assumes an English-educated audience, and exudes what one might call a 'cantonment' culture in articles, reminiscences and stories, and takes for granted that many middle class Indian families now have close relatives settled abroad, it is much less sophisticated in its content and production values than magazines like *Femina* and *Savvy* that are its closest rivals in the market.[5] Nonetheless, curiously, *WE* has more than held its own with these smarter publications in a very competitive field, claiming itself to be the largest-selling English-language magazine in the Indian market. Puzzling over the popularity of *WE* a few years earlier, the Trinidadian writer V.S. Naipaul had concluded that it must be its very *ordinariness* that commended the magazine to its regular readers: it didn't try to 'intimidate' them, he suggested, but sought instead to assist women to cope with the multiple and complex demands of everyday life through simply-written instructional articles and fictionalized portrayals of life-like dilemmas with which they could easily identify (Naipaul 1990:409; Singh and Uberoi 1994:98-9). Other commentators have suggested that *WE* is at least *consistent* in its homely conservatism on gender issues, where *Femina*, for instance, increasingly presents a 'confusion' of the conservative and the risqué to garner attention. Several informants stressed that *WE* is widely regarded as 'safe,' wholesome and useful leisure time reading for the women and girls of the family.

CONSTRUCTING THE PROBLEMATIC

Very little has so far been written on the nature and role of romance fiction in contemporary India,[6] and the task of mapping this *terra incognita* is much complicated by the huge volume of output on the one hand, and the fragmentation of Indian linguistic sub-cultures on the other. However, a preliminary foray into this field, an analysis of a small set of romantic short stories published in *WE* in 1988-9, revealed some interesting features, the most notable being the preponderance of tales of the development of romantic relationships *after* marriage (see Tyagi 1989; Singh and Uberoi 1994). This was both surprising, given the models of romantic fiction that the writers apparently followed (i.e., the format of stories in English magazines like *Women's Weekly* and *Woman's Own*, and *Mills and Boon* and *Harlequin* romances), and yet not totally unexpected, given the continued prevalence of the practice of arranged marriages in India.

In sum, the stories of post-marital romance reviewed in that earlier study - and I can see little change in their structure over the intervening years - characteristically begin with a newly married couple experiencing problems in their relationship. An event then occurs to put these problems in a new light. Adjustments are made accordingly, and the conjugal relation put on to an even keel. Whatever the immediate cause of marital tension proposed in these stories (and it is interesting that the dreaded mother-in-law was rarely in fact the villain of the piece), the real problem threatening conjugal harmony was what is called in common parlance an 'ego hassle': that is, the husband and wife had got themselves into a situation of mutual confrontation in which one or the other has to give in or both have to compromise if the marriage is to be saved. Typically, if not invariably, the fictional resolution of this conflict involved an asymmetrical 'adjustment' on the part of the wife, who was often assisted in coming to terms with her reality by the advice or example of a kindly person in authority. Conversely, the wife's failure to make such adjustment in good time, as in the 'real-life' confessional tales of marital breakdown also published in *WE* in these years, led inexorably to that most disastrous of outcomes - divorce.

These tales of post-marital romance were the most consistently formulaic and structurally predictable of the *Woman's Era* love stories; and they almost always ended happily. They conformed in a sense to an expected model of romantic fiction - with the not insignificant difference that they *began* with marriage and *ended* with love, rather than the other way around. They were also, clearly, cautionary tales, consistent ideologically with the overall social attitudes of the magazine in which they featured. Needless to add, the recommendation of 'adjustment' makes sound practical sense in the context of the sexual politics of Indian marriage (see for example, Kapur 1970), disappointing though it may be to a feminist sensibility.

The tales of romantic courtship in this archive were also, if in a different way, cautionary tales, but they were narratively much more varied. In fact, only half followed the classic romantic formula, from first encounter through difficulties to a declaration of love and a proposal of marriage. The remaining stories scarcely qualified as 'true romance,' either ending unhappily, or concluding with one of the protagonists marrying a *third* person - an old flame, for instance, or the person their parents had already selected for them. Lacking the compulsory fairy-tale happy ending (Bettelheim 1978:26), these stories of pre-marital romance suggested a marked authorial ambivalence regarding the practice of courtship. This fictional ambivalence was endorsed in the *WE* instructional and advice columns which were similarly equivocal on the question of 'love marriage,' neither approving nor disapproving it *per se*, yet hedged with caution.

As romantic stories, the tales of romantic courtship appeared to us at the time less emotionally satisfying than those of post-marital romance, as well as analytically much more intractable. My earlier analyses therefore set these texts aside and focused instead on exploring the more regular narrative structures of the tales of conjugal love, and on documenting the substantive ethnographic details regarding the sources of marital conflict that these stories disclose. But in this paper, taking courage in hand, I return to the theme of romantic courtship, recognising that the heterogeneity of narrative formulae in these stories and their unsatisfactory endings - though no doubt offensive to the analyst's sense of order - *themselves* testify to a significant area of anxiety, uncertainty and conflicting norms and expectations in contemporary Indian social life.

There is reason enough for this anxiety. The stories speak of a phase of the female life cycle, between sexual maturity and its containment within conjugality, for which there is, cognitively speaking, no legitimate space under the traditional order (see for example, Yalman 1963). Where the norms of the traditional system, required that girls be married before or immediately after puberty, the social changes of the last century or more have entailed that girls of the class of *WE* readers remain unmarried well after maturity. Yet they are still expected to enter marriage as pure virgins. If once 'sexualised' outside the context of legitimate marriage, the girl's chances of a 'decent' marriage are severely impaired.[7] The mature sexuality of the adolescent girl is thus a source of immense danger, both to herself and to the reputation of her guardian and family. As *WE* warns readers of its aptly-named 'Teenache' column: 'A wrong decision or indiscreet move can spell disaster and ruin a life!' A recent *WE* story, 'No beating about the bush,' parodying its own thematic of the virtues of plain speaking, states the dangers of adolescent sexuality quite bluntly. I paraphrase:

Leela and Bhanu, the young college-going daughters of Susan and Ragunath Menon, are resentful and defiant of their mother's restrictions on their movements. Realising that she is getting nowhere with her daughters, Susan appeals to their father, well-known for his plain-speaking approach to life, to do some plain speaking with his own daughters. Primed to his task, Ragunath confronts the girls:

'What's all this I hear, eh?.'...
'Did you say that you expected to be treated on a par with young men of your age?.'...
'And Bhanu, did you say that in the United States, boys and girls enjoy live-in arrangements when they cross 18 and it would be a good idea to introduce that system in India?.'...
'Listen, ' ... 'do you want to get pregnant by some foolish overstepping...?'
'Yes, that's what will happen if we give you unlimited freedom. You wouldn't know when and where to say 'no' What would be the consequences then? ...'
'We want you to get married as virgins. Understand? Without any premarital sex experience. Understand? No man will marry you, if you are experienced. An Indian groom wants an untouched woman. Understand ...'
'Do you want to lead the life of an honourable housewife or that of a dishonourable harlot? It is impossible to remain an unmarried woman in our Indian society. Or as a single mother. Never!'
The girls bowed their heads in shame ...'Actually,' sighed Bhanu, 'Daddy is right. It's all right to complain about our parents to friends and talk about wanting more freedom - but we all know in our heart of hearts that our parents have only our welfare in mind when they make rules for us!'‘
The girls then apologise for their defiance and their mother is overwhelmed with relief' (*WE* 494 [July 1994, II]:128-9).

The forthrightness of this story on a delicate theme is actually quite unusual. Perhaps the bluntness is made excusable by the story's supposedly humorous tone, or by its sound - if somewhat embarrassing - common-sense. For the most part, though, the *WE* love stories (whether of the pre- or post-marital variety) avoid direct mention of sex. On one occasion, a sexual touch was actually a lustful assault on a divorced woman; on another, the hero avoids a sexual encounter by deeming it dishonourable. When sexual attraction and arousal are mentioned, they are usually hinted at indirectly in phrases such as 'sensuous lips,' 'fiery eyes,' 'glowing skin,' 'trim body,' 'tumultuous emotions,' etc.: 'His touch had sent her heart strings vibrating'; 'his electrifying touch had sent a thrill down her spine.'.. are some of the phrases used to describe a situation which, fleeting though it might be, often marks a turning-point in the heroine's mind and in the story-line.

Displacing the problem of sexuality to the personal columns, whose very existence bears witness to a pathological breakdown of normative order, the *WE* stories of romantic courtship propose and seek to resolve an entirely different dilemma. This is the conflict between the lovers' duty towards their families and their desire for each other, between conformity to social norms and expectations and individual freedom of choice, between the wisdom and experience of age and the impetuousness of youth - in all, between the enduring, if now threatened, values of Indian family life and the individualist values of the West (cf. Uberoi 1997; n.d.[a]). This conflict is manifested as a problem of choice between the alternatives of 'love marriage' (that is, self-arranged marriage) and 'arranged marriage' (alliance settled by family elders, with or without the express approval of the young couple). The perfect solution to this dilemma is that articulated by the hero of the 1994 blockbuster Hindi movie (at the time the most successful Hindi movie ever made), *Hum Aapke Hain Koun* (Rajshri Productions). The hero is asked by his elder brother's wife what sort of marriage he wants: an 'arranged marriage' or a 'love marriage'? Seeking the best of both worlds, the 'traditional' and the 'modern,' he replies without hesitating, an 'arranged-love-marriage,' and thereupon reveals to his sister-in-law that he has fallen in love with her younger sister and wants to marry her. The remainder of the film is dedicated to making this fantasy come true, despite the formidable obstacles that have to be overcome before individual desire and family responsibility can be satisfactorily reconciled (see Uberoi n.d.[a]).

NARRATIVE TRAJECTORIES

We now look in greater detail at some of the typical trajectories of the *WE* tales of romantic courtship, paying particular attention to their conclusions - happy, unhappy or open-ended - and noting the factors and circumstances that characteristically determine these contrastive outcomes.

MAKING LOVE RESPECTABLE

A number of the *WE* love stories follow, in general, a rather standard romantic formula - albeit in an impoverished or restricted transformation: (i) a young couple are thrown together by circumstances and fall in love with each other; (ii) there are certain seemingly insuperable obstacles to their union; (iii) an event occurs that crucially transforms the situation; and (iv) the young couple are united to live, presumably happily, ever after (cf. Radway 1987:133-4).

A typical example, of the several we came across in this set, was the story entitled 'The resignation':

> Aruna was a smart and pretty twenty-six year old pharmacist, who wanted to pursue her career and was averse to marriage. Her boss of two years, Deepak, an eligible but 'confirmed' bachelor, has become attracted to her, but hesitates to declare his affections because of her known views concerning marriage. After consulting his brother on the problem, Deepak adopts a policy of alternate bossiness and consideration. This unnerves Aruna.
>
> Her nerves were on end. Of late, Deepak had disturbed her peace of mind and she could not understand why. The answers lay in her heart, but her ego refused to accept them.' She decides to quit her job, and Deepak appears to endorse this, insisting that 'a woman's place is in the home' and that she has no need to work if she gets married.
>
> Meanwhile, however, Aruna has to accompany Deepak to a business conference, and they go sightseeing together on a lake. Aruna falls into the water and is rescued by Deepak: 'His touch had sent her heart-strings vibrating.' Deepak proposes to her, but Aruna rejects the proposal. She later regrets her action and confides in her mother.
>
> Next day at work, Aruna hands her resignation letter to Deepak. Deepak begins to apologise for his earlier behaviour, but Aruna reveals her real motivation: she knows he doesn't expect *his wife* to work after marriage! Aruna's parents invite Deepak's parents and relatives to meet them (*WE* 496 [August 1994, I]).

There are certain conditionalities for a happy ending in narratives of this kind. The first is that the partner should be of appropriate class status, with the man, if possible, in a position of relative authority or seniority (cf. Singh and Uberoi 1994). For instance, as is often the case in these stories, the relation may be that of employer and employee. Second, though the match may be self-arranged, it should be of the kind that the young couple's parents would have arranged for them. If there seem to be problems in the match, from the viewpoint of social compatibility or physical desirability, the story line is geared to showing these problems to be irrelevant or illusory. For instance, a lame girl who is self-conscious of her limp walks 'almost normally' once her beloved declares his intentions ('Miss Tamerlane,' *WE,* June 1994, I); or a girl with a nasty skin allergy has merely to seek proper dermatological treatment ('An unforgivable omission,' *WE,* December 1994, I). An Anglo-Indian girl in love with her German employer, but hesitating to marry him because of the cultural difference between them, is delighted to find that her fiancé's beloved 'mother' (i.e. step-mother) is actually an *Indian* woman: he's really an Indian at heart, that means. Another young girl with a rather dark complexion discovers that her German boss is less colour-conscious than her Indian fiancé, who is in any case two-timing her with a fairer friend. Cultural differences in this case fade into the background, compared to the young man's superior human qualities.

Such fictional devices for neutralising apparent mismatch in physical attributes or social status do not, however, carry over into real life, as the personal columns of *WE* fulsomely attest. On the contrary, the personal columns do not offer much encouragement to couples with very diverse backgrounds, especially - significantly - where the woman is of a higher status or economically better off than the man. Inter-community affairs are handled cautiously, depending on the maturity of the couple. A twenty-one year old college student from a conservative family who has fallen in love with her American pen-friend is given a stern warning and advised not to 'mess up' her marriage prospects:

> Your plans are risky and impractical.... American society and its values and expectations are extremely different from ours. Since you have led a conservative and sheltered life, you will be completely at sea in it.
> Westerners feel that Indian women are docile, obedient and accommodative - refreshingly different from their own independent minded, assertive womenfolk. This tempts many of them to marry Indian women, often with disastrous consequences due to the vast disparity of culture, principles and thinking (*WE* 491 [May 1994, II]:89).

The second conditionality is parental approval of the relationship. It is rarely sufficient for the couple to simply melt into each other's arms as their misunderstandings are dissolved. An elder is usually around to bless or authorise this solution: the couple's parents step into the act and arrange to meet each other; the bride-to-be touches the feet of her prospective mother-in-law; and so on. Without parental approval, it is difficult to make a marriage work, as the *WE* counsellors constantly advise all but the most mature and economically well-established of correspondents.

In answer to an eighteen year old girl who was worried that her twenty-four year old boyfriend might not marry her in the face of strong parental opposition, the advisor queried:

> Why are both your families against the relationship? Do bear in mind that it is not an easy matter to marry without family support. Setting up a home, rearing children and looking after a family need a loving family infrastructure.
>
> The disapproval of elders can cause rifts in a marriage with each spouse holding the other responsible for the unhappy state of affairs (*WE* 495 [July 1994, II]:50).

There is also the real material problem of setting up house independently, without the fallback resources of the joint family.

The final conditionality is that the love relationship should preferably not have a sexual expression. Sexual intimacy prior to marriage raises the suspicion that the relationship is primarily a carnal one, unlikely to translate into the enduring 'love' relationship of Indian marriage. The only happy solution in such cases is that the relationship should be formalised and sacralised in marriage - providing, that is, that the partners are otherwise well suited to each other. Two stories of our set address this theme explicitly. One, 'Making commitments' (*WE* 494, 495 [July 1994, I & II]),

> is about a young man, Varun, who returns from the U.S. along with a live-in American girlfriend, Suzy. His conservative parents are horrified, and his mother gives Susan a dressing-down in which she reminds her of the cherished values of Indian marriage and family life, and insists that living together without marriage can only do harm to all concerned. Suzy and Varun see the wisdom of all this, and decide to get married after all.

Another story, ('Changing perceptions') concerns an established career woman, Jaya, who has a live-in relationship with a successful executive, Kashyap:

> They 'make love when the urge takes them,' but otherwise live in different worlds and cherish their individual freedom. In the course of a long train trip, observing her fellow passengers (a loving middle-aged couple) and reflecting back on the satisfaction she felt while caring for a friend's young daughter, Jaya realises that her life lacks something. She now sees that her relationship with Kashyap is a form of escapism from the responsibilities of family and home. Jaya decides that she and Kashyap should now make a proper commitment to each other, without necessarily jeopardising their respective careers (*WE* 525 [October 1995, II]:20-5).

Elders do not actively intervene here, but it is the example of a caring middle-aged couple on the train that sets Jaya's thoughts in motion in the first place.

Varun and Suzy, and Kashyap and Jaya, could hope to put a sacramental seal on their sexual relationship because they were, in any case, suitably matched. Were it not for the corrupting influence of alien values and life-styles they would surely have been married. But the same is not true of the majority of examples of pre-marital sex that are aired in the agony columns of *WE*. Very often a lack of commitment has already been shown, the boy perhaps breaking off the relationship and leaving the girl to face the dire consequences in terms of her reputation that *WE* constantly warns of.[8] Worse still, many of the sexual involvements aired in *WE* are actually incestuous. Disturbingly, the counsellors in such cases, as also in the numerous rape cases reported, often blame the girl for leaving herself open to such a disaster.

PUTTING LOVE INTO ARRANGED MARRIAGE

A surprising number of stories in the set of stories looked at deal with a young couple who are already engaged to each other, but one or the other of the parties feels uncomfortable with the arrangement, boding ill for the success of the marriage. It requires a dramatic (indeed, melodramatic) event, or some wise counsel, to reconcile the young couple with each other. These stories structurally mimic the narrative structure of the tales of post-marital love already described. A good example of such a story is 'Hidden depths':

> Aina is resentful of the fact that, though an educated girl, no-one had thought of asking her opinion when her 'autocratic' father had fixed her marriage to a good-looking and eligible young man, Chaman.
> 'Why should she toe the line and accept him just because her family wanted it? Had she no right to a will of her own? Shouldn't she decide for herself with whom she wanted to spend her life? It certainly wasn't fair!'
> What is worse, she did not care for Chaman's manner and comportment. A reserved person herself, she found Chaman flippant, frivolous and supercilious, and was irritated by his constant chatter and bantering. Her mother urged Aina to give herself time to understand him and appreciate his 'hidden depths.'
> One day Aina's sister-in-law collapses and has to be taken to hospital. Aina is alone with Chaman, who handles the emergency calmly and efficiently, and with sensitivity to her anxiety. When the news is broken that the sister-in-law is not seriously ill but merely pregnant, Aina rushes into Chaman's arms shedding tears of relief. Despite herself, Aina's attitude to Chaman begins to change.
> Soon after, Aina discovers that she has 'uterine' problems. Realising that she might never be able to have children, Aina tries to break off her

engagement to Chaman, but he nobly refuses to do so:

'Aina lay wondering how she could have been irritated with such an adorable man. Yes, she loved him and he really and truly loved her. But she would not marry him if the operation [hysterectomy] was performed. She cared too much to spoil his life. But would he be able to live without her?'

As it turns out, a second medical opinion confirms that Aina does not need an operation after all. Chaman throws himself on the bed crying. Aina 'cuddles his head,' and they laugh and cry together.

Shortly afterwards, they get married, Chaman 'completely mesmerised by her bridal finery'! (WE 510 [March 1995, I]:52-8).

'Hidden depths' suggests two distinct problems in arranged marriage, at least from the women's subjective position. The first is that of reconciling to the loss of autonomy involved in having someone else - e.g. the 'autocratic father' - choose one's marriage partner for one. As Aina's affectionate sister-in-law chides her in this case: 'You do enjoy [Chaman's] company, Aina. You are just averse to the idea of your father deciding whom your husband should be. You don't have anything personal against Chaman!' To this Aina's mother adds the conventional assurance that: 'We have your interests at heart, child. We love you and will do the best we can for you.' Indeed, it is widely believed that family elders will be wiser than the young people when it comes to mate selection, since the latter's judgement may be impaired by passion or based on frivolous considerations. In 'Hidden depths' the parents' judgement was indeed correct, but Aina had to be made to realise this through the unfolding of events.

Parents and elders who fail to take the initiative in arranging their wards' marriages in good time, or who find fault unreasonably with all proposals, are shown to be doing a disservice to their children. This is all the more so since respectable young women are not expected to be out in the market finding husbands for themselves.[9] In the only story of our set which deals with this issue, 'Speed breakers' (WE, December 1994, I), the girl is commended for boldly making her own choice, regardless of whether the man meets all the different criteria laid down by her unreasonably fastidious family. This is not a welcome situation, clearly, but it is the best that circumstances allow, and certainly preferable to spinsterhood![10]

The anxiety attendant on the failure of parents to arrange their children's marriage is reflected in the following letter to the personal columns of WE:

I am a 25 year old working girl hailing from a respectable family. I am earning a good salary. My parents do not at all seem concerned about getting me married. Till now they have not seen a single boy for me. Due to this, I remain very worried. I have now started hating my bhabhi [brother's wife], who is of my age and who is not only enjoying the bliss of married

179

life, but is also going to have a baby very soon. Please tell me what I should do (*WE* 508 [February 1995, I]:123).

Significantly, the writer is not advised, as she might be in a 'courtship' culture, to be more sociable, join a club, make herself more attractive to men, etc. Rather it is suggested that she make an ally of her sister-in-law to bring the question of her marriage to the parents' attention.

The second problem is that of ensuring the personal compatibility of a couple whose marriage has been arranged on the entirely different considerations of matched social and class status, perhaps astrological suitability, or a contract of material exchange (dowry). This is complicated by the fact that once the initial decision has been made, further negotiations regarding the marriage typically put the girl and her family (the 'wife-givers') in a disadvantageous bargaining position vis-à-vis the boy's family (the 'wife-takers').

Young women are extremely sensitive with regard to personal shortcomings which, if known to the boy or his parents, may affect their marriage prospects or their acceptability in the eyes of the chosen partner. They are also aware that not admitting to these defects beforehand may be a cause for complaint later. Drooping breasts and weight problems are persistent preoccupations in health, beauty and personal columns. So, too, is short-sightedness. Writes one young woman to 'Teenache':

Next month I am getting married to a man whom I have not yet met. It is an arranged match. I am short-sighted and wear specs at home. When I go out, I use contact lenses.

I will meet my fiancé soon. I keep wondering whether I should tell him about my short-sightedness. I am worried that he and his family might not like this fact. Do you think they will feel cheated if I hide this from them before the wedding?

The advisor recommends honesty as the best policy here:

You could, when conversing with your fiancé, mention casually that you use contact lenses. Do not sound apologetic, guilty or fearful. Just be matter-of-fact. It is unlikely then that he will make a big issue of this.

Of course, you are not obliged to declare all your shortcomings to your fiancé: but if you are frank and open, you will enjoy a relaxed relationship. Your fiancé will be gratified to find that you are an honest person who does not keep any secrets from him. This could also encourage him to trust you with the truth at all times (*WE* 492 [June 1994, I]).

A broken marriage in the parental generation can also prove embarrassing and threaten marriage prospects. This is the theme of a story entitled 'Family reunion':

> Amrita and her husband Pritesh had divorced many years ago, and Pritesh and their son had subsequently moved to the States while Amrita remained with her daughter Meghna in India. Looking back, Amrita realises that 'she could have, with a little patience, easily salvaged her marriage.

> Now Meghna's marriage to Neel is almost fixed, and the young people too have taken to each other. But Neel's parents are still unaware that Meghna's mother and father are divorced. Meghna's family are concerned that Neel's parents may not agree to the marriage when they come to know of it, Neel's mother being most 'particular that her daughter-in-law comes from a good family.' Even if Neel insisted on the marriage in defiance of his mother, it would be bound to create ill-feeling and land Meghna with a host of problems.
> As it happens, Pritesh and his son are visiting at this time, and Pritesh proposes the obvious solution - to remarry Amrita and 'become one happy family again.'
> Now wiser, Amrita vows not to ruin this 'second chance' in life, 'to pick up the broken threads' and to 'build ... dreams anew.' Neel is suitably impressed by the family's warmth and mutual affection' (*WE* 496 [August 1994, I]:98-104).

The ultimate stigma, needless to say, is a broken hymen. The *WE* counsellors argue reassuringly that an intact hymen is not a foolproof indication of virginity, since the hymen may be ruptured naturally, through menstruation: only a doctor can tell the difference, they insist. But sexually experienced girls on the brink of marriage fret, nonetheless, and continue to inquire about the possibilities of reconstructive surgery. Beneath the anxiety shown by readers on account of their looks or self-presentation lies the usually unasked question: is sexual attraction and arousal a necessary element in making a viable marriage? A letter in the 'Teenache' section of *WE* brings this problem into the open:

> Q: Can love be created? My marriage was fixed a few years ago and now we are soon to be married. But I find that whenever we are together he does not arouse romantic emotions in me. In fact, I quite often fantasise about another boy and weave romantic dreams about him, although I have not even exchanged a single word with him. Please help.

The *WE* answer seeks to distinguish the lasting 'love' of an arranged marriage with the 'so-called love' that is merely infatuation, but leaves the question of sexual compatibility within marriage unaddressed:

Love in arranged marriage grows with time. Affection, concern, caring and tenderness are all preludes to a deep and abiding love which stands the test of time growing between husband and wife. The so-called 'love' you are feeling towards this other boy you only see but do not speak to is simply an infatuation based on imagination. Make a sincere effort to get to know your fiancé, learn to care for his feelings, hopes and dreams - and you will soon find that you love him too (*WE* 510 [March 1995, I]).

This was obviously what Chaman was trying to tell Aina when, half-jokingly, half-threateningly, he said: 'You will like me when you live with me and have no option but to remain with me, for I hate divorce.'

Though sexual attraction is discounted as a *grounds* for marriage, it is clear from the hints provided in the *WE* stories, and from other ethnographic evidence (see Uberoi 1995:334-42), that sex *within* legitimate marriage, or specifically the sexualisation of the virgin-wife in marriage, is expected to mystically transform into the enduring attachment of regular conjugal love. (A pathological example of this reasoning is to be found in a letter from a frustrated young man who wants to know whether he should 'force [his girl-friend] to have sexual relations with [him] so that she knows that she belongs only to [him] and nobody else!' [*WE* 508 (February 1995, I):26]). It is therefore of a qualitatively different order to the infatuated quasi-love that physical intimacy generates outside marriage.

While structurally similar to the tales of post-marital romance, these stories have their own specificity. For one thing, an engagement does not have the *sacramental* status of a marriage. Thus, for a married couple, the problem is simply one of clearing misunderstanding and ensuring the couple's accommodation to each other. In the case of an engaged pair, however, the issue is somewhat different, namely, to decide on whether, and under what conditions, the marriage should go ahead as planned. Breaking an engagement is a serious matter, not to be undertaken on trifling grounds or personal whim, and certainly not on grounds that the couple fail to feel attraction for each other!

WE advice columns are cautious, steering a delicate path between upholding parental authority and family reputation, and endorsing the progressive social values (as on untouchability and secularism) that the magazine claims to espouse. For instance, advising an educated Muslim woman whose fiancé doesn't want her to take employment after marriage, the counsellor suggests: (i) clearing the air on this before entering marriage, lest there be frustration afterwards; (ii) taking elders into confidence; and (iii) coming to a compromise on the issue, namely, 'working till the birth of your first child when you should start devoting your full attention to family and home.' 'Children need full attention and care from their mother,' the advisor adds in explanation ('Teenache,' *WE* 508 [February 1995, I]:26).[11]

182

In another representation to the personal advice column, a young girl writes that her fiancé had found fault with her nose and suggested she have cosmetic surgery done on it. The girl's parents were furious when told, feeling that the young man should never have agreed to the match in the first place if he found his fiancé's nose ugly. The boy's mother had apologised on his behalf, but the girl feels that she has now lost respect for him. The counsellor advises breaking off the engagement, not merely on the grounds that 'the boy has displayed a hidden desire for beauty' which may resurface after the marriage, but more on grounds that 'there has already been a heated exchange of words between the two families and that does not augur well for a good relationship.' Moreover, the boy's 'ego is already bruised' by the reaction of the girl and her father, 'and there is every possibility that he may create problems after marriage.'

In another instance, an engaged girl from a 'very orthodox family' reports her regret and worry at angrily dashing off a letter of protest to her fiancé when his parents demanded a Rs.50,000 dowry. The advisor is reassuring, and counsels discretion:

> Although demanding dowry is considered a crime nowadays, many boys' parents ask for it to help the newly-wed couple get a good start in their life. Since you have found this family to be a decent one, extortion may not be their intention. .... Do not make your parents unnecessarily anxious by confessing your deed. Relax and look forward cheerfully to your wedding (*WE* 495 [July 1994, II]:50).

CONCLUSION

The stories of romantic courtship presented in *WE* in the period under discussion follow multiple and complex trajectories which this short paper has been able to indicate only in the briefest of detail. But beneath the profusion of details and outcomes is a very persistent anxiety and a consistent philosophy. The institution of Indian marriage and the Indian family system are seen to be under threat from an alien value system and a powerful and irresponsible feminist movement. While it is allowed that 'love marriage' is something consistent with a 'modern' and democratic way of life, these stories confirm that sexual attraction in itself is regarded as a fickle basis for marriage. In the fantasies of *WE* readers, love marriage is viable and desirable only to the extent that it is simultaneously 'arranged-love-marriage.' Alternatively, engaged and married couples are invited to inscribe 'love' more actively into their relationship. But in no case is courtship and marriage an affair between two souls: they are merely units within the wider family to which they belong, and their desire must be subordinated to their responsibility to the family collectivity.

NOTES

*   Acknowledgments: My thanks are especially due to Yasmeen Arif and Aradhya Bhardwaj for their help in the preparation of this paper. Some of the material presented here is included in Chapter 7 of my forthcoming book on gender and family in Indian popular culture (Uberoi n.d.[b]).

1   *Woman's Era* has the appropriate acronym, *WE*. Altogether twenty issues of *WE* were examined, and a total of ninety-eight complete short stories or novellettes. About three quarters of these were what one might term 'romantic' stories about a man-woman relationship, the majority being of husband-wife relations. Our focus here is on the twenty-eight stories that deal with love relationships prior to marriage.

2   On the general characteristics of this magazine, see Singh and Uberoi 1994: 98-99. Shailaja Bajpai (1997) has recently discussed *WE*'s profile in relation to its nearest competitors among Indian English-language women's magazines, *Femina* and *Savvy*, in the wider context of the post-liberalisation explosion of publications in this 'niche' of the popular magazine market. She concludes that *WE* has maintained an overall consistency through the years, despite the competition from its glossier rivals.

3   A quick glance at the matrimonial columns of *WE* will confirm, however, that very few clients availed of these discounts!

4   Editorial, 'Lib and liberation,' *WE* 489 [April 1994, II]:7), emphasis added. See also the publisher's similar comments as reported in an interview with Trinidadian writer, V. S. Naipaul (1990:418); also Bajpai 1997.

5   For instance, in September 1995, *WE* announced features on: 'Make-up tricks that make you look gorgeous'; 'Delightful dahlias'; 'What price sex without marriage?'; 'Beware of viral infection in pregnancy'; etc. *Femina* (a *Times of India* publication) sought to entice readers with: 'Is boredom wrecking your marriage?'; "'I never do things just for the money,' Claudia Schiffer bares her soul'; 'Swapna Sundari, learning dance from the 'devadasis''; 'Kavelle Bajaj's multi-million dollar enderprise'; and the lead article, 'You can save your city from dying.' The September issue of the somewhat more daring *Savvy* (Magna Publications) advertises: 'TBZ's Yamini Zaveri on the gory goings-on in a traditional jeweller family' (in their series of confessional statements by women socialites); 'Hitting the highway' (on the car preferences of glamorous celebrities); 'Sex after 4O: who has it, who doesn't'; 'Do you know your lipstick?'; '*Savvy* takes on Lakshmi Parvarthi and Pramod Navelkar'; 'Nuns get a kick out of karate'; 'Hope for multi-handicapped children'; and 'Cook-book filled with sour power.' For a similar profile two years later and a comparison of these

magazines with the new and more cosmopolitan entrants into the market, see Bajpai 1997.

6 But see, on woman's magazines in general, Bannerji 1991; Media Action Group 1997; Shukla 1991; Sita Chanda 1991; Wolf 1991. For the role of women's magazines as an important resource for Indian social history, see Minault 1998.

7 The useful term 'sexualization' is from Veena Das' discussion (1996) of the sentencing structure in cases of child rape.

8 See the article, 'Chastity till marriage,' *WE 519* [July 1995, II]). This theme continues to be reiterated in one form or another.

9 In one story on this theme, 'Hunting hearts' (*WE* 498 [September 1994, I]), a father despairs of finding grooms for his three strong-willed daughters, and challenges them to find their own husbands, adding the catch that he will not pay a paise in dowry either. The three girls rise to the challenge - 'the hunt so far initiated by the males of the species had been taken over by the members of the fair sex' - and eventually nail their young men. This unconventional approach to matchmaking was obviously redeemed by the jocular tone of the story - and by the girls' ultimate good choice of the sort of young men their parents might have chosen for them.

10 See P.H. Prabhu's discussion (1995:150-1) of the position of the Hindu classical legal texts on this question. The texts propose that if a girl's parents fail to arrange her marriage within three years of her attaining puberty. 'it is permissible for such a young lady to take the whole responsbility on herself of choosing her life-mate and enter into wedlock with him.'

11 The situation reported here is a tricky one, given *WE*'s overall gender and communal politics. On the one hand, *WE in general* endorses women's education, while giving homemaking firm priority over careers outside the home. On the other hand, *WE* editorials are constantly solicitous on behalf of Muslim women, especially on issues of triple *talaq* and polygamy.

REFERENCES

Bajpai, Shailaja (1997) 'English Women's Magazines,' in Media Advocacy Group 1997, pp. 1-38.

Bannerji, Himani (1991) 'Fashioning a Self: Educational Proposals for and by Women in Popular Magazines in Colonial Bengal,' *Economic and Political Weekly* 26:43, pp. WS 50-62.

Bettelheim, Bruno (1978) *The Uses of Enchantment: The Meaning and Importance of Fairytales*, Harmondsworth: Penguin Books.

Das, Veena (1996) 'Sexual Violence, Discursive Formations and the State,' *Economic and Political Weekly* 31: 35-7 (Special Issue), pp. 2411-23

Kapur, Promilla (1970) *Marriage and the Working Woman in India*, New Delhi: Vikas.

Kumar, Suhas (1997) 'Hindi Women's Magazines,' in Media Advocacy Group 1997.

Media Advocacy Group, ed. (1997) *An Analysis of Women's Magazines*, New Delhi: Centre for Advocacy and Research.

Minault, Gail (1998) 'Women's Magazines in Urdu as Sources for Muslim Social History, *Indian Journal of Gender Studies* 5: 2, pp. 201-14.

Naipaul, V.S. (1990) *India: A Million Mutinies Now*, London: Minerva Paperbacks (India).

Prabhu, P.H. (1995) *Hindu Social Organization: A Study in Socio-Psychological and Ideological Foundations*, 2nd ed. Bombay: Popular Prakashan.

Radway, Janice A. (1987) *Reading the Romance: Women, Patriarchy and Popular Literature*, London: Verso.

Shukla, Sonal (1991) 'Cultivating Minds: Nineteenth Century Gujarati Women's Journals,' *Economic and Political Weekly* 26: 43, pp. WS 63-6.

Singh, Amita Tyagi and Patricia Uberoi (1994) 'Learning to 'Adjust': Conjugal Relations in Indian Popular Fiction,' *Indian Journal of Gender Studies* 1: 1, pp. 94-120.

Sita Chanda, P. (1991) 'Birthing Terrible Beauties: Feminisms and 'Women's Magazines,'' *Economic and Political Weekly* 26: 43, pp. WS 67-70.

Tyagi, Amita (1989) 'Courtship and Conjugality: A Sociological Study of the Man-Woman Relationship in Indian Popular Fiction,' unpublished M.Phil. dissertation, Centre for the Study of Social Systems, Jawaharlal Nehru University, New Delhi.

Uberoi, Patricia (1995) 'When is a Marriage not a Marriage? Sex, Sacrament and Contract in Hindu Marriage,' *Contributions to Indian Sociology* 29: 1 & 2, pp. 319-45.

--(1997) 'Dharma and desire, freedom and destiny: Rescripting the man-woman relationship in popular Hindi cinema,' in: Meenakshi Thapan (ed.) *Embodiment: Essays on Gender and Identity*. Delhi: Oxford University Press, pp. 147-73.

--n.d. (a) 'Imagining the family: An ethnography of viewing *Hum Aapke Hain Koun...!,*' in: Rachel Dwyer and Chris Pinney (eds) *Pleasure and the Nation: The History and Politics of Popular Culture in India*. forthcoming.

--n.d. (b) Dharma *and desire, Freedom and Destiny: Gender and Family in Indian Popular Culture*. forthcoming.

Wolf, Gita (1991) 'Construction of Gender and Identity: Women in Popular Tamil Magazines,' *Economic and Political Weekly* 26(43), pp. WS 71-3.

Yalman, Nur (1963) 'On the Purity and Sexuality of Women in the Castes of Ceylon and Malabar,' *Journal of the Royal Anthropological Institute* 93(1), pp. 25-58.

CHAPTER 10

COMPARATIVE MODERNITIES:
OTTOMAN WOMEN WRITERS AND WESTERN FEMINISM[1]

REINA LEWIS

For centuries, the image of the secluded, polygamous Oriental woman has fascinated the West. The masculinist vision of the harem as a sexualised realm of deviancy, cruelty and excess has animated some of the West's best known examples of dominant Orientalism from fine art paintings to popular literature, whilst for nineteenth-century feminists the plight of the harem inmate functioned as a metaphor for women's oppression in Britain (Zonana 1993; Lewis 1996). But the veiled, secluded Oriental woman was not always represented as a hapless victim.

Some Western sources, women travellers in particular, were concerned to debunk such stereotypes: from Lady Mary Wortley Montagu in 1763 onwards, there was a strain of women's writing that explained the relative freedoms available to women within a segregated world, freedoms (like the ability to own property) that sometimes outweighed the rights of their European contemporaries (Melman 1992). Whilst the real or imagined status of Oriental women came to operate as an index of female liberation for Western discussions of emancipation, women positioned as Oriental were themselves, of course, actively concerned with their own status and liberation.

This chapter is concerned with how Oriental women, Ottoman Turkish women in particular, presented their struggle for emancipation in the early twentieth century to these Western onlookers. In connection with these, I shall be referring to the writings of the British feminist and journalist Grace Ellison, notably her book *An English Woman in a Turkish Harem* (1915). It is clear therefore that my source material is from a slightly earlier period than most of the chapters in this book. But I hope it will also become clear that many of the issues and themes discernible in later material are adumbrated in this earlier sample. Early-twentieth-century Western images of Orient - a realm whose flexible geography was always imaginary (Said 1978) - were already constituted in relation to a well-established represen- tational tradition operating across the visual arts, the print media, the performing arts and material culture (see for example MacKenzie 1995). This dialogical relationship also held true for those like Grace Ellison who self-consciously positioned themselves as a challenge to what we might, as a form of shorthand, call dominant Orientalist discourse. It was also a major factor in the writings and self imaging of those who were positioned by the West as Orientalized objects cf Orientalist discourse - the 'Oriental' women writers of my sample.

All these accounts of Oriental female life were designed to counteract prevalent assumptions about Oriental female life. The sources I shall be discussing here were written in English by self-identified 'Oriental' women and were intended primarily for an Occidental European and North American audience. Their writings provide what is in effect a reverse or counter discourse; an insider account of segregated life, written for an audience of outsiders. The texts construct an addressee who is assumed to be familiar with and informed by dominant Orientalist knowledges and stereotypes. But this is not to say that I think that we should read these sources simply as the realistic transcripts of an untroubled authorial intent, speaking 'authentically' from a usually silenced position. Rather, I want to look at how the struggle to create a narrative voice that can speak as an Oriental and as a woman without being subsumed under the various stereotypes in operation, is itself part of the political fight for emancipation at home and understanding abroad.

The three authors I am concentrating on today were all Ottoman subjects and hailed initially from Istanbul, but their life experiences and politics were very different. I have discussed elsewhere the non-fixity of the designation 'Oriental woman' (Lewis 1999), so let me just signal here that this is a shifting term whose geographical terrain varies for the West according to different periods and geo-political interests. All the sources I am covering here name themselves as Oriental women, and this is my starting point for discussing them as such. This shifting classification is important here, as we shall see, in relation to the internal, local differentiations between Oriental women which these authors often assume will be invisible, unless explained, to their Western readers.

So, for example, Halide Adivar Edib who identifies herself as Oriental is a Turkish Muslim who starts off her life as an Ottoman subject and becomes a Turkish citizen with the establishment of the Republic in 1923. Halide Edib comes from an elite background and was given a Western education by her progressive minded father. As a child she was dressed in European clothes although by and large she moved in a segregated world. Her two volumes of memoir were published in London in 1926 and 1928. My second author, Demetra Vaka Brown, also calls herself Oriental and Ottoman yet she, though born and raised in Turkey, is of Greek-Christian descent. Although Vaka Brown professes great affinity with segregated life, she is not Muslim and knows segregated society only as a visitor to Muslim houses. Vaka Brown wrote two volumes about Turkish women, both penned on the occasion of protracted visits back to Turkey after her emigration to America. The first *Some Pages from the Life of Turkish Women* published in 1909 is largely an account of her reunions with childhood friends and their circle, including an Istanbul feminist group. The second, *The Unveiled Ladies of Stamboul*, was published in 1923 after her second return visit. This second volume documents the changes in gender relations already visible in the new Turkish republic that mark the beginning of a period of accelerated social change. My third author, or set of authors, are the sisters who style themselves Melek and Zeyneb Hanum who travelled to Europe in 1906. Their correspondence with Grace Ellison was published under her editorship in 1913 as *A Turkish Woman's European Impressions*.[2]

Whilst Vaka Brown presents herself to her Occidental readership as an authentic and reliable source, Halide Edib directly disputes her version of harem life and her romanticization of polygamy. Writing bitterly of the misery that polygamy brought to her (Halide Edib's) childhood when her father took a second wife, she says

> Although this dramatic introduction of polygamy may seem to promise the sugared life of harems pictured in the 'Haremlik' [the American title of Vaka Brown's *Some Pages*...] of Mrs Kenneth [Vaka] Brown, it was not so in the least ... On my own childhood, polygamy and its results produced a very ugly and distressing impression ... (Halide Edib 1926: 144-5).

Halide Edib includes this in the first volume of her memoirs, written whilst in exile in Britain, having fallen out of favour with the Ataturk regime. Halide Edib's authority rests on her experience of segregated life and her involvement in revolutionary politics. For her, the problem of being close enough to the object of study without being rendered unreliable by a lack of objectivity (see Melman 1992) is resolved through her obvious contribution to changing sexual politics in Turkey: other women are represented as retaining allegiances to old outmoded customs but not she. Her journey towards emancipation - which she, like Vaka Brown, stresses must be developed in specifically Turkish terms - chronicles her changing consciousness. In 1908, even as she was writing for the radical Unionist, ie. constitutionalist newspaper *Tanine*, she was still 'not emancipated enough to go to the newspaper office' (Halide Edib 1926:265).

RE-WRITING THE HAREM

The condition of Oriental women was inevitably discussed in relation to the harem. This system of segregated living was for a long time common to many different ethnic communities in the Middle East, but by the last decades of the Ottoman Empire it had come to be associated almost entirely with Islam in the minds of the West (Keddie 1991). Segregated life was central to both the dominant Western Orientalist fantasy and the challenges to it provided by Oriental women. There are four reasons for this. firstly, the mythic sexualised harem was the pivot of a well-established Western fantasy of Oriental depravity, that was both proof of the Oriental's inferiority and source of much pleasurable and envious contemplation. Secondly, this was well known to Oriental women, whether or not they identified as feminist, who in their various ways set out to debunk this myth and present the harem as a home not a brothel (see for example Said-Ruete 1888). The primacy of the harem myth is illustrated by Grace Ellison's determination to challenge the Orientalist reification of the term. Arguing that the 'Turkish woman is not what Europe generally imagines her to be' (Ellison 1915:16) she cites the philanthropic and educational activities of Turkish women as they move towards their own version of modernity. She writes specifically about how 'harem' operates as a sign within Orientalist discourse, giving this account of her first discussion with Halide Edib, by then an acknowledged leader of the emerging Turkish feminist movement:

> I asked Halide-Hanum, perhaps the most active and best known of modern Turkish women, in the name of one of our prominent suffrage societies, how we English women could help the Turkish women in their advancement. 'Ask them,' she said, 'to delete for ever that misunderstood word "harem," and speak of us in our Turkish "homes." Ask them to try and dispel the nasty atmosphere which a wrong meaning of that word has cast over our lives. Tell them what our existence really is.' (Ellison 1915:17).

Thirdly, it is clear that whilst the phantasmagorical harem plagued Oriental women in their dealings with the West (witness Melek Hanum in 1872 and Said-Ruete, 1888) the harem as an experiential domestic system of segregated living was the very real terrain on which Turkish women fought for liberation. So when Ottoman women write about their domestic lives in English, they are simultaneously trying to encode themselves as Oriental women in a way that wrests their image back from the 'misrepresentations' of dominant Orientalism *and* to argue their case against the forces of conservatism at home. The construction of an alternative female Oriental subject is thus a project of reincarnation that has a dual axis: in the struggle for self-definition and autonomy the Oriental woman is contesting her subordinated position in relation to both Western imperialist knowledges and local Oriental gender relations.

Fourthly, the harem system in particular and the status of women in general had since the *Tanzimat* reforms of the nineteenth century (1839-76) become a central issue in the fight for modernisation against the Sultanate and in the subsequent national liberation struggle. As in many national and development struggles all sides tried to make the status of women their particular property. Attitudes to female emancipation shifted regularly in the intense factionalism of Turkish politics between the *Tanzimat*, the second Constitutional period instigated by the Young Turk revolution in 1908 and the formation of the republic. For intellectuals and politicians of quite diverse political persuasions the West featured large in discussions of modernity, of which female emancipation was considered an element, whether the Western model were to be emulated, adapted or rejected.[3] It is important to read women's discussions of changes in female life in relation to this wider intellectual and political current.

The battle over the changing image of Turkish women was played out in a dialectical relationship to perceived notions of modern Western femininity. The Turkish woman, whether coded as a guardian of tradition or an emblem of modernity, became increasingly crucial for the projection of a distinctive national identity (especially as the end of the Ottoman empire required collective identities be reconfigured from imperial to national, see below). We see throughout these discussions an interiorised dialogue with Western Orientalism in which Ottomans evaluate themselves in relation to the West's essentialised image of the Orient whilst at the same time projecting onto the West a series of similarly stereotypical characterisations of Western female life and morals. In this dialectic both sets of assumptions are informed and created interactively, each often relying on the figure of woman as a central indicator - be it of change, stability, morality or immorality. This set of dynamics, identified variously as Occidentalism (Nader 1989) or ethno-Orientalism and ethno-Occidentalism (Carrier 1992), is also present in women's writing. Thus, just as Oriental women writers reject some elements of the Orientalist stereotype and valorise others (replacing soporific odalisques with noble and calm Turkish women who compare favourably to the frivolity of Western women), so too does Ellison re-evaluate the 'protection' offered by the apparent confinement of the harem system in relation to the travails of Western 'freedom'. So the image of the West which haunts Ottoman discussions of modernity is both produced by and productive of Ottoman discourses of gender, nation and culture just as the image of the Orient is imbricated within Western discourse.

But none of these constructed images were ever static. In the Ottoman empire the initially pro-Western thrust of *Tanzimat* modernising reforms shifted in the late nineteenth century as Islamists developed a defense of Islamic law and custom regarding women (that was more or less apologist) and pan-Turanism constructed an imagined past that figured female emancipation as an indigenous pre-Islamic Turkic tradition (Kandiyoti 1991). Niyazi Berkes characterises the rule of Sultan Abdulhamit II (1876-1909) as a period in which imperial policy tried to adopt elements of Western modernity that it could consider 'material,' such as electricity and locomotives, without being tainted by what it considered 'moral,' or rather immoral, such as prostitution, divorce and so on (Berkes 1964). During the second constitutional period (1908-19), Young Turk policy was increasingly influenced by Ziya Gökalp's Turkist sociology and his theories on gender equality and the modern family. When Mustafa Kemal (Ataturk) emerged as a visible leader with the collapse of the Ottoman empire in 1918, the Hamidians' imaginary division between the material and the moral was discarded as he forged ahead with a policy of nation building and modernisation that specifically emulated a secular Western model, within the context of an emerging Turkish nationalism (Berkes 1964). Predictably, the religious leaders who had already opposed the reforms of the Young Turks' Family Code in 1917 continued to oppose the newer reforms of the National Assembly and the adoption of the Swiss Civil Code in 1926.[4] The Civil Code made marriage a purely civil matter, gave equal divorce rights to men and women and specifically prohibited polygamy, something which had only been discouraged in the 1917 Family Code. But Kemalism was not without internal divisions and significant criticism was raised in relation to both Westernist and secularist policies (Berkes 1964).

It is within this matrix of competing definitions of what was truly Oriental, Ottoman and Turkish and how to ameliorate women's conditions that early-twentieth-century Ottoman women writers represented the 'old' and 'new' woman of what came to be called modern Turkey.

THE PROBLEMS OF THE 'MODERN WOMAN'

The conservative Vaka Brown and the revolutionary Halide Edib have quite different politics, but they both stress the need for a specifically Oriental route to female emancipation. Simply copying the West will not do. This view is shared by Melek and Zeyneb Hanum.

Whatever their political differences, all the writers I have looked at begin by challenging the stereotype of the Oriental woman as docile, ignorant, inactive and uneducated. Writing from elite backgrounds they are all at pains to stress the noble characteristics of Turkish womanhood: they may be unlike their European or North American sisters in many ways, but the difference may often be to the Oriental's advantage. Without denying the disadvantages of the Oriental attitude of fatalism and *mektoub* (tomorrow will do, everything is God's will ...) these writers emphasis the Oriental women's active role in philanthropy (Halide Edib), their legendary hospitality (Vaka Brown and Ellison) and great 'natural' nobility. Vaka Brown in particular, poses the natural grandeur and justice of the Oriental woman against the false sophistication and misguided passions of the over-educated European 'New Woman'. Her cruel characterisation of the Occidental feminist grows as the book develops:

> There was so much of the sublime in them [Turkish women], which is so lacking in our European civilization. I felt petty and trivial every time I found myself facing one the conditions which they understood so well. It is true that in Europe and America there are, and have been, women who sacrifice their lives for big causes. But as a rule it is a cause to which glory is attached, or else some tremendous thing that they half understand, and to which they give themselves blindly because of its appeal to that sentimentality which is so colossal in European women. And through their self-abnegation they [Turkish women] were reaching heights unknown to us of the Western world (Vaka Brown 1909:128).

The image of the Western 'New Woman' recurs again and again in all these sources. For Vaka Brown, the Occidental modern woman is often depicted as intemperate, overeducated and misguided with all the advantages accruing to her more natural Oriental sister. The pitfalls of blindly mimicking the American way are indicated in the account of her meeting with Houlmé, an elite Ottoman woman who was given an 'enlightened' Western style education, only to find that she cannot settle for a segregated life. Raised by her grandfather, 'a Turk of the new school, which believes women ought to be educated to be the companions of men' (Vaka Brown 1909:137) Houlmé was betrothed to her cousin Murak with whom she had played and been educated until she took the *tcharchaf* (a heavy form of face veil in use during this period) at fourteen. Promised to him as his only wife, she nonetheless begs her grandfather to send him away to Europe for three years so that she may really be sure that, having seen the world, he chooses only her. Now, of course, she is missing him desperately and feels all the evils of her transitional situation, caught between Western ideas and Eastern life.

Since they let us share your studies they ought to let us lead your lives and if this cannot be done, then they ought not to let us study and know other ways but our own (Vaka Brown 1909:147).

Houlmé's problem is that she now thinks that a man

must be to his wife what she is to him, all in all. Is this not what Occidental love is? I did not use to think this way till I read your books. I wish I had never, never known (Vaka Brown 1909:148).

The impact of Western print media, notably novels and romantic fiction, is illustrated by the contrast provided by Houlmé's sister Djimlah who, though also raised with a Western education, seems unaffected by it. To this point Houlmé responds, 'True... my sister is educated as far as speaking European languages goes but she has never been touched by European thought [she still believes that] her husband is her lord, the giver of her children'. It is not knowledge of Western languages, then, that is the problem so much as familiarity with Western literature. Vaka Brown repeatedly limits the impact on Turkish women of Western ideas to a concern with men and romance. Whilst this also fits in with her support for the refusal to export American feminism wholesale in favour of an indigenous development over time, it also allows her to trivialise Turkish women's aspirations somewhat. By keeping discussion of liberation firmly within the bounds of the domesticated realm of romance, Vaka Brown is able to appear marvellously contemporary and journalistic (a selling point) whilst simultaneously weaving in a popular narrative of love stories. She thus captures the market both for popular romance and the exotica of harem travelogues.

Although I think that Vaka Brown presents this obsession with romantic love as a childish distraction from the real issues of female emancipation and social change, opposition to arranged marriages was indeed something that greatly concerned progressive Turkish men and women in the years prior to 1908. The complex signification of love as an ideological idea even if not matched by actual practice shifted, as Alan Duben and Cem Behar have shown (1991), in the years between the *Tanzimat* and the formation of the republic. The individualism spawned by the liberal ideas of the *Tanzimat* led to a valorisation of love among the political elite in the 1860s and 1870s. During the years of Abdulhamit's rule, when political free expression was severely censored, many opponents of the Hamidian regime turned to the expression of personal liberty, often focused on the issue of free as opposed to arranged marriages, as a stand-in for the political self expression they were denied. The role of Western, mainly French, literary culture in the development of this political discourse cannot be ignored.

Love, or *amour*, as it was often referred to by privileged Ottomans (after the French literary and political writings that inspired them), came to stand for so much more than just an intense personal relationship. It came to be associated with a political passion ... *Amour* and *liberté*, then, went hand in hand in a wave of intellectual liberalism ... (Duben and Behar 1991: 88).

Despite Vaka Brown Brown's critical overlay, the pull of romantic love evidenced by the Turkish women in her account marks, I think, the legacy of this earlier period, especially as I would date her visit back to 1900 or 1901.[5] The women that Vaka Brown interviews are depicted as her contemporaries in age (she was born in 1877), and would have been, therefore, young enough to have spent their pre-marital years in the repressive Hamidian era when love 'was often a euphemism, perhaps one might say a displacement, for liberty' (Duben and Behar 1991:92). So they can be expected to have experienced the heightened trauma of the conflict between modernising expectations and traditional practices. Houlmé, who as we shall see shortly is relatively conservative in her attitude to changing gender roles, does not believe that the Westernising experiment leads to personal happiness. When Vaka Brown asks her how she would raise any daughters she were to have, Houlmé's response calls for moderation - attempting to make the change in one generation is too fast.

> I do not think Turkish parents have any right to experiment with their children. I should not like to give my daughters this burden of unrest. I should like to bring them up as true Osmanli women.' 'Then you disapprove of the modern system, of education that is creeping into the harems? Were you to be free to see men and choose your husbands would you still disapprove?' 'Yes. It took you many generations to come to where you are ... we ought to have [the new thought] come to us slowly and through our own efforts. Mussulman women, with the help of Mahomet, ought to work out their own salvation, and borrow nothing from the West. We are a race apart, with different traditions and associations (Vaka Brown 1909:148-50).

In contrast to Houlmé's conservatism, her other friends are ardent feminists who want 'immediate freedom' and look upon her 'with mistrust as if [she] were a traitor' (Vaka Brown 1909:150). Their urgency is evidenced by their choice of the French anarchist Louise Michel after whom they name their group (Vaka Brown 1909:151-2).

Houlmé takes Vaka Brown to a meeting of the 'suffragettes of the harem' and Vaka Brown is quite scathing. The women's plans are in her opinion ill-thought of and immature and betray more about the potential of bored young women for self dramatisation than any grasp of real world politics. With dripping sarcasm she notes that the women attend the meeting wearing grey veils - to symbolise the new dawn - only to unveil and change into contemporary French fashions the minute the meeting ends. Clearly, the veils are simply there to create a gratifying sense of mystery and conspiracy (Vaka Brown 1909:167). After giving the whispered password 'Twilight' Vaka Brown and Houlmé are ushered into the meeting room:

> In a large hall stood the rest of the gray [sic] symbols of dawn all so closely veiled as to be unrecognisable ... It was all very mysterious and conspirator-like. The nine windows of the room were tightly shuttered, that no unromantic sunlight should fall upon the forerunners of the new epoch.

> I was utterly disgusted at the whole meeting. I might just as well have been in one of those silly clubs in New York where women congregate to read their immature compositions. These were totally lacking the sincerity, the spontaneity, and the frankness which usually characterises Turkish women (Vaka Brown 1909:163-6).

After the meeting, at which point most of the women reappear in Paris fashions for lunch, the discussion continues and Vaka Brown is asked for her views. Again, much of the discussion centres on the relations between the sexes. Vaka Brown starts by challenging their illusions about the liberated lifestyle of American women, telling them that young American women are also chaperoned and that whilst divorce may be legally available, it is nonetheless avoided by respectable women. On the subject of the non-polygamous man, she challenges their vision of the romantic Western hero who meets every female need.

> 'Few men are women's companions intellectually.' I said ... 'The only men who are the companions of intellectual women are half-baked poets, sophomores, and degenerates. Normal men, nice men, intelligent men, never talk the tomfoolery women want to talk about. They are too busy with things worth while to sit down and ponder over the gyrations of their souls. In fact, they don't have to worry over their souls at all. They are strong and healthy, and live useful lives without taking time to store their heads with all the nonsense women do.

Those forty women breathed heavily. To them I represented freedom and intellectual advancement and here I was smashing their ideals unmercifully. I pretended not to notice the effect of my words and continued: 'If you expect real men of any nationality to sit down and talk to you about your souls, you will find them disappointing. As for American women, they are as different from you as a dog from a bird. Whatever they do cannot affect you. They are a different stock altogether ...' (Vaka Brown 1909:169).

Vaka Brown repeatedly emphasises that the differences between Occidental and Oriental women mean that their liberation must follow a separate path. Picking up on Houlmé's lament that her unrealistic expectations and subsequent suffering were prompted by the uncritical consumption of Western fiction, Vaka Brown stresses that Occidental liberation is not always as easy as it appears to be in the French novels from which she deduces the suffragettes have derived many of their immature ideas. As an antidote to this literary 'malady' she recommends them to take advantage of the benefits offered to women by Islam and to go about campaigning for change in a more moderate and 'sensible way'.

> Then, instead of closeting yourselves together behaving like imitation French anarchists, you ought to have your meetings in the open. Since you all wear your veils, you can invite the men who are sympathetic to your movement, to take an interest in it. Little by little, more men will come, and also more women ... What you want it to be free to mingle with men. Since you want it, you had better have it, though you are overrating the privilege. There is a great deal of poetry and a great deal of charm in your system; but if you don't like it, you don't like it ... (Vaka Brown 1909:175-6).

Now as we shall see, other women note the constraints and deficits of the so-called freedom in the West, but I want to stop for a moment and think about Vaka Brown's admiration for the traditional harem system. This is a woman who now lives in America, at this time not yet married, and who works as a teacher, journalist and editor of Greek and English language American papers. She went on to travel and write political journalism (some with her husband) about the Middle East and the Balkans, as well as to be a prominent member of several American-based Greek relief and philanthropic organisations. Yet she treasures the luxury and grace of elite harem life. Although she is quick to note that she could not stay in the Orient - 'he who tastes of American bustle can never again live for long without it' (Vaka Brown 1909:221), she cannot condemn it out of hand. Her fondness for *konak* life (the grand wooden houses typical of the multiple/extended family living of the Istanbul elite) means that she cannot recognise the predilection for romance as a burgeoning discourse of individual rights.[6] In contrast to the pro-Westernism of many progressives, Vaka Brown's need to commodify the East as a recognisable Orient for her Western readers in conjunction with her own mainly conservative politics works against a recognition of the value of social and political change. Although Westernisation was contested by many who also opposed Hamidian autocracy there is something very peculiar about Vaka Brown's need to defend a system which her American modernism might well render unappealing. This resistance is driven by her investment in elements of Orientalism (Lewis in Jones and Stephenson 1999). Whilst part of her selling power is her ability to reveal the inside of harem life to an Occidental audience and although, as a self-identified Oriental woman, she clearly has an investment in challenging some negative Orientalist stereotypes, Vaka Brown does not really want to see the changes in harem life. Hence, her critique of the Turkish feminists' idealisation of romantic love, whilst also an accurate indication of the idealisation of the West typical of many strands of Turkish Westernism over the late Ottoman period (Berkes 1964), allows her to patronise her Turkish hosts and assert a Western superiority to which she as a hybrid subject can subscribe. As we shall see shortly, Turkish women were also critical of the limits of Western 'liberation,' but Vaka Brown's rendition of the feminist meeting allows no such sophistication to those who wish to end their *konak* lifestyle.

In contrast to Vaka Brown's nostalgia for the charm and luxury of the elite harem Halide Edib presents it as a stifling environment. She left her first husband when he took a second wife and challenges all romanticisation of polygamy.

> I have heard polygamy discussed as a future possibility in Europe in recent years by sincere and intellectual people of both sexes. 'As there is informal polygamy and man is polygamous by nature, why not have the sanction of the law?' they say (Halide Edib 1926:144).

Without stinting in her criticism of the supposed superiority of Western Christian marriage, Halide Edib rejects this idea. Whilst she also wants to assert the benefits of a specifically Oriental emancipatory politics, and has no objection to the export of valuable Oriental qualities or habits (selflessness, patriotism, lack of elitism), polygamy is not an example she would have the world follow. Notably, she removes polygamy from the privatised realm of individuated romance and locates it within the social unit of the household which includes children, servants and relations. Here, the hurt is even worse than the injury done to a wife who shares her husband with a 'temporary mistress'.

> Whatever theories people may hold as to what should or should not be the ideal tendencies as regards the family constitution, there remains one irrefutable fact about the human heart, to whichever sex it may belong. It

is almost organic in us to suffer when we have to share the object of our love, whether that love be sexual or otherwise. I believe indeed that there are as many degrees and forms of jealousy as there are degrees and forms of human affection. But even supposing that time and education are able to tone down this very elemental feeling, the family problem will still not be solved; for the family is the primary unit of human society, and it is the integrity of this smallest division which is, as a matter of fact, in question. The nature and consequences of the suffering of a wife, who in the same house shares a husband lawfully with a second and equal partner, differs both in kind and in degree from that of the woman who shares him with a temporary mistress. In the former case, it must also be borne in mind, the suffering extends to two very often considerable groups of people - children, servants, and relations - two whole groups whose interests are from the very nature of the case more or less antagonistic, and who are living in a destructive atmosphere of mutual distrust and a struggle for supremacy.

On my own childhood, polygamy and its results produced a very ugly and distressing impression. The constant tension in our home made every simple family ceremony seem like a physical pain, and the consciousness of it hardly ever left me ...

And my father too was suffering in more than one way. As a man of liberal and modern ideas, his marriage was very unfavourably [sic] regarded by his friends ... Among the household too he felt that he had fallen in general esteem, and he cast about for some justification of his conduct which would reinstate him. 'It was for Halide that I married her,' he used to say ...

The wives never quarrelled [sic], and they were always extremely polite, but one felt a deep and mutual hatred accumulating in their hearts, to which they gave vent only when each was alone with father. He wore the look of a man who was getting more than his just punishment now ... (Halide Edib 1926:144-7).

Halide Edib clearly abhors polygamy and has no allegiance to the veil. For her, Vaka Brown is dealing with fantasy, not reality. To Halide Edib, represented as the voice of the modern woman of the Turkish Republic and writing some years after Vaka Brown's first publication, the harem produced a state of mind that was not healthy. The end of the old ways that Vaka Brown sees as the sad Ottoman decline, Halide Edib celebrates as a new, modernising order. But she is torn: she also wants to represent all that is best about Muslim women of the old order (their contribution to the war effort and so on).

Halide Edib was one of the founder members of the first women's club in Istanbul, but her presentation of Turkish feminism is very different from Vaka Brown's. For Halide Edib, this momentous event in the annals of female emancipation is subsumed under the wider national crisis of the Balkan Wars. Female emancipation is located almost entirely within the fight for a wider social and crucially national emancipation. In the winter of 1913, Istanbul was flooded with refugees and wounded troops as the Bulgarian army advanced South. Many families in her circle left the city, but Halide Edib remained, having sent her servants and children to safety elsewhere. This is how she introduces the club:

> I stayed in Fatih [Istanbul] at Nakie Hanum's house and worked with the women of the Taali-Nisvan Club for relief and nursing. We, with some teachers and some educated Turkish women, had formed that first women's club. Its ultimate object was the cultivation of its members. It had a small centre [sic] where the members took lessons in French and English. It also opened classes for a limited number of Turkish women to study Turkish, domestic science, and the bringing up of children... There was a feministic tendency in the club, but as a whole it kept within the bounds of usefulness and philanthropy, and we tried to maintain a quiet tone, avoiding propaganda, which becomes so ugly and loud and offers such an easy way to fame for any one who can make sufficient noise.

> The club organised and opened a small hospital with thirty beds in Istamboul [sic]. A young surgeon and a chemist, both husbands of club members, volunteered to help ... We took only privates. As the Balkan war saw Turkish women nursing men for the first time, any little human incident became a tremendous scandal (Halide Edib 1926:334-5).

Halide Edib's disapproval of attention-seeking feminists is of a quite different register to Vaka Brown's. For Halide Edib, personal emancipation is presented as part of national emancipation, and publicity seeking might distract from that. Also, by the 1920s when Halide Edib was writing, an individualist emphasis on love had been recomplexioned as reactionary in favour of a view that registered the modern Western family as the foundational unit of the new republican society. Tracing the political travails of love, we can see how the nuclear family and individualism which for late nineteenth-century Ottomans represented a progressive-minded attack on the old order and its associated repressive family and state structures had shifted. By the time of the Young Turks in the early twentieth century such individualism had, as Duben and Behar demonstrate, come to 'be associated with anti-nationalism, moral corruption and even treason' (Duben and Behar 1991: 94). By the end of World War One the discursive terrain had shifted again as the companionate nuclear family was reactivated by Kemalism as a national model.

It is worth considering how Halide Edib's account is partly determined by the changing status of feminism in Kemalist politics. Women's emancipation was taken up as a standard in the fight for the republic, and was central to Ataturk's anti-religious social reforms. Some commentators have argued that Kemalism wanted to control the boundaries of feminism, too much of which would be seen as a distraction (Jayawardena 1986) and it would certainly seem that the early republic preferred a centralist 'state-sponsored' feminism to the development of an autonomous women's movement (Kandiyoti 1991:42, see also Abadan-Unat 1981, Tekeli 1989). One illustration of the repositioning of women's demands a part of a national, rather than only a gender, issue is Halide Edib's endorsement of women's contribution to the world of work. This is in contrast to writers published in the early years of the century like Vaka Brown and, as I shall discuss shortly, Zeyneb Hanum. Although most commentators agree that Turkish feminism began with elite and governmental initiatives and not as a grass roots movement, women had already taken on a limited involvement in work outside the home before Ataturk emerged as a leader at the end of World War One. He inherited previous measures permitting women's public labour from the Young Turk era when Imperial *irades*/decrees permitted women to work during the First World War in factories (munitions, textiles, food) and nursing, although their dress and demeanour was strictly policed (Kandiyoti 1991). Apart from the economically crucial nature of this female labour, modern and educated women were also a sign to the West of Turkey's progress and modernisation. So, for the Kemalists the cultural capital of women's new and, crucially, public working lives was immense but then so was the primacy of women's role as mothers of the nation, and hence guardians of the new ways. In light of these changes, we can see the tensions in Halide Edib's work between an overarching nationalist rationale, that provides as an alibi for feminism, and a very personal account of her own response to the limitations of the old order and the sometimes frightening challenges of the new.

Her memoirs cover the painful period of her divorce from her first husband (occasioned by his determination to take a second wife) and stand in contrast to the mould-breaking heroines of some of her earliest fictions. The tensions involved in trying to represent a mode of female emancipation that did not transgress all moral codes indicates the struggles women experienced as they sought to construct and participate in an acceptable version of modernity. Halide Edib was unable to demand a divorce in her own right (this is precisely the situation that the wife's right of veto on a second marriage in the 1917 law was intended to ameliorate) and so had to prevail on her husband. She is circumspect on the subject of his other affairs and says little about the ending of the marriage. By now a published novelist and journalist Halide Edib presents a dignified front as she attempts to overcome the unwanted notoriety the divorce brings. Fast-living and modern (or, as many saw it low) morals are not for her. Halide Edib's self-presentation is as a wronged woman suffering for her principals. It is very important at this stage in her narrative, which comes after her first indictment of polygamy in the account of her father's experiences, that Halide Edib differentiates her desire for a modern, Western-style nuclear family from the excesses and immoralities associated in the press with scandalously Westernised young women. At the time of Halide Edib's divorce and through years of the Balkan and First World Wars, the Turkish press continued to worry that for some women the allure of a Westernised lifestyle was based on a desire for decadence in which freedom was equated with a lack of any moral code or restraint. A quote from 1926 gives a sense of this prevailing panic: 'these days women have become alienated from many of their responsibilities. They want neither to look after their children, not do anything else! These women are the daughters of men who raised them in dance halls ... A misunderstood modernity has made women lazy... perhaps this situation results from their rather sudden emergence from seclusion into a free style of life'.[7] It was this concern about decadence and low moral tone that Ziya Gokalp set out to transform with his concept of an essentially moral and Turkish experience of modernity (Berkes 1964). The attendant sacrifice of self and emphasis on women's and men's involvement in child-rearing as part of their contribution to the new nation can be found in Halide Edib's autobiography where she presents herself devoted to motherhood and immersed in a busy domestic life. This is in contrast to her earlier fiction where as Saliha Paker (1991) points out female liberation is sometimes clearly linked to sexual liberation: in *Seviye Talib* published in the same year as her divorce, Halide Edib's eponymous heroine takes a lover as a route to self-fulfilment. This and her emphasis on female choice in marriage even led to death threats (Paker 1991:282). Paker identifies subsequent novels, like the tales of nationalist women *Aleslen Gomlek* (1923, English translation *Shirt of Flame*, 1924) and *Vurun Kahpeye* (*Strike the Whore*, 1923) which explore the tensions faced by professional women in a still changing society, as those texts which produced what came to be seen as the typical Halide Edib protagonist: the heroine who subordinates all personal desire to the national cause.

In her memoirs it is notable that Halide Edib's version of Western influenced modernity and egalitarian gender relations is one that includes a strong moral code. In this Halide Edib distances herself from representations in the Turkish media of free-living Turkish women and from her own sexually 'deviant' female characters, as well as from the radical advocates of free-love among European utopians and feminists. Instead, she aligns herself with a feminist tradition that sought to reform marriage with a moral agenda. As Lucy Bland makes clear in relation to British feminism in the years prior to World War One, from the late 1880s onwards most feminists whilst bitterly opposed to the inequities of marriage law and custom were determined to reform rather than abolish the institution and saw their campaign in distinctly moral terms (Bland 1995). Men would be encouraged to overcome the 'beastly' sides of their natures whilst women would, through legal change and sexual education, learn to assert their own rights over their bodies.[8] Halide Edib's memoir illustrates the conflict for women between living out their politically ascribed role as modern and educated and the tenacity of traditional attitudes to female sexuality. As Durakbasa deduces from memoirs and interviews with professional women alive at the early years of the republic, women were required to adopt a public demeanour in keeping with traditional concepts of 'modesty' whilst also manifesting 'modernity'. Their professional status was designed to make them equal to men without shaking off the 'patronage' of their 'fathers and Kemal Ataturk, the symbolic father of all the nation and especially of women' (Durakbasa 1987 in Paker 1991). She notes that in the fiction of the 1930s onwards, active participation in left politics is often the preferred route out of female frustration, rather than the depiction of an all too dangerous active female sexuality as was sometimes presented in Halide Edib's early fiction.[9] The moral tone of Halide Edib's memoir, then, distances her from the disreputable modern misses of Istanbul balls and from the free-love ideology of those European feminists who sought to dismantle the very model of the nuclear family that Turkey was trying to adopt.

STATUS: DOES EMANCIPATION REQUIRE LOSS OF CLASS OR RACE STATUS?

The West was central to women's consideration of female emancipation too, although it just as often figured as a disappointment as a positive model. A clear exposition of how Turkish women perceived the constraints of Western liberation is given by Zeyneb Hanum's account of her journey through Europe in 1906 with her sister Melek. The letters from Zeyneb

Hanum that I am quoting here make it clear that, like the feminists Vaka Brown represents in 1909, she and her sister started out with an elevated idea of European female life. But these illusions were soon challenged:

> It seems to me that we Orientals are children to whom fairy tales been told for too long - fairy tales which have every appearance of truth. You hear so much of the mirage of the East, but what is that compared to the mirage of the West, to which all Orientals are attracted?

> They tell you fairy tales, too, you women of the West - fairy tales which, like ours, have all the appearances of truth. I wonder, when the Englishwomen have really won their vote and the right to exercise all the tiring professions of men, what they will have gained? Their faces will be a little sadder, a little more weary, and they will have become wholly disillusioned ...

When in Turkey we met together, and spoke of the Women of England, we imagined that they had nothing more to wish for in this world. But we had no idea of what the struggle for life meant to them, nor how terrible was this eternal search after happiness. Which is the harder struggle of the two? The latter is the only struggle we know in Turkey, and the same futile struggle goes on all the world over' (Zeyneb Hanum 1913:186-8, letter dated 1908).

The emphasis on the tiring pursuit of dubious pleasures is constant in Zeyneb Hanum's letters. The sisters miss the quiet ease and companionship of Turkish social life, and are bemused by the ceaseless and, to them, pointless and graceless, activities of the European upper and middle classes (sports, skating, soirees etc.). Her negative depiction of women's entry into the professions speaks to their privileged Oriental background which, formed without a Northern Protestant work ethic, does not see wage labour as an ennobling event. This fits with much of what Vaka Brown, who is similarly conservative, reports from the Istanbul feminist meetings: that Turkish women crave emancipation in terms of education, freedom of movement and sexual politics, rather than for a right to work. The ways in which Zeyneb Hanum's gendered identifications are class- and race-specific are highlighted by Zeyneb Hanum's next lines where she argues that concepts of happiness are culturally specific.

> Happiness - what a mirage! At best is it not a mere negation of pain, for each one's idea of happiness is so different? When I was fifteen years old they made me present of a little native from Central Africa. For her there was no greater torture than to wear garments of any kind, and her idea of happiness was to get back to the home on the borders of Lake

Chad and the possibility of eating another roasted European (Zeyneb
Hanum 1913:186-8, letter dated 1908).

Having previously discussed the myths or mirages that the East and the
West hold about each other, Zeyneb Hanum now deploys a stereotype about
the 'South' that presumably transcends the East/West divide. The stereotype
of the cannibalistic African primitive was a staple of Western popular
imperialism well before the late nineteenth and early twentieth centuries
(Hulme 1986). In Oriental sources, which make clear distinctions between
Orientals and non-Arab Africans, reference to cannibalism also occurs,
though infrequently. Halide Edib makes joking reference to being told such
tales as a child, also in relation to a young enslaved African (Halide Edib
1926 p166-8). Clearly, Zeyneb Hanum uses this image as a tongue in cheek
joke for her European audience but it is also part of her own Oriental
lexicon of racialised division, something that she and her Occidental readers
can share. Tellingly, neither she nor her English editor Ellison see any need
to remove or explain it (and Ellison does use footnotes elsewhere to explain
what she sees as Zeyneb Hanum's misapprehensions about European life).
The figure of the naked African cannibal does what she is meant to do: she
simultaneously exemplifies the non-universality of human happiness, thus
naturalising the different aspirations of Turkish and English women, whilst
also uniting the Turks with the Europeans and separating them from the
Africans. This supports Zeyneb Hanum's (and Ellison's) argument for a
separate Oriental route to female emancipation. But, because the African
slave represents the worst of human depravity, the differences between
Occident and Orient are minimised: Turkish women, although different
from European women, are far more like them than they are like the
uncivilised savage. Although it is not clear whether for the purposes of the
cooking pot a Turk would count as European, the story certainly serves to
separate Turkey from the more primitive-coded others of imperial Europe
without merging her as one with Europe. The humorous tone with which the
slave's cannibalism is invoked, deflates the threat that such alleged practices
provide for Europeans and reinforces the African's subordinate position.
Enslaved, young and uncivilised, without the power to enact her revenge,
the African's inferiority elevates and unites the Occidental readers and
Oriental writer.

The need to be separated from these 'primitives' occurs infrequently in
the text but another separation - between herself and the European working
class - is frequently constructed. It is clearly imperative for Zeyneb Hanum
to be recognised as a lady and seen as distinct from a primitivised working
class. She regularly remarks on Western activities that seem to her
unladylike (sporting exercise that leaves women with red cheeks and

disordered clothes for example) and is traumatised by the possibility of not being 'taken for a lady'. It is this potential loss of class status that colours her response to English feminists. In this account of a feminist meting, differences of class rather than nationality are paramount.

> Since I came here I have seen nothing but 'Votes for Women' chalked all over the pavements and walls of the town. These methods of propaganda are all so new to me. I went to a suffrage street corner meeting the other night, and I can assure you I never want to go again. The speaker carried her little stool herself, another carried a flag, and yet a third woman a bundle of leaflets and papers to distribute to the crowd. After walking for a little while they placed the stool outside a dirty-looking public-house ... When the other lady began to speak quite a big crown of men and women assembled: degraded-looking ruffians they were, most of them, and a class of man I had not yet seen. All the times they interrupted her, but she went bravely on, returning their rudeness with sarcasm. What an insult to womanhood it seemed to me, to have to bandy words with this vulgar mob. One man told her that 'she was ugly'. Another asked ' if she had done her washing,' but most of the hateful remarks I could not understand, so different was their English from the English I had learned in Turkey.

> Yet how I admired the courage of that woman! No physical pain could be more awful to me than not to be taken for a lady, and this speaker of such remarkable eloquence and culture was not taken for a lady by the crowd, seeing she was supposed 'to do her own washing' like any woman of the people.

> The most pitiful part of it all to me is the blind faith these women have in their cause, and the confidence they have that in explaining their policy to the street ruffians, who cannot even understand that they are ladies, they will further their cause by half an inch. I was glad when the meeting was over, but sorry that such rhetoric should have been wasted on the half-intoxicated loungers who deigned to come of the public-house and listen. If this is what the women of your country have to bear in their fight for freedom, all honour to them, but I would rather groan in bondage (Zeyneb Hanum 1913: 89-191, letter dated 1908).

Gender emerges as an identification calibrated by class. Changes in women's status achieved at the cost of losing the class-specific privileges of their position as ladies may not be worthwhile. As Zeyneb Hanum later concludes:

I do not pretend to understand the suffragettes or their 'window-smashing' policy, but I must say, I am even more surprised at the attitude of your Government ... I cannot tell you the horrible impression it produces on the mind of a Turkish woman to learn that England not only imprisons but tortures women: to me it is the cataclysm of all my most cherished faiths. Ever since I can remember, England had been to me a kind of Paradise on earth, the land which welcomed to its big hospitable bosom all Europe's political refugees. It was the land of all lands I longed to visit, and now I hear a Liberal Government is torturing women. Somehow my mind will not accept this statement (Zeyneb Hanum 1913:236, letter dated 1912).

CONCLUSION

Compared to Europe, Turkey may not be so bad. It is clear that Oriental women writers evaluate female status in the West in relation to their own home conditions, just as European women had long looked East for a comparison or contrast. For Oriental women, the gaze is reversed as they examine European social mores in relation to their own changing situation. Since the nineteenth century, Oriental women had been puncturing myths about the relative evils of Occidental and Oriental marriage even though the polygamy that so gripped the West was uncommon by the late nineteenth century and even rarer by the twentieth. In the twentieth century, whilst clearly still concerned with the practice and representation of polygamy, Oriental women widen the discussion to cover the conditions for the emergence of social and political emancipation in both East and West. And, as we have seen, the West does not always come out on top when it comes to desirable visions of modernity for women. In contrast to the negative treatment of suffragettes in England, ranging from rudeness to brutality, Turkish women have the advantage of substantial and active male support, something which Ellison after her British experience finds 'still almost incomprehensible' (Ellison 1915:65). For the avowed feminist Ellison, the contrast with Turkey makes the limits of Western freedom all the more keenly felt.

I came here with perhaps just a little of the 'downtrodden woman of the East' fallacy left, but that has now completely vanished. To me, as an Englishwoman, there are sides of this life which would irritate me into open rebellion [the veil, separate transport, etc.] ... But then, after all, is not everything relative? ... If we in the West possess what is known as the 'joy of liberty,' have not so many of us been deprived of the blessing of protection? If the Moslem women are 'possessions' they are 'cherished possessions' and treated as such (Ellison 1915:195-8).

NOTES

1 An earlier version of this article appeared as 'Writing the Racialized Self? Ottoman women writers and Western feminism' in Cohen, Phil (ed) *New Ethnicities, Old Racisms*, London: Zed press 1999. I am grateful to the editor and publishers of that volume for permission to reproduce this second version.

2 Allegedly the inspiration for Pierre Loti's *Les Désenchantées*, the two women's real names were possibly Nouryé and Zennar. See Syliowicz 1988.

3 For historical overviews and different interpretations of the political significance of Westernism see Berkes 1964, Shaw and Shaw 1994 and Kandiyoti 1991.

4 The Family Code of 1917 brought marriage under state regulation, rendering a religious ceremony alone insufficient for legal recognition. It also made limited provision for women to initiate divorce, notably in relation to polygamy which a woman was now able to stipulate against and over which she was entitled to a divorce if her husband married again against her will.

5 Although the book was published in 1909, I estimate that the visit on which it is based occurred in 1900 or 1901 since Vaka Brown reflects back on her 'six years' in America. She emigrated in 1894 so this would put the visit to Istanbul at the start of the twentieth century. Further, references to her unmarried state also date the visit several years prior to publication and certainly no later than early 1904, in the April of which she married Kenneth Brown. This puts her in Istanbul before the second constitutional period began in 1908.

6 Alan Duben and Cem Behar (1991) note how in Turkish novels of the period and in their interviews with elderly people in Istanbul the phrase 'the end of *konak* life' came to signify the end of an era, typified by gracious living and multiple family dwellings. The emergence of a 'modern' nuclear family on a Western model based on companionate love marriage was not just about individual choice, it also drastically re-ordered the previously patriarchal and cross-generational structure of family and civic society.

7 Feridun Necdet in *Sevimli Ay* 1926 in Duben and Behar 1991:197.

8 Though some wings of British feminism did advocate free unions, where marital relations should be privately contracted outside of state legislation, this was opposed by most British feminists. (Some though saw free union as a future ideal.) The stigma of unrespectability was considered intolerable and ill-advised by the largely middle-class feminist grouping. Interestingly, Bland (1995) notes that whilst

advocates of free-love or free-union saw relationships as ideally monogamous and long-term many critics, feminist and otherwise, worried that men would use free-love as a way to access more than one woman. European feminism is, then, haunted by the spectre of polygamy and concubinage as a potential threat of male sexuality the world over.

9 On reasons for the belated rise of individualistic or 'autonomous' feminism in Turkey, following the 1980 military coup see Yesim Arat 1994.

REFERENCES

Arat, Zehra F. (1994) 'Turkish Women and the Republican Reconstruction of Tradition,' in: Göçek, Fatma Müge and Shiva Balaghi (eds) *Reconstructing Gender in the Middle East: tradition, Identity and Power*. New York: Columbia University Press.

Abadan-Unat, Nermin (ed.) (1981) *Women in Turkish Society*. Leiden: E.J. Brill.

Berkes, Niyazi (1964) *The Development of Secularism in Turkey*. Montreal: McGill University Press.

Bland, Lucy (1995) *Banishing the Beast: English Feminism and sexual Morality 1855-1914*. London: Penguin.

Carrier, James G. (1992) 'Occidentalism: The World Turned Upside-Down,' *American Ethnologist*, 19(2), pp. 195-212.

Duben, Alan and Behar, Cem. (1991) *Istanbul Households: Marriage, Family and Fertility, 1880-1940*. Cambridge: Cambridge University Press.

Edib, Halide Adivar (1926) *Memoirs of Halide Edip*. London, John Murray.

Ellison, Grace (1915) *An Englishwoman in a Turkish Harem*. London: Methuen.

Hulme, Peter (1986) *Colonial Encounters: Europe and the Native Caribbean, 1492-1797*. London: Methuen.

Jayawardena, Kumari (1986) *Feminism and Nationalism in the Third World*. London: Zed Books.

Kandiyoti, Deniz (ed.) (1991) *Women, Islam and the State*. Basingstoke: Macmillan.

Keddie, Nikkie (1991) *Women in Middle Eastern History: Shifting Boundaries in Sex and Gender*. New Haven: Yale University Press.

Melek-Hanum (1872) *Thirty Years in the Harem: or the Autobiography of Melek-hanum, Wife of H.H. Kibrizli-Mehemet-Pasha*. second edition, Calcutta, Lewis and Co., 1888.

Lewis, Reina (1996) *Gendering Orientalism: Race, Femininity and Representation*. London: Routledge.

--(1999) 'Cross-Cultural Reiterations: Demetra Vaka Brown and the Performance of Racialised Female Beauty,' in: Jones Amelia and Stephenson Andrew (eds) *Performing the Body/ Performing the Text*. London: Routledge.

MacKenzie, John M. (1995) *Orientalism: History, Theory and the Arts*. Manchester: Manchester University Press.

Melman, Billie (1992) *Women's Orients: English Women and the Middle East, 1718-1918. Sexuality, Religion and Work*. Basingstoke:Macmillan

Nader, Laura (1989) 'Orientalism, Occidentalism and the Control of Women,' *Cultural Dynamics* 2(3), pp. 323-55.

Paker, Saliha (1991) 'Unmuffled Voices in the Shade and Beyond. Women's Writing in Turkish.' in: Helena Forsås-Scott (ed.) *Textual Liberation: European Feminist Writing in the Twentieth Century*. London: Routledge.

Said, Edward W. (1978) *Orientalism*. Harmondsworth: Penguin.

Said-Ruete, Emily (1981) *Memoirs of an Arabian Princess: Princess Salme bint Said ibn Sultan al-Bu Saidi of Oman and Zanzibar*. London, East-West Publications.

Shaw, Stanford J. and Ezel Kural Shaw (second edition 1994) *History of the Ottoman Empire and Modern Turkey, vol.2 Reform, Revolution and Republic*. Cambridge: Cambridge University Press.

Szyliowicz, Irene L. (1988) *Pierre Loti and the Oriental Woman*. Basingstoke: Macmillan.

Tekeli, Sirin (1989) 'Emergence of the Feminist Movement in Turkey,' in: D. Dahlerup (ed.) *The New Women's Movement: Feminism and Political Power in Europe and the USA*, London: Sage.

Vaka Brown, Demetra (1909) *Some Pages from the Life of Turkish Women*. London: Constable.

--(1911) *In the Shadow of Islam*, London: Constable.

--(1923) *The Unveiled Ladies of Stamboul*. Boston: Houghton Mifflin.

Zeyneb Hanoum (1913) *A Turkish Woman's European Impressions*. London: Seeley, Service Co.

Zonana, Joyce (1993) 'The Sultan and the Slave: Feminist Orientalisms and the Structure of *Jane Eyre*,' *Signs* 18(3), Spring.

Printed in the USA/Agawam, MA
July 30, 2014

594230.012